ABOUT THE AUTHOR
OF THIS BOOK

About fifteen years ago, Byron Dalrymple began to concentrate full time on outdoor writing and he has become the best-known author in this field. Columns and features by him run regularly in *Sports Afield, Outdoor Life, Field & Stream* and *Man's* magazines. His output of over a thousand articles has covered almost the entire range of magazines.

This book is a revision of *All You Need to Know About Fishing, Hunting and Camping,* published originally by Pocket Books, Inc., in 1950. It was the first paperback book in the outdoor field. Dalrymple is the author of half a dozen other books on fishing and hunting and has contributed to most of the major reference works in this field, including the *Encyclopaedia Britannica.*

A lifelong outdoor enthusiast, Dalrymple has hunted and fished in every state, in Canada and in Mexico. He travels more than 25,000 miles a year gathering material for his books, articles and columns. When not traveling, he can be found either at his home in northern Michigan or at his second home in the Texas hill country.

Other books by Byron Dalrymple

FISHING IN THE UNITED STATES
ICE FISHING FOR EVERYBODY

THE FUNDAMENTALS OF

Fishing and Hunting

•

BYRON DALRYMPLE

Illustrated by
PAUL ORBAN

PERMABOOKS • NEW YORK

This Permabook is a revised edition of *All You Need to Know About Fishing, Hunting and Camping,* originally published by Pocket Books, Inc. It is printed from brand-new plates made from completely reset, clear, easy-to-read type.

The Fundamentals of Fishing and Hunting

POCKET BOOK edition published April, 1950

PERMABOOK edition published July, 1959
1st printing.........................May, 1959

PERMABOOK editions are published in the United States by Pocket Books, Inc. and in Canada by Pocket Books of Canada, Ltd.—the world's largest publishers and distributors of low-priced books for the entire family.

CONTENTS

Part 1. Fishing

Chapter		Page
One	Fresh-Water Fishing Tackle and How to Use It	3
	Bait Casting	5
	Fly-Fishing	13
	Spinning	23
	Bait- and Still-Fishing	28
	Miscellaneous Equipment	31
Two	Fresh-Water Fish and How to Fish Them	33
	Game Fish	36
	Pan Fish	50
	Rough Fish	59
Three	Ice-Fishing	65
Four	Salt-Water Tackle and How to Use It	79
	Surf Tackle and Its Use	88
	Salt-Water Trolling	92
	Other Types of Salt-Water Fishing	94
	Salt-Water Baits	96
	Playing Salt-Water Fish	98
	Salt-Water Fishing Services	100

CONTENTS

Chapter   *Page*

Five Salt-Water Fish and How to Fish Them 103

    Big-Game Fish 106

    General Game Fish 110

    Bottom Fish 123

Part 2. Hunting

One Hunting Equipment and How to Use It 133

    Rifles 136

    Shotguns 151

    Safety with Guns 161

Two Dogs and Their Training 164

    General Training 166

    Hunting-Dog Breeds 169

    Field Training 174

Three Hunting Upland Game Birds 184

    The Quails 187

    The Pheasant 192

    Partridges 196

    The Grouses 198

    The Woodcock 207

    The Wild Turkey 209

    The Doves 212

Four Hunting Lowland Game Birds 218

    The Ducks 221

CONTENTS

Chapter		Page
	The Geese	230
	Waterfowl Guns	233
	Hunting Methods	235
	Rails and Rail Hunting	243
Five	Hunting Small Game Animals and Varmints	245
	Rabbits	246
	Squirrels	249
	Night Hunting	253
	Bobcats and Foxes	257
	Varmint Hunting	260
	Crows	264
Six	Hunting Big Game	267
	Deer Hunting	270
	Other Horned and Antlered Game	277
	Bears	290
	Mountain Lion	293
	Wild Hogs	294
Seven	Calling Predators, Pests, and Game	296
Eight	Hunting with Bow and Arrow	301
	Bibliography	311
	Index	315

THE FUNDAMENTALS OF

Fishing and Hunting

Part 1

FISHING

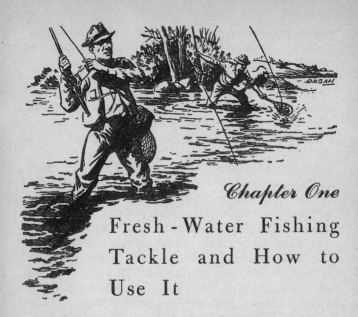

Chapter One

Fresh-Water Fishing Tackle and How to Use It

The mere mention of fishing, to anyone, whether or not he has ever fished before, immediately suggests a picture of cool lakes and streams, people forgetting the workaday grind, engrossed, excited, partaking of the best, most healthful sport imaginable. We have, in fact, so heartily taken to fishing, as a nation, that it is today our top American participant sport, with one person out of every five doing at least some fishing every year.

You might wonder how there could possibly be any fish left. But luckily, even with the tremendous amount of fishing being done, our active, alert, and thoroughly schooled conservation departments do, all told, an excellent job of keeping the potential catch continuously abundant. Theirs is a worth-while work, for fishing is a means toward more happiness, and better health, for all of us.

There is no better relaxation or hobby, nor any more exciting and satisfying. And, since in our fast-paced civilization we *need* satisfying and relaxing hobbies, everyone should know how to fish. Never has there been a person who took up this sport and was sorry for it. Perhaps the reason is that fishing is something everyone can do—*successfully!*

Once you start, you soon learn why U. S. anglers are so noisily enthusiastic about what our tens of thousands of fresh-water lakes and streams and our seemingly endless salt-water seacoasts offer. Our fish species are so fabulously diverse that methods of angling have had to follow suit. Not only are there fish of kinds to please every sporting taste, but ways of catching them to suit every individual, from the complete dub who laughs at his own inexpertness to the fine angler whose precision with his tackle is a high art beautiful to witness.

Since most of us live closer to fresh fishing waters than to salt, fresh-water angling accounts for the greater portion of our line-wetting endeavors. Its tackle and the methods used for each fish species vary widely. They also greatly overlap. Though actually it is unnecessary to have more than hook, line, and can of worms to catch fish, the use of modern tackle makes it tremendously more exciting.

For example, take the fellow, carrying line and hook, who goes to a stream, cuts his pole, finds a frog, and catches a bass. He is to be commended for his ingenuity, and certainly there is nothing wrong with his method. It is, in fact, good sport. But the point is, he can have *more* sport by using, let's say, light tackle such as a whippy fly rod and an artificial bass bug. And, since he can catch the fish just as surely as with his frog, why not avail himself of the better opportunity? By learning to use modern tackle, which has come to an extremely high state of development directly for the purpose of making it possible to catch more fish and have more fun, he does himself a favor, and he passes on to his youngsters the same idea. He assists the fine hobby of fishing for generations to come, and he makes his fishing actually *easier,* and more interesting.

After he has begun one method, such as fly-fishing, or plug casting, he soon realizes that knowledge of and proficiency with *all* the various kinds of tackle lead to the ultimate of satisfaction and success. The following sections, therefore, separate the several methods of fresh-water fishing and their tackle, and give compact, easy-to-follow, detailed information about how to choose and use each outfit. For the beginner, it should serve as a complete guide, and for the old hand an easy reference and a refresher course.

BAIT CASTING

THE METHOD known somewhat confusingly as "bait casting" nowadays takes second place to spinning but is still useful and popular. It takes in a very wide scope of activity, but it does *not* mean the casting of *live* bait exclusively. Modern bait-casting tackle was developed first so that live bait such as frogs and minnows might be cast, or thrown out, longer distances and into more likely spots than could be reached by the long hand pole. If you have fished with a long pole from lake or stream bank, you know how disappointing it is to see some spot where a lunker must surely lie in wait, and yet not be able to get your bait to him.

Later, after live and natural baits were being tossed around enthusiastically by users of this new invention, artificial lures which were fairly heavy began to be developed more and more. The "bait-casting" outfit proved perfect for them, allowing an angler not only to throw them exactly where he wished, but also to impart lively, fish-teasing motion to them as he reeled in.

Thus, bait casting took its name from its origin, but has been developed primarily as a means of casting artificial lures too heavy to manipulate otherwise. Today it is really streamlined, a most simple, yet exciting and intriguing, manner of fishing. It also gets sensational results, especially with the larger game species. And the battles to be had with such fish taken with bait-casting tackle are in the top bracket for thrills.

A brief description of every necessary item of bait-casting tackle follows. It tells you concisely everything you need to know, about the tackle and its uses, in order for you to become a successful bait caster.

BAIT-CASTING RODS, though extremely diverse in length, weight, and action, are made nowadays almost without exception of glass. Lengths run from 4 to 6½ feet. Short rods are best for crowded or brushy casting conditions.

The shorter the rod, the stiffer. Longer rods can be had, however, in various actions, from very light to stiff. Stiff actions, whether short or long, are best suited to casting for pike, muskies, etc., because of the heavy lures and the power of the fish. Extra-light action is nowadays unnecessary for light-lure casting. The spinning rod—which we will discuss later—has eliminated the need for it. Long rods cast lures more accurately than short, stiff ones. But an all-round good choice for average uses is 5½ feet, medium action, glass or hollow-drawn alloy.

BAIT-CASTING REELS are of two general types: single action, meaning one turn of handle equals one turn of the spool; quadruple multiplying, which means each turn of the handle equals four turns of the spool. For modern fresh-water angling, the single action is worthless. Multiplying reels are of three types: free-spool, meaning the reel handle does not turn as the lure is cast; anti-backlash and level-wind (reels with devices [1] to avoid a line tangle on the reel when the lure fails to carry the line as fast as the momentum of the reel spool; [2] to lay the line evenly on the spool during the retrieve); open-spool—that is, reels lacking the previous devices.

For all general purposes the level-wind, anti-backlash multiplier is best. Most bait-casting reels have capacities of 100 yards of 15- to 20-pound test line. A few are larger, some smaller. The average is entirely adequate.

LINES are made of several materials, nowadays mainly of the newer synthetics. Silk, once popular, has been replaced by nylon and Dacron, both braided, and even by nylon monofilament. The synthetics are little affected by moisture, even by salt water. Nylon stretches somewhat, taking up some pressure when a fish is played or

7

when a lure is snagged. These synthetics are also less bulky, for their strength, than old-fashioned lines.

Bait-casting line sizes are named by poundage test. The test needed depends upon rod action, kind of fish expected, weight of lures to be cast. For all average fresh-water casting, for bass, walleyes, pike, etc., 12-pound test is ideal. Fifty yards of line are adequate for all average purposes. For very large fish, 100 yards heavier test are preferable.

Trolling—that is, fishing from a moving boat with the lure running some distance behind—calls for heavier lines than casting. It is a very productive method to which the bait rod is perfectly adapted. But the line gets hard wear. Tests of 20 to 30 pounds will give best service for this purpose.

For extremely deep trolling, metal lines are available. They eliminate the need for sinkers, and sink deep without "bowing," thus making a straight pull possible .at the strike of a fish.

LEADERS are sometimes advantageous in bait casting, for they are invisible, or nearly so, to a fish. Thus they give the fish the illusion that the lure has "no strings attached." When working lures slowly, a three-foot length of nylon monofilament at line's end often helps get strikes. Too-long leaders that come back onto the reel are a nuisance, and unnecessary.

Short wire leaders, swiveled on either end, and with snaps for attaching and changing lures, are generally used. They avoid having fish teeth cut the line, and they greatly facilitate swift changing of lures.

LURES are of infinite variety, and it is here that the bait-casting enthusiast can have almost as much fun—in buying them, guessing how productive they'll be, and in simply looking at them—as he'll have fishing. Their gaudy colors in combination seemingly without end, their shapes, which range all the way from streamlined, shiny items of real beauty to laughable inventions which appear to be the last thing any fish would want to strike, are so appealing that usually a fisherman starts out conservatively with three or four and winds up with his tackle box stuffed and looking like a toy store at Christmas time. Indeed, in bait casting the lures are as intriguing and exciting as what may be done with them and what they will do.

But don't underestimate those gaudy colors and those artistic or crazy shapes. Modern bait-casting lures of quality are scientifically designed, and tested over long periods for results before they're marketed. The majority of them, under proper fishing conditions, are killers on the fish for which they are individually intended.

All bait-casting lures may be placed in two general categories: wooden (or plastic) plugs; metal spinners and spoons. Some are a combination of the two, or of spinner and fly. Their weights, which must be considered according to the tackle with which they are to be cast, fall into three general divisions: up to ⅜ ounce;

Balanced Tackle Chart

	LURES	LINE	ROD LENGTH	ROD ACTION
1.	to ⅜ oz.	6 to 9 lb. test	5½ to 6 ft.	Extremely light
2.	⅜ to ⅝ oz.	9 to 12 lb. test	5 to 6 ft.	Light
3.	⅝ to 1 oz.	12 to 18 lb. test	5 to 5½ to 6 ft.	Medium
4.	1 oz. & over	18 to 30 lb. test	4 to 5 ft.	Stiff

from ⅜ to ⅝ ounce; above ⅝ to approximately 1¼ ounces.

If you are buying bait-casting tackle for the first time, you can't go wrong by following the chart on page 9 in your selection. If you think you might also take up the new sport of spinning which has recently swept the U. S., you should consider Line No. 1 in the chart obsolete, for the spinning rod replaces it. If you cannot afford more than one outfit, you should choose the third listing above. It is the perfect all-purpose rig. However, if most of your fishing will be on open-water locations, such as from a boat, or open banks without obstructions, choose the longer rod lengths. They make casting easier. For cramped conditions, short rods are best.

Basically, all the hundreds of artificial bait-casting lures are of two kinds: floating and sinking. There is, however, great variety of actions among them—for example, wiggling, whirling, diving, gurgling.

FLOATING LURES are classed as follows: *Strictly surface lures:* These float during retrieve, either with gurgling or "popping" noise, or with fore and aft spinners revolving. Such lures should be fished slowly. Cast, let the lure lie motionless momentarily, retrieve in short jerks of varied motion, or by slow, steady reeling. These are excellent for surface-feeding bass and pike.

Shallow-running floaters: These float when motionless, dive and wriggle when reeling, from one to three feet below the surface, depending upon the speed of retrieve—i.e., the faster, the deeper. These are the most popular lures to meet average conditions. They take surface-feeding fish and also often bring curious or hungry fish up from somewhat deeper water.

Deep-diving lures: Exactly like the former, but with metal lips or other devices which cause them to run from three to six feet deep. For use when fish are at or somewhat below those depths, around steep drop-offs, and deep weed beds. All of the diving lures, deep or shallow, can be utilized as surface lures by extremely slow retrieve, pausing and jerking motions, etc.

SINKING LURES, which include both certain plugs and all the spoons and spinners, are of two kinds: slow sinkers and fast sinkers. The former are effective when you are certain fish are not near the surface but you are unsure of their exact depth. The latter are for use when fish are consistently lying deep. Slow sinkers can be fished over deep-lying weeds, bars, etc., and are easily manipulated to avoid snagging. Use the fast sinkers only in unusually deep spots where space restrictions make quick sinking desirable. All spoons and spinners are in this class. Many have "weedless" hooks. When properly used, they are deadly.

Best colors and types of lures can never be forecast. Every tackle box should therefore carry a selection of each previously described general type, in various sizes and colors. It is not, however, necessary to have scores. For average purposes, a dozen is adequate. Tantalizing motion imparted by the angler often makes up for lack of a particular lure. Colors should run from red-and-white combinations, through yellows or oranges, striped and spotted, scale finishes, etc., to dark browns, greens, and black, to meet light conditions, clear or cloudy water conditions, etc. Frog finishes, lures imitating natural foods, are also good.

And so we come to the time to put all this tackle together and see what we can do with it. Certainly there's nothing difficult about putting it together. But most would-be fishermen, seeing the array of shiny gadgets for the first time, are a little awed at the prospect of just what's going to happen when they try to make it work. Have no fears! Bait casting is so simple to learn that an hour after you purchase the tackle you can be flinging flashy lures around with the best of them—and catching fish, too. By the end of your first season, if you consciously try to improve your technique, there's no reason why you cannot be a real expert.

To use bait-casting tackle, hold the rod in your right hand, thumb on the reel spool (line) to hold reel from turning, lure dangling about six inches below rod tip. Bring the rod straight up and back over the shoulder, swing it sharply forward. On this forward sweep, when the rod reaches vertical, release thumb from reel spool. The lure momentum thus carries line from the reel. The rod is brought on forward as the lure sails out. The lure is stopped by thumb pressure on the spool.

To avoid tangles (backlashes) it may be necessary with some reels to keep light thumb pressure on the spool during the cast. Most reels have set-screw devices, however, for adding or subtracting pressure of a built-in drag. This is adjusted according to the weight of the lure being used.

At the end of the cast, the rod is transferred to the opposite hand, and reeling is begun. For beginners, if trouble comes from the lure plunging downward directly in front of you, imagine on the next cast that you are going to attempt throwing the lure straight up and outward with the cast.

Side casts, and underhand casts, sweeping the rod

around from waist height, or below, also have their uses. It is bad form, but at times advantageous for placing the lure in spots under brush or obstructions. In all bait casting, emphasis should be upon accuracy rather than distance—very long casts are seldom necessary—and upon manipulation of the lure in a manner to entice the fish. Try all variations of lure action, cast accurately to the best spots for fish to be lying—and you cannot possibly avoid becoming a *successful* plug-rod angler!

FLY-FISHING

FLY-FISHING is unquestionably the most artistic form of angling, for it requires the lightest, most dainty tackle. How many times you'll hear a nonfisherman say, as he watches an expert fly caster, "If I were going to fish, that's what I'd like to do." Or, very often, you'll hear people who've been fishing for years say, "I'd give anything to fly-fish, but I don't believe I could ever learn."

It is true that the equipment of the fly caster looks extremely complicated, and that his work appears to call for a fine and expertly precise hand. But it is also true that there has been in past years much snobbery among fly-fishermen, especially in the East. They have propagandized the sport as prohibitively difficult for all but the few. This is pure nonsense. There is no more thrilling or satisfying fishing method, nor one in which the catch can prove more exciting. Fly-fishing gets the most out of a fish. It makes little fish seem big. And though it is more difficult than other angling, it is only a little more so. It takes closer attention to detail and more careful and thoughtful practice. That's all.

13

First you have to understand, *basically,* how fly-fishing differs from other angling. To say it simply, here's all there is to it. First, a heavy line, ordinarily designed to float, is used. Second, the *line,* not the lure, is cast. This is necessary—and is the reason for the heavy line—for the lure is almost weightless. Therefore the line must carry it to its destination.

Obviously, with such a setup, it is tremendously important that tackle be properly *balanced;* otherwise casting would be either terribly difficult or impossible. Though each portion of the tackle should be in fine proportion for best results, the most important item is proper line size and weight as related to rod weight and action.

Now, keeping those elementals in mind, let us look briefly at the various individual items of tackle.

FLY LINES are of two kinds: level (same size throughout) and tapered. Single-taper lines become gradually smaller, therefore lighter, on one end only. Double-taper lines become gradually smaller for about 12 feet on each end. Special purpose lines have several tapers at various points. Most popular of these is the torpedo-head, with an extra-heavy section preceding the final taper to handle heavy, wind-resistant flies, such as bass bugs. For all other average purposes, double taper is best. When one end wears, it can be reversed on the reel.

Fly-line sizes are indicated by letters, i.e., size "A" (heavy) down to "H" (very light). Tapered lines thus are lettered, for example, "HDH." Synthetics (nylon, etc.) have about replaced enameled silk. Many of these new lines float without greasing ("dressing"), are cheaper, wear better than the older silk.

FLY RODS nowadays are mainly of glass (excellent, economical) and split bamboo (usually expensive). They weigh from 2½ to 7 or 8 ounces, are 6 to 9½ feet long. The longer, heavier ones are in modern disfavor. Rods differ greatly in action, from very limber throughout, to limber only at the tip, to stiff. A good all-round rod is 8½ feet, 4½ ounces. For heavy bass bugs or small spinners some anglers prefer a heavier, longer rod.

Matching Line To Rod				
ROD	LINE			
	TAPERED	LEVEL	TAPERED	LEVEL
4 to 5 ozs., 8½ ft.	Stiff action: HDH	E	Soft action: HEH	F
3½ to 4¼ ozs., 8 ft.	" HEH	F	" HFH	G
2½ to 3½ ozs., 7½ ft.	" HEH	F	" HFH	G

For heavier, longer rods, compute accordingly. If extra-heavy lures are to be cast, boost line size one letter, but be sure rod will stand the weight.

LEADERS also are level or tapered. Popular lengths are 7 to 9 feet. Limp nylon is the most used material. Heavy

Leaders	
SIZES	TENSILE STRENGTH, NYLON
8/5	5 lbs.
9/5	4½ "
0x	3½ "
1x	3 "
2x	2¼ "
3x	1¾ "
4x	1¼ "

bugs require level leaders, light flies call for tapered leaders. The chart on page 15 gives average breaking strength of most modern leaders.

There are larger, and smaller, sizes. The ones given are most popular. Sizes of tapered leaders are named from the smallest, or tippet, section of the leader. With proper handling of tackle, a 3x tippet will land a much larger fish than its tensile strength indicates. The smaller the flies used, the finer the leader tippet should be.

The purpose of leaders is to be inconspicuous to a fish. When fish are extremely wary, or water is low and clear, leaders up to 12 feet, very fine tippet, are used to eliminate line shadow near the fish. They are, however, more difficult to cast. Leaders have a loop at the end that is to be attached to the line. A similar loop should be made at the end of the line. Attach the leader by: (1) shoving line loop through leader loop; (2) then bringing opposite end of leader through line loop, and pulling until the two loops are tight.

FLY REELS are of two kinds: single action and automatic. They serve only as storage space for the line. Fish are not reeled in by them but played in carefully by stripping in line with the left hand. The single action is lighter, holds more line, and balances better. The automatic takes up slack line with the press of a lever. Choice is a matter of personal opinion, but automatics rarely hold more than 30 to 35 yards (lengths of tapered lines). When "backing" (spare bait-rod line beneath the fly line to allow long runs of large fish) is needed, a large single action reel is necessary.

FLIES and their innumerable patterns are the items

which lend romance to fly-fishing. At first they may seem confusing, but after you've become acquainted with their names and their exciting histories—who invented them, how they happened to be tied in those particular patterns, etc.—they become more than dainty and beautiful bits of feathers. They become rather personal possessions, with much sentiment attached to their ownership and use, and to the memories of fine catches and exciting battles that match each size and pattern.

Here, as with fly-fishing in general, it is necessary to understand first the fundamentals of fly patterns and their uses. Supposedly, of course, flies match natural food forms, and thus they fall into two general categories: dry and wet.

Dry flies are simply floating flies. For stream fishing, they are usually fished upstream. Fly dressing—a very fine oil or mixture of paraffin and naphtha which can be purchased in any tackle store—is lightly daubed on the fly to help it float. After each upstream cast, a coil of line is taken in by a winding motion of the last two fingers, then the thumb of the left hand. Thus, slack line is taken up as the fly floats back toward the caster. Winding motion should match speed of stream's flow. Current "drag" on the line must be avoided, or the float of the dry fly will look unnatural to a fish. Between casts, the fly is dried by several "false casts." When it begins to become waterlogged, first dry it carefully by pressing cleansing tissue around it, then re-dress it. When purchasing dry flies, look for stiff, abundant hackle. These float best. Wingless dry flies are especially excellent floaters.

Wet flies are underwater flies, tied more sparsely than

17

dry flies. They are usually fished downstream. There are several types. Regulation wet flies represent drowned mature insects. Nymph flies represent the immature of water insects. Streamers and bucktails look in action like small minnows.

The usual procedure is to cast the fly down and *across* the current. The fly then tumbles down, circles on a tight leader toward stream center, then is retrieved in short jerks by "stripping in" line. The majority of strikes come as the fly straightens out in the current. In dry-fly fishing, the strike is *seen,* and the fisherman sets the hook. With wet flies, the strike must either be felt, or the line must be closely watched at the point where it enters the water. The fisherman must then strike at the slightest evidence of a tightened line. With all flies, the strike should be dainty, quick but firm, otherwise the leader will be snapped.

Streamers are fished like regulation wet flies, but the line is stripped in to imitate the action of a small minnow working against the current. Nymphs should be allowed to tumble loosely through the pools.

All wet flies can be productively fished upstream. They should merely be allowed to tumble. But this is difficult. Strikes are hard to detect. Best results with all flies come from fishing them slowly, covering the water thoroughly, and *quietly*.

When fly-fishing on lakes, all action either of dry or wet flies obviously must be imparted by the caster, for there is no current. Dry flies, from tiniest to large "popping" bugs for bass, are cast, left inert for a few seconds, then twitched enticingly. Wet flies are allowed to sink, then worked tantalizingly as in stream fishing.

There are hundreds of standard, named fly patterns.

A good range of colors from light to dark and a good range of sizes from large to small are all any fisherman needs. Rules of thumb: light flies for dark days, dark flies for light days; gaudy flies on little-fished waters, somber, conservative flies on heavily fished waters; match as nearly as possible in size and color the food fish appear to be taking, or the food in greatest abundance; keep a few large, gaudy flies handy, but let your stock in trade be small flies in light and dark grays, browns, grizzles, and yellows.

Probably the greatest initial puzzle for fly-fishermen is getting the fly properly attached to the end of the leader. Fishing books describe and picture all kinds of fancy knots. Don't let these confuse you. Just remember that by using a fine, tapered leader and trying to cast properly you are setting out to do everything possible to keep a fish from guessing that this bit of food has a catch in it. Thus, don't spoil it by a big, crude knot that will stand out plainly as a warning.

There is one simple knot which is the best you can find. Others may allow the fly to be removed and changed more easily, but they will also weaken your leader tippet in the process. So, since this fly knot is going to be the difference very often between getting your fish or breaking your hair-fine leader as you strike or having a fish snap it as he wildly leaps and bends your rod, tie it on as follows and you'll have no worries. Run the leader tippet through the fly eye. Now tie a standard slipknot in the tippet. Push the fly through it, and pull the loop tight on hook shank back of eye. Carry a pair of snippers for cutting flies free in changing, and for trimming excess leader left when you tied the slipknot.

Line Dressing is important for lines requiring it. The line is strung out, wiped clean with a soft cloth, then lightly greased. The dressing is then worked in with the fingers and the excess wiped off. When, in casting, the line begins to sink, get out of stream or boat, stretch the line out, dry it a few minutes, wipe it, and re-dress it.

Playing Fish on fly tackle is a careful art. Suppose you are fishing a dry fly. Suddenly there is a splash as a small trout or a bluegill sunfish grabs at the fly. You set the hook. Your long rod immediately bends in a whiplike arc. Indeed, catching an average sized sunfish with such light tackle can be as thrilling as hooking a five-pound bass on heavier tackle. And the fish fights longer because you dare not put too much pressure on him. He must be allowed to wear *himself* out.

That is what makes playing your fish a careful business. Your rod should be held in position to take the pressure with its bending—but not all on *tip*. The line must always be kept taut, but with no undue pull or quick jerks to snap the fine leader. When the fish runs, give line. When he eases up, strip quickly. The trick is never to let the fish get a breather but to keep on him only such light pressure as the leader will bear. Eventually he wears himself out. By expert handling, even four-pounders can be landed on tiny 4x leaders. Never attempt to lift a fish from the water by the leader. Use a landing net—but only after he is thoroughly beaten. Otherwise he'll run when you're holding line and rod with one hand and putting net down with the other. Thus he can snap the leader. And remember always to net fish *headfirst,* and carefully. Many a dandy is lost because the net was splashed and scooped carelessly, or because the net touched his tail first and "spooked" him.

MISCELLANEOUS NECESSARY ITEMS of fly-fishing equipment are as follows. Fly boxes: of plastic, aluminum, or cedar, some even with magnets to hold flies when the box is opened in the wind. Leader boxes: either of aluminum with pads for moistening gut leaders or simply poplin pouches with divisions for leaders of various sizes. For stream fly-fishing, creels: of wicker or canvas. The wicker creel keeps fish best, but is awkward and heavy to carry. Canvas creels are perfectly adequate, and much less cumbersome. Landing net: for stream fishing should have short grip, deep, waterproofed bag, front of the hoop squared rather than rounded. The landing net is slung over the shoulder on an elastic cord. Collapsible landing nets with light metal frames serve well and handily.

HOW TO CAST FLIES—that is the big question which makes the beginner quake in his waders. He's certain he'll never be able to get it going smoothly. And many an old hand has for years had trouble with his casting. The beginner should first put aside his fears, for he thereby removes a big psychological hurdle. Fly-casting is simple if thoroughly understood, and practiced. The old hand with fly-casting troubles undoubtedly is doing some one thing wrong, from habit, and is thereby spoiling an otherwise smooth and perfect cast. Follow the simple basic technique outlined below, and you cannot possibly go wrong.

The rod, not your arm, must do most of the work.

21

Your left hand always holds and manipulates the line. With your right hand grip the rod butt firmly, thumb extended *on top,* reel below the hand. Keep elbow low and fairly close to body. Strip off line with left hand, keep bringing rod up and forward in false casts until about 25 feet of line are lying out in front of you on the water.

Now take in enough line with the left hand so that the line lies straight. Keep the rod pointed straight ahead and raise it to about a 30-degree angle. With speed and power increasing during the upswing, sweep the rod up with *wrist* motion, *imagining* that you are going to *try* to throw the line straight up (an impossibility). Thus you avoid a too-low backcast and the fault of bringing the rod too far back. Its tip at the end of the backcast should be above and behind you at no more than a 20-degree angle—in other words, little more than directly above and behind your shoulder —and its motion should stop *abruptly.*

Pause now until the line sweeps back in a high U and almost straightens out behind you. The forward cast must begin at that instant. Push the rod up a bit, outward in front of you, and forward, beginning the motion firmly but slowly, increasing speed and wrist power, aiming *above* where you wish the fly to alight, thus straightening the line in the air, and dropping it lightly, without splashing. Cast should end with rod in the position from which backcast began. Don't bring it too low to the water. Practice timing the pause properly between backcast and forward cast; be sure the forward push is with the wrist, that the spring of the rod is throwing the line, that you are not attempting to throw it yourself—and in short order you will have mastered the exciting art of fly casting. That's honestly all there is to it!

SPINNING

DURING the past few years spinning has found such favor among American anglers that it has all but swept away the bait-casting or plug-casting outfit in many areas and has made tremendous inroads also into the world of the fly fisherman. Most beginners nowadays start with spinning. It is actually an old method, introduced from France and England. It is an exciting and deadly way of taking all game fish.

The way in which spinning came about, and the reason it has so appealed to American anglers since its introduction, not only makes interesting reading but helps you to understand what this fine sport is all about. It has long been known that the largest, oldest, and wisest fish would often more readily strike small, deep-running minnow-like lures and natural (live) baits than either flies or large plugs and spoons. The problem for American anglers has always been how to cast successfully these "in-between" lures. They are far too light to be really efficiently handled even by the longest and most limber of bait-casting rods. And though many of them have been advertised as "fly rod" lures, these tiny plugs, small metal spinners, spoons, and minnows of the spinning enthusiast are actually much too heavy to be properly fished with the fly rod.

Spinning, therefore, is a method—introduced from Europe—for doing the job properly. A cross between bait and fly casting, it is based upon the use of an extremely light bait-casting line, a very limber rod longer than the bait rod, shorter than the fly rod, with soft action *throughout* instead of only in the mid and tip sections, and with a near-frictionless reel whose spool does not revolve but from the *end* of which the line runs off at the slightest pressure, as from a conical thread bobbin.

The spool of the spinning reel, therefore, must have its axis pointing *along* the rod rather than at right angles to it. The line is put back on the reel during the retrieve by a metal finger, activated by a turn of the reel handle, which grips the line, revolves about the spool, guiding the line smoothly into place for the next cast. There are variations of this principle in some of the late spinning reels. But originally the procedure as described was, and is, the foundation of spinning.

You may be wondering now, just what advantages such crazy fishing tackle can possibly have. Why should it be better for its purpose than any other tackle? The answers make pleasant news for anglers everywhere. For example, since the line runs off the reel with almost no friction, backlashes—those tangles of line on reel which often occur just when the fish are hitting best, and which take an exasperated angler valuable minutes to straighten out—are virtually impossible. In addition, extra-long-distance casts are easy, a life saver when trout streams or bass lakes are low and clear, or for covering big water thoroughly. Besides, you can get pinpoint accuracy even at long distances, for your casting is nearly effortless, giving you opportunity to concentrate on dropping a lure exactly where you want it. Such accuracy adds fish to the creel. The big ones, logically, always lie in the spots most difficult to get a lure into. As if these advantages were not enough, it may be added that the deepest holes, always big-fish hangouts, may be fished by lures whose actions are not inhibited by sinker weights used to take them down deep. And this sort of fishing may be done with less chance of snagging.

Obviously, by now, you're going to want to try your hand at spinning one of these days. Following are compact descriptions of the various items of tackle you'll need.

SPINNING RODS are almost all made of glass nowadays. They are either one-handed (6 to 7½ feet, 3 to 7 ounces) or two-handed (for heavy work or for salt water, longer and heavier than the former). They have either a straight cork grip with reel-locking rings (for open-faced reels) or offset grips made to take so-called closed-face reels. Rod guides, especially the butt guide, are very large to eliminate friction.

REELS are of two main types, open-faced and closed-face. The first usually is cranked left-handed, has spool in sight, with bail pick-up. The second usually cranks right-handed, operates by a push-button device under the caster's thumb, has the spool covered. Both types have a slip brake with adjustable tension to avoid line breakage when playing a fish. Spinning-reel spools are easily changed. Extra spools, fitted with lines of differing sizes, may be had for making quick changes to heavier or lighter lines. Reel capacities differ, usually running to about 200 yards of 6 or 8 pound test line. Spool should be filled only to the lip. Closed-face reels generally take less line, 75 to 100 yards if it is fairly heavy.

Spinning, or "Thread," Lines run from 2-pound test on up. Some are braided (example: of fine nylon filaments), some are of single-strand (monofilament) nylon. Choice is an individual matter.

Leaders are not ordinarily necessary with spinning lines, but some anglers use a length of *heavier* material near the lure to absorb wear. Some also use short leader with swivel at each end to avoid line twist, a hazard of sorts in spinning.

Lures are of infinite kind and variety, most of them metal, many of them revolving, or with heads which revolve. When these last are used, they should be bought in pairs, one revolving left, one right. By changing from one to the other, ruining of the line by twisting is offset. All small "fly rod" plugs and spinners, as well as small fly-and-spinner combinations may be considered spinning lures. Spinning lure weights are from ⅛ to ½ ounce. Choices should be made as with flies and plugs—a good sprinkling from small to large, colors ranging light to dark, actions varied. No one can guarantee which will be best at any given time. Only by trial and success can the most effective ones for any given circumstance be chosen.

One of the advantages of spinning tackle which should make it appeal to a very wide audience is that it is perfectly adapted to the casting of natural baits such as frogs, worms, minnows, crawfish. Thousands of anglers enjoy fishing with real bait much more than they do with artificial lures. But trying to get the bait to the best places, or to cast it and reel it in slowly— a most effective method—has until now always been extremely difficult, if not impossible, to accomplish properly and easily.

MAKING THE CAST is rather similar to bait-rod casting, except motions are more delicate, and whip of rod rather than lure weight does the most work. Procedure: Hold rod in right hand; disengage line pickup; grip line against rod with right forefinger (or hold thumb on push-button, depending on reel type); raise rod and with quick light flick of wrist make the cast, releasing line at end of sweep. With left-hand reels, the rod is not shifted to left hand at end of cast. Most closed-face reels require the same shift as in bait casting. Left-hand reeling, though awkward at first, soon becomes easy. Cast length is controlled by lifting rod tip and turning reel crank, which activates bail or gear to take up line. Hook setting should be done with delicacy in ratio to the lightness of the line.

Tackle Chart

LURE	ROD			LINE		
	FEET	WEIGHT, OZ.	ACTION			
to ¼ oz.	7 -7½	3¾-4¾	medium	3-6 lb. test,	75 yds.
¼ to ⅜ oz.	6½-7½	6 -6½	stiff	6-10 " "	125 yds.

For large fish the heavier tackle should be used, regardless of lure size.

There is just one caution to be observed if you are new at spinning. Don't expect that it is going to be absolutely infallible. It has been much publicized as a foolproof fishing method. But we anglers are a little inclined toward exaggeration! Spinning isn't foolproof, but it is unusually productive, exceedingly sporty, and most exciting.

BAIT- AND STILL-FISHING

THERE ARE many anglers who look down their noses these days at the fellow with the cane or brush-cut pole. But bait-fishing, whether with the bait in motion or dangled motionless from bank or boat, is just as enjoyable today—and just as solidly productive—as it was hundreds of years before artificial lures became popular. It must be admitted, too, that the old-timers with their bank poles, or drifting slowly around the lakes in their old scows with long poles thrust overside, very often come in at dusk with a bigger string and bigger fish than the fancy anglers with heaps of paraphernalia.

Surely everyone knows the traditional tackle for still-fishing: the long cane or hand-cut pole; the braided ("salt-and-pepper") line about the same length as the pole; the light float or bobber of cork, wood, or plastic and easily adjustable for depth; the sinker; the baited hook.

With no aspersions cast at this fine old outfit, it might be well for its advocates to note that still-fishing with bait is often more effective, and unquestionably more sporty, when the cane pole is replaced by bait-casting, spinning, or fly rod. As has been said, spinning rods now allow easy casting and retrieving of natural baits. Plug rods are excellent for trolling bait or the effective, wriggling cut pork chunks or strips which can be purchased in tackle stores. Fly rods are excellent for still-fishing either from bank or boat.

Though almost everyone knows at least a little about

still-fishing, it might be well for us to review its mentals briefly. In still-fishing, a quiet approach oars and when dropping anchor is, along with knowledge of the habits of the fish sought, the first requisite. Proper depth is paramount. Rule of thumb: Bait should be fished just above bottom or weed beds. Or try various depths until bites materialize. Drift fishing—i.e., drifting until bites occur, then dropping anchor—is a refinement. "Skittering" baits along the surface or "plunking" them among lily pads, etc., at the end of the long cane pole is also extremely effective. Slow-motion trolling, with bait dangled several feet below surface by bobber and trailing fifty feet or so behind boat, is a killing method.

Many still-fishermen fail to choose proper sized hooks for the fish they're after. Hooks should always be selected according to the mouth of the fish sought, and its size and strength. Bass, pike, walleyes, catfish, crappies, and yellow perch have large mouths compared with their size. Trout have medium-large, narrow mouths. Sunfishes of all species have small mouths.

Hooks are of many styles. Choice is a matter of personal opinion. Standard, long, and short shanks can be had in most hook styles. Standard, heavy, and light hooks of any size may also be had. This means the wire used is either of standard size, heavier than for that size, or lighter. Always buy good hooks. See that they are sharp. A small hone is an excellent addition to the tackle box.

There are larger, and smaller, hooks. They are numbered and measured accordingly. See next page for proper hooks for average fresh-water bait- or still-fishing.

Sinkers also go by numbers, and are of many types.

Hook Sizes, Standard Length Shank
(Hook eye is not measured)

HOOK NO.	DIAM. OF WIRE, INCHES	LENGTH, INCHES
12	.021	7/16
10	.024	9/16
8	.027	11/16
6	.030	13/16
4	.033	15/16
2	.037	1⅛
1	.039	1¼
1½	.041	1⅜
1/0	.043	1½
2/0	.045	1⅝

The best are: light, split shot of various sizes, which is pinched on the line; medium or heavy, clincher type, also pinched on line; adjustable, equipped with rings for spacing adjustment; bell (dipsey), for casting, trolling, etc., fitted with swivel; keel type, weight off balance to avoid line twisting when trolling with spoons and spinners. Rule of thumb: Place sinker one foot above bait and use short nylon monofilament leader or, for toothed fishes, wire leader.

The bait-fisherman should be sure to place his bait properly on the hook for best results.

Natural Baits

BAIT	HOW TO HOOK
Minnows	under back fin; through *both* lips
Angleworms	under collar, then loop and let dangle
Frogs	through both lips, or use patented frog harness
Crawfish	through tail
Grasshoppers	threaded, tail first; vertically through back
Crickets	same
Aquatic nymphs	under collar

(These last are hellgrammites, dragonfly larvae, etc., found under stones in running water.)

There are many other natural baits, including all manner of larvae and grubs. Rule: Use bait most abundant in vicinity; try off-trail baits when standard ones fail.

MISCELLANEOUS EQUIPMENT

STREAM FISHERMEN should have waist or armpit waders, either boot-foot type or stocking-foot type. The first is most popular, least trouble. Hip-boots are nearly worthless in many streams but are good equipment for bank and boat fishing under wet or stormy conditions.

For very large fish, a gaff hook replaces the landing net. The fish is simply brought alongside and hooked with it. A "tailer" (device with handle and wire slip noose for landing fish by tail) is more humane.

Every fisherman, regardless of his methods, will want a tackle box. See that its bottom is seamless, therefore waterproof, and that its lock has a catch to save spilling contents when you forget to fasten the snaps and pick it up by handle. Every fisherman also needs a good supply of sinkers, hooks, swivels, leaders, floats, etc., in various sizes and of various types. Small plastic boxes (available in the stores) for each of these collections keep the tackle box neater and the items where you want them.

Pliers, knife, hook disgorger, wire cutters are *must* items for the tackle box. Reel oil and reel pouches keep reels in good condition. Mosquito dope should always be in the box. For boat fishermen a fish stringer keeps catch in top condition. Sunglasses and long-billed cap are valuable comfort items, and a kapok life preserver cushion for boat fishing is good accident insurance.

31

There are literally thousands of other gadgets advertised and displayed for the fresh-water fisherman. Though many are handy and useful, those covered in this chapter, plus a thorough knowledge of the fish and their habits, are all anyone needs to put fish in the skillet, photos in the album, and priceless memories in the mind!

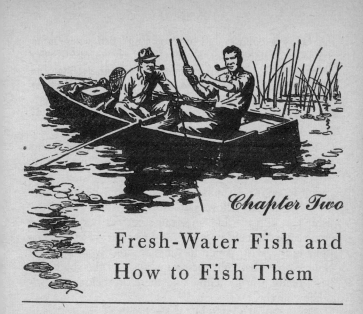

Chapter Two

Fresh-Water Fish and How to Fish Them

There are some six hundred species of fresh-water fish in American waters. The more the tyro might dwell on that matter, the more he might begin to have misgivings. How could anyone ever know the habits and prejudices of *that* many species? And surely he would need such knowledge in order successfully to attach any of them to his line.

Luckily, by far the greater share of those six hundred species are merely forage fishes. They serve as food for the larger sporting and eating fishes. There are a few of these, of course, such as chubs, dace, the sprightly and swift little fall fish, which are what might be termed "in-between" species. They fill a big gap at times, serving many a country lad as "catching" fish when none better is available. Yet, all told, they are hardly worthy of being called true sport fishes. Some others, such as the several herrings and whitefishes, though excellent "eating" fish, are not well adapted to summer rod-and-line fishing and are therefore rarely fished, and seldom considered true game fish.

The salt-water shad, however, one of their distant relatives which runs up fresh-water streams in the East to spawn each spring, was found some years ago congenial to taking a sunken fly with colored beads strung ahead of it. This fellow is an awesome battler, and shad fishing, a difficult and uncertain sport at best, has become an extremely popular fad in very restricted locations in the East. Again in some coastal rivers the salt-water striped bass fills the spring place of the shad. But he is really a briny fellow and therefore belongs in another chapter.

Thus, out of that total of six hundred species, only fifty-odd species in the U. S. form ninety-nine per cent of the annual fresh-water catch, and these are the gamesters this chapter will briefly touch. To make fishing seem still more simple for the beginner, of these fifty-odd species not more than twenty are of top importance —but among these few are found the very best gamesters to be had anywhere in the world! And for that reason we as anglers, whether expert or inexpert, can well be proud of them.

The easiest way to get to understand our various sport fish and to get a quick line on how best to catch them is to divide them into general categories. These classes, of course, have nothing to do with science but are merely for the sake of an angler's convenience.

Thus, we can split up all the so-called "angler's fishes" into three general classes, as follows: game fish; pan fish; rough fish. It must be understood, too, that this lumping of species together in such a manner is not meant to be derogatory to any angler's favorite. There are many fishermen who consider the catfish, for example, to be just about tops. In our three classes, however, he would not be placed in the game fish division. That's no insult to him. The classes serve only as a simple means of separating our species as to size and general tenacity.

NOTE: *It must be understood, too, that fishing methods greatly overlap among these three categories. The bass, for instance, which falls among the game fishes, is often caught in the same manner as the bluegill, a pan fish, and vice versa. Brief fishing-methods sections are given for each fish or group of closely related fishes. But to avoid constant repetition, methods are designated only generally. For example, fly-fishing and still-fishing differ greatly from plug casting (or so-called "bait casting") and spinning. But bait casting and spinning, which often utilize the same types of lures, are fundamentally much alike. Thus when* plug-casting tackle *is mentioned, it can be taken to mean either bait casting or spinning. Likewise, if both spinners and flies are mentioned, the reader is expected to assume they may be used with any outfit that will cast them and is preferred. Bait fishing or, by the same token, still-fishing can be accomplished with any outfit the angler likes best to use.* Heavy plug-casting rods (*see* Pacific Salmons: Methods) *can also be construed as* two-handed spinning rods.

GAME FISH

As GENERALLY used, the term "game fish" refers to the *larger,* more *active* and voracious species which strike both natural bait and artificial lures avidly and viciously, and whose muscular stature, swimming ability, and tenacious spirit cause them to fight valiantly when hooked.

THE SALMONS undoubtedly head the game-fish list for superlative sporting qualities. To every angler, the possibility that he may one day have an opportunity to fish them is an awesomely glamorous thought. Their restricted ranges, however, keep them actually relatively unimportant to all but a small minority.

Atlantic Salmon: Found in coastal streams from Cape Cod north. Streamlined, muscular, bluish above, silvery below, with x-shaped black spots. Deep-notched tail. As with all trouts and salmons, small head, spineless fins, fleshy adipose fin above near tail, scales very small. Food mainly small fish. Lives in sea, fished during its runs up fresh-water streams spring and summer to spawn. Averages to 20 pounds.

Methods: Fly-fishing, with large streamers, and at times large, or small, dry flies. When purchasing flies, specify salmon flies, for the several special patterns are best. Outfit must be fairly heavy. Special sturdy salmon rods may be purchased. Gaff, or tailer, is needed, also plenty of backing line on reel. Fish with extreme caution, in the deep pools. Don't strike too fast. This is a careful, persistent angler's game.

Landlocked Salmon: Sebago, or Lake Salmon; simply the landlocked form of Atlantic Salmon. Back usually darker; spots *double*-x'd; fins, scales, eyes larger. Averages to 10 pounds. From northern New England north, in deep, cold lakes. Food mainly smelts; some insects. A smaller subspecies in northernmost portion of range.

Methods: During insect hatch periods fly-fishing with dry flies is successful, for the fish then feed near surface. Mainly, however, deep trolling, using plug-casting tackle, Monel metal line, a live smelt for bait, with or without metal spinner ahead of it, is the ticket. Troll very slowly, with bait right on bottom. Don't strike quickly. Let fish take bait and run. Fishing is usually best just after ice goes out in spring.

Pacific Salmons: These include the Chinook (King), Silver (Coho), Blueback, Dog Salmons, and several others. First two most important to sport fishermen. Both range from northern California north. Chinook: averages to 50 pounds up. Bluish black-spotted above, silvery-pink to reddish below. Top of head very slightly concave. Silver: averages to 10 pounds. Color similar but fewer fin, head, and tail spots. Head more convexly arched. Both taken during spawning runs up coastal fresh-water streams. Food, mainly fishes.

Methods: The big Chinook are fished in salt-water bays, brackish river mouths, and torrential fresh-water coastal rivers. *Heavy* plug-casting rods are needed, preferably with light salt-water reel, and 150 to 200 yards line at least 30-pound test. Lures, large spinners and spoons, blades 2½ to 3½ inches long. River trolling is done by attempting to row upstream, zig-zag. Current actually forces boat *downstream,* slowly. Lure is maneuvered into likely holes and pools, current giving it motion. In bay and river-mouth fishing, bait—herring, smelt, strip of salmon belly—trolled, or cast slowly and retrieved, deep, often works successfully.

Silver salmon are fished by the same methods, but tackle can be much lighter, either regulation bass plug-casting outfit, or fly rod of about 7 ounces with large-capacity reel holding 50 yards of backing in addition to fly line. Spinners and spoons can be smaller also, though 2½ inch blades are satisfactory.

Although the fabulous Chinook is a wonderful thrill to an angler, he does require special, heavier tackle and a lot of know-how. The smaller Silvers, on the other hand, furnish some of the most exciting and amazing fishing it is possible to find in the U.S., and for a great many average anglers. For anyone living on the West Coast, or having vacation access to western salmon waters at the proper times, this sport should be a *must*.

THE TROUTS are extremely active fishes of cold, clear waters, predominantly swift streams of the northern U.S. There is probably no angler anywhere who does not aspire at least to become a trout fisherman, and who does not think of this group of fish as the most romantic and exciting of any which can be caught. But many anglers, hearing that trout are extremely wary, exactingly selective and temperamental in feeding habits, and just plain difficult to deal with, hesitate to try. It is true that trout are as described above. They can be the most exasperating of fish, or again they can in a twinkling decide to favor the most careless angler. That is what makes trout fishing such sport. Too, the scenic beauties of the trout streams add much to the heady pleasure of this endeavor. The careful and well-schooled trout fisherman will always take more trout than the novice, but that should not keep the novice from fishing for trout, for if any angling might be described as glamorous, this is it!

Though trout may be readily taken with bait, spinning lures, and, when large, on spoons and plugs, they are the pride and pets of the fly-fisherman. Trout are spectacular fighters, extremely beautiful, and delicious. Light-tackle trout fishing is, without exaggeration, exactly as it has always been publicized—the most fascinating and thrilling of all fresh-water fishing endeavors, whether the game be seven-inch brook trout or ten-pound steelheads.

Brook, or Speckled: When small, deeply notched tail; when old and large, tail squared. These latter often called "squaretails" and "coasters." Swift, cold streams, some lakes; from the Smoky Mountains north, New England, Michigan, Minnesota, etc. Planted from California northward. Back mottled black-green, brilliant blue-circled red dots on sides, belly fins often crimson or orange, with white edge. Averages 7 inches to several pounds. Food mainly insects and small minnows.

Rainbow: California and Rocky Mountain states to Alaska, planted widely throughout brook trout range. Habitat same, but will tolerate warmer waters. Greenish (pale) above, silvery below, many black dots on head, back, sides, tail; diffused pinkish swath laterally on sides. Color varies greatly. Averages 7 inches to 10 pounds. Food as above.

Brown, or Loch Leven: Introduced many years ago from Europe. Present range about like Rainbow, but tolerates still less congenial habitats. Size, food, methods as for Rainbow. Dark greenish-brown with brick-red to orange spots. Color varies light to dark.

Cut-Throat: Black-spotted Trout. From California north. Color variable, much like Rainbow, but with red stripe, from whence name comes, under jaw.

Dolly Varden: Red (or red-spotted) Trout. From upper California north. Close relative of Brook Trout. A dark fish, brownish and greenish, with pale back spots, red side spots white encircled. Belly fins with white edges. Most voracious; less selective than other trout. Averages a pound; grows to 20-odd.

Western Trouts and Races: There are dozens of trout *races* about which scientists are uncertain. Some, like the Golden of the Sierra, have been named as actual species. Most are considered simply variations of the Rainbow, Dolly Varden, or Cut-Throat, which have developed race color characteristics because of isolation in certain lakes and streams. Examples: Piute, Rose, McCloud River, Silver Trouts. Some, again like the Golden, inhabit only extremely high altitudes. Food, general habitats, average size are about the same as for previously described species.

Methods: The dry fly is undoubtedly the most popular and exciting method. It works best during those weeks when insect hatches are at their peaks. Success with it depends upon using a fly which closely resembles the surface insects upon which the fish are feeding at the moment. This can be ascertained by watching rising trout, noting the kind of insects on the water, and matching them in size and color of fly. Sometimes trout feed in the pools, sometimes in swift, shallow runs, sometimes over sandy, unrippled shallows. Note where the majority of rises are, fish that type of water, casting over the "rises."

Wet flies often take more, and larger, trout, for the

large, old trout feed predominantly near bottom. Wet flies, streamers, nymphs, are also usually the best bet very early, and late, in the season.

Bait, most often angleworms, sometimes small minnows, will catch all kinds of trout. It is successful when water is high, or roily, since at such times flies often are useless. The very largest trout are most easily taken thus, either with bait alone or with a small spinner a few inches above the bait. Split shot sinkers are used, pinched on the leader, and the bait cast quietly into holes and pools. Grasshoppers and other insects also make good bait.

In addition to slow, patient, careful, quiet fishing, a thorough knowledge of trout habits is the most important item toward success. They always lie head to current, take advantage of every smallest hiding place and current break—behind rocks, at log ends, under bank edges, etc. When trout fishing, observe minutely every detail of the particular stream and the habits of the fish in it and you will add to your success.

Steelhead and Kamloops: Doubtful if either is a true species. Probably only variations of the Rainbow. The first denotes the very pale, silvery Rainbows which have gone to sea and returned to fresh-water streams for spawning; usually large, 3 pounds to well above 20, and exceedingly strong from salt-water environment. The Kamloops is mainly a lake fish, of the upper Columbia River basin. Both look rather similar to true Rainbows. The Kamloops has recently become famous as a planted fish in Lake Pend Oreille, Idaho, where it grows to upwards of 40 pounds.

Methods: The Steelhead is a tough, wild battler, the "Atlantic Salmon" of the Pacific Coast. A spawning run occurs in one or more rivers almost every month in the year. Fly-rod tackle: 9-foot, 6- to 7-ounce, firm-action rod; large-capacity reel; torpedohead taper line about size GAF, with 75 to 100 yards backing; leader at least 8-pound test; flies wet and streamers in good variety, for fish often very selective. Patterns preferably local favorites. Fishing is done in orthodox wet-fly manner. Bait of salmon eggs also excellent method. Fly-fishing tackle can be used during runs of smaller fish, up to 5 or 6 pounds. In winter, the steelhead runs are of larger fish. Tackle: 6-foot plug-casting rod, stiff; large-capacity reel; 15-pound test line; 2-foot level nylon leader; hook size No. 2 to 4, baited with salmon eggs, which can be purchased, bottled. Artificial lures: spoons, spinners, cast, as with bait, down and across current, retrieved slowly.

The big Kamloops trout is fished in lakes by trolling with heavy plug-casting tackle, using spoons and spinners, or bait of live smelts, etc., fished deep.

Lake: Togue (New England), Mackinaw (Great Lakes), Namaycush (Canada). New England, Great Lakes, north and west all the way to Alaska. Dark grayish, with paler mottling. Large, cold, very deep lakes. Will eat almost anything. Averages 3 pounds, to 50 up.

Methods: In very early spring, at ice-breakup, and again in fall spawning, lake trout are near the surface. They can then be taken by shallow trolling with large spoons and spinners or bait of smelt or other small fish. The remainder of the year lake trout live in *extremely* deep water, where trolling as above but using Monel metal line and heavy sinkers is indicated. Tackle should be heavy, rod very stiff, reel large-capacity. A "fisherman's thermometer," for taking water temperature at various levels, is essential. The laker stays in water of 40 to 45 degrees. Fish precisely at that level, and you will catch him. Another good method is to ascertain the 40-degree level, let down a large spoon to that depth, jig it erratically up and down.

Graylings: Closely related to the trouts. Two species: Arctic and American, the first from British Columbia north, the second (once abundant but now extinct in Michigan) mostly in Montana, Idaho. Mountain streams. Food, mainly insects. Troutlike in shape, but scales prominent, mouth small, tender. Color bluish above, paler to gray downward, iridescent bronze-blue; a few dark spots; beautiful, high dorsal fin colored and spotted with red, green, purple, orange. Averages a pound.

Methods: There is little grayling fishing left in the U. S. proper. Alaska, however, is excellent. Light trout tackle is used, with dry flies preferable. The grayling is one of the finest of dry-fly species, but he calls for a discerning fisherman, for he takes the flies very lightly. Flies should be small, and for the most part dull in color, fished quite as in average trout fishing. These fish offer one of angling's highest thrills, not only because of their rarity nowadays, and their striking beauty, but because of the spirited battle they give.

THE BLACK BASSES rank on the whole next to the trouts. To be sure, many anglers would place them above the trouts. There has long been a friendly but loud debate between the two angling factions as to which should have top place. The black basses are actually *more* important than the trouts to the average angler because of their wide distribution, variety of habitats, non-selective feeding habits, and readiness to strike any and all lures at almost any time. The wide range of the bass is in particular responsible for his popularity among a great majority of anglers. The basses are spiny-finned, elongated, but deep bodied, silvery and green-ish to bronze, and belong to the sunfish family. They are excellent eating, except in a few instances when taken from lakes where too much decomposition of plant life on the bottom may lend them a rather muddy taste.

Largemouth: "Trout" or "Green Trout" in the South. Almost all of the eastern half of U. S., Gulf states, widely planted on West Coast. All manner of fairly warm, weedy lakes and large, slow streams. Food mainly fishes, insects, frogs. Not particular. Averages 1 to 4 pounds in North, anywhere up to 20 in South. Distinguished from Smallmouth by upper jawbone, which extends well past eye.

Smallmouth: Present, greatly by planting, in all but Gulf states; color often more bronze than above, and with diffused mottlings; clearer, colder waters than Largemouth, more often in streams and large, rocky lakes. Average size about the same as Largemouth, but never grows to as large a maximum. Upper jaw extends no more than even with back of eye. Food, as above, but due to general habitat shows preference for craw-fish.

Strains and Races: There are several other basses, about which scientists are often undecided. These in-clude the Kentucky, or Spotted, Bass, and the Red-eyed Bass. The average fisherman will have no reason to distinguish them from the two main species.

Methods: Bass food is so varied, and the fish so voracious that many successful methods may be used. Plug casting is by far the most popular, for the most part with surface and shallow diving plugs, except in very hot weather, when the fish lie deeper and deep divers and sinking plugs are necessary. Even in hot weather, however, if fished at night, when the bass come into shallows to feed, surface plugs are perfect. Cast near weed and lily pad beds, around stumps, logs, overhanging trees; try various types of retrieve, slow, fast, erratic.

Fly-fishing with large dry flies and especially with cork-bodied "bugs" called "popping bugs" is sensationally successful. Early morning and late afternoon and evening are best for both plugs and bugs. The bug requires tackle as follows: 5- to 7-ounce rod, forward taper (torpedohead) line. Cast as with plugs, let bug lie momentarily, then twitch it enticingly.

Bait-fishing, with frogs, crawfish, minnows, night crawlers (large angleworms), big grasshoppers, etc., is also most productive. In the South, 5-inch shiners, fished three or four feet deep with a bobber, using a casting rod, still-fishing near water hyacinths, is a killer method. In ordinary bait-fishing, the boat is moved slowly, quietly along the weed beds, the bait "plopped" near the weeds in short casts and retrieved slowly.

When bass lie deep, often spinners and spoons, with or without bait or pork chunk attached to the hooks, will do big business. However one chooses to fish them, they are always game, and their leaps and "tail-walking" make them sensational battlers.

THE PIKES, though not especially good eating, have for centuries been favorite prizes of anglers around the world because of their size, viciousness, readiness to smash bait and lures of many kinds, abundance, wide distribution, and brutal battling qualities. They are long, slender but heavy-bodied fishes, with huge, wide, cruel-toothed mouths, and the dorsal fin set far back toward the tail, strong swimmers who rove widely but are given to lurking in weeds and rushing their prey.

Muskellunge: (spelled variously), colloquially "Muskie." Mainly ranging in New York, Michigan, Wisconsin, Minnesota, and into Canada. Largest (in U. S.) of the pikes. Brownish to greenish, with dark mottlings on lighter background and with lower half of gill cover scaleless. Averages 10 pounds up to 50 or more. A lone wolf of cold, clear (but weedy) lakes and slow rivers. Food mainly fishes, large suckers preferred.

Methods: The muskie is the tiger of fresh water. And what a thrill he is for those who get a chance at him! Heavy-duty casting or spinning rods are usual, with line of 15- to 18-pound test. Muskies are caught by casting large plugs, spinners, spoons, or spoon and large bucktail-fly combinations over bars, underwater logs, along the reedy shallows near deep drop-offs, etc. In streams, muskies often lie over sand bars in the current, awaiting food. These are good places in which to cast. Trolling is as popular as casting. Bait-fishing is perhaps more popular and effective than using artificials. Good-sized suckers are the preferred bait. They are either cast, slowly trolled, or fished in likely places from a drifting boat. Be sure to have plenty of line: the muskie is a fabulously strong, hair-raising battler. He also has sharp teeth, which means a short wire leader is required to keep him from cutting the line.

Northern Pike: Many colloquial names, but this is

the only *large* true *pike* of American waters. Across most of northern U. S. and Canada and Alaska. Dark greenish above to silvery below, with light spots on dark background (a subspecies in Minnesota silvery without spots), fins often reddish. Averages 1 to 10, up to 40 or more pounds. Great variety of waters, deep and shallow, rocky and weedy. Seldom in swift streams. Food mainly fish.

Chain Pickerel: Eastern Pickerel, Jack. Maine to Florida to Texas, planted elsewhere. Averages up to 5 pounds. Greenish gold, with darker "chainlink" markings on sides. Weedy lakes, ponds, slow streams. Food, minnows and frogs mainly.

Barred and Mud Pickerels: Eastern half of U. S. and lower Canada. Neither is important as a game fish, but listed simply to avoid having them confused as young of other pikes. Dark or light greenish. The first has definite dark vertical bars, the second dark scrawled, wavy lines. Each grows only to about 1 pound weight, 14 inches length. In weedy ponds, swamp streams, etc., but often in waters with the larger pikes.

Methods: The pikes have been much maligned as game fishes in many quarters, but actually are excellent fighters, vicious strikers, and, except for many small forked bones, good eating. Tackle should be about the same as for bass, a bit heavier in waters where very large pike lurk. Lines of 12- to 15-pound test are adequate, and short wire leaders should be used. Fairly large, minnowlike plugs, various metal spinners, spoons, and spinner-bucktails are the best lures. Pike are almost always found in, near, or over weed beds. Diving lures and sinking lures take more fish than surface lures. The erratic retrieve often used when bass

47

fishing is not necessary with pike. The lure should move enticingly but fairly slowly and steadily, either when casting or trolling. Trolling is especially success-ful, for it allows coverage of a great deal of water where the lone-wolf pike may be lying in wait.

Bait-fishing is very effective. Frogs, even worms, will catch pike, but minnows of good size are by far the best bait. These can be trolled, cast, drifted from a boat, or simply still-fished. An excellent method on small lakes is to place a bobber about four feet above the big min-now, pay out thirty or forty yards of line behind the boat, and row slowly. In bait-fishing, pike often mouth a minnow for some time before attempting to swallow it. Thus, never set the hook immediately when the bob-ber goes down. Often, in still-fishing a wait of five min-utes is necessary before the fish takes down the bobber and keeps it down. In waters where pike do not run above five pounds or so, great fly-fishing sport may be had, using a large streamer fly, sunk deep and retrieved in long, slow sweeps. In handling landed pike, be care-ful of their vicious teeth.

Don't be misled by snobbish anglers who disdain the pike as a game fish. No finer sport has ever come along in the world of angling than fighting it out with a string of these old tackle smashers when they're hitting. There is no reason whatever for any angler to make excuses for his enthusiasm for the various pikes as game fish.

Walleyed Pike and Sauger: Not pikes, but members of the perch family. Included under this heading simply because they are among the larger game fishes. Ex-tremely difficult to distinguish between Walleye (Pike-perch, Blue, Green, Yellow Pike, Pickerel, Jack Salm-on), and the Sauger (Gray, Sand Pike). The Sauger averages about a pound, the Walleye 1 to 8, up to 20. Elongated, chunky fish, greenish or yellowish to gray with diffused mottling. Spiny and soft portions of dorsal separate. Strong teeth. Unmistakably identified by "bleary," "blind-appearing" eye. Clear, cold, large, deep waters, over most of Canada, eastern and midwestern U. S., south to Alabama. Food 90 percent fishes; mainly nocturnal feeders. A delicious "eating fish."

Methods: Walleye fishing is best in spring and fall, on dark, windy days, or at night. Sometimes in the evening walleyes come into shallow water over sand bars to feed on minnows. They may then be taken with spinners or even fly-rod and streamer flies. By and large, however, walleye fishing is most successfully done by drifting or trolling with plug-casting outfit of bass weight, using deep running spinners and spoons, with or without bucktail or a bait of night crawlers. Or, as is perhaps most popular of all, trolling, drifting, or still-fishing very deep with minnows up to four inches long. Bait, or lure, should be kept near bottom, over bars, gravel bottoms along deep weed-bed drop-offs, etc. When one fish is caught while drifting, trolling, or casting, the spot should be fished hard, for walleyes are school fish. Often a limit can be taken without moving.

Walleyes and saugers are a lot of fun to catch, and some of them put up hair-raising battles. As a rule, however, these fish are inclined to hit and then sulk on bottom until brought alongside by force. At that moment, though, look out. One may decide to run. Many a line has been broken thus!

PAN FISH

MORE PAN FISH are caught annually than all others combined, yet there is no good definition of a pan fish. In general, the term means our smaller, more easily caught species, the mainstay of still-fishermen. This should not, however, reflect upon their stature as sport fishes. Several are most exciting diminutive battlers on light tackle. All are superbly abundant, and excellent eating. The majority belong to the sunfish family.

THE TRUE SUNFISHES make up the main body of this family and are by and large our most important pan fishes, having among their numbers several species swiftly becoming recognized as startlingly doughty gamesters when properly fished. All are short, compressed, extremely deep-bodied fish, old, large specimens appearing almost "round." Of the 35-odd U. S. species, the majority are too small or rare to be important. Six species, however, go from ½ pound to 1½ pounds in weight, are very abundant, wide-ranging, and exceedingly game. All roam in small loose schools; where one is caught a limit may usually be taken.

Bluegill: Bream, Redbreast; Great Lakes region throughout Mississippi Valley, widely stocked. Color variable, dark greenish, darker vertical stripes, throat rust to yellow, ear flap long, squarish, and black. All manner of lakes, sometimes in slow streams. Averages up to a pound, 8 to 12 inches. Food predominantly insects.

Common Sunfish: Pumpkinseed; eastern half of U. S., stocked elsewhere. Color variable, but brilliant, throat yellow, wavy blue cheek lines, body dark greenish flecked with yellow, ear flap short with long red spot below. Same habitat as bluegill but more often in sluggish streams, weed-choked ponds. Averages a bit smaller than bluegill. Food more worms and tiny crustaceans than bluegill but some insects.

Yellowbreast: Tobaccobox, etc., Maine to Florida and Gulf states, casually around Great Lakes. Greenish-black, paler belly, throat yellow, long, narrow black ear flap. Large eastern streams and bayous. Averages to a pound. Habits similar to bluegill.

Long-eared Sunfish: Mississippi Valley, North Carolina, southward, extremely abundant in Kentucky. Throat and belly yellow, body dark with much blue and orange in spots and lines, ear flap very long, wide, and with either blue or red border. Large, clear streams, clear lakes and ponds. Averages to a pound. Food predominantly insects.

Shellcracker: Red-eared Sunfish; most abundant in South—Florida, Alabama—but also west to Rio Grande, north to Illinois. Runs larger than other sunfishes (maximum to 2 pounds or more); body predominantly blue or green, ear flap with wide scarlet border. Large, warm lakes, streams, bayous. Food mainly small mollusks, crustaceans, also insects, minnows.

Green Sunfish: Creek, or Blue Sunfish; most of eastern half U. S., stocked on West Coast. Brownish to green, blue cheek spots, pale border to black ear flap, often with thin crimson border. Favors small creeks, although also in lakes, ponds. Smaller than the other sunfishes given here, maximum 8 inches, ½ pound. A good "fill-in" pan fish where others may be scarce.

Methods: These sunfishes are popularly still-fished with cane pole and worms. Catching them is a simple matter of finding a spot near weed beds, usually in no more than four to fifteen feet of water, where the small, loose schools congregate. Early morning and from midafternoon until dusk are usually the best times. Other baits that are just as good, often better, than worms include small grasshoppers, crickets, bee larvae, catalpa worms, etc. Since these fish have small mouths, hook size should be small. For this kind of still-fishing, usually done with a small bobber, replacing the cane pole with a fly rod and dispensing with bobber adds greatly to the fun. A short nylon leader and split-shot sinker will make for better fishing by fooling the large, wise old specimens.

Lately many fishermen have discovered that these sunfishes are also excellent little game fishes when fished with light fly-rod outfits. Bluegill, pumpkinseed, yellowbreast, long-eared sunfish, all take flies, both wet and dry, with alacrity and fight brilliantly. Small "popping bugs," especially those with rubber legs, are particularly deadly. In the North, spring brings the best bug fishing. In the South, it is often good the year around.

Wet flies and tiny spinner-and-fly combinations are productive early in the season and when the sunfishes are feeding deep. These, cast, allowed to sink near stumps, logs, weed beds, and channels where the schools swarm, then retrieved very slowly, will make good catches. In the North, when the sunfishes have retired to offshore waters during hot weather, wet flies work well, especially spider patterns. Let them sink slowly and naturally, watch the line carefully and strike at the slightest twitch of it.

The southern shellcracker, being entirely a bottom

feeder, is difficult to catch on flies but is a fine fighter who is easily caught on worms or small pieces of fish. An excellent method of making good catches of this large sunfish and several others in the South is to push the boat into floating hyacinth and "wild lettuce" beds and beat the tops of the vegetation with an oar. Small crawfish and worms are in their roots. These are shaken loose and sink. Now, with an oar, sweep a fishing hole in the floating vegetation and drop a baited hook into the hole. Regulation weighted ice-flies as used in northern winter fishing, jigged up and down near bottom in such a location, will catch fish when bait is unavailable.

All told, a tremendous amount of high sport can be had with the sunfishes if light tackle is used. Truly, they are *game!*

THE SUNFISH FAMILY, a very large one, includes several other important pan fishes not numbered among the *True* Sunfishes. All have the generally typical "sunfish" outlines, and are gregarious, small-school fish.

White Crappie and Black Crappie: Known by more than fifty colloquial names; extremely abundant and important to thousands of anglers; White Crappie native from Great Lakes to Gulf, more abundant southward; Black Crappie range likewise but more abundant northward. Widely planted, even to West Coast. Narrow, deep-bodied, "fan-finned" fishes, greenish and silvery flecked with green-black spots, the Black Crappie much darker. Mouths large, but tender. Two species distinguished as follows: Black, snout length roughly equals eye diameter; White, snout length greater than eye diameter. Tolerant of muddy, weed-choked waters, but found in all manner of lakes, ponds, bayous,

large or sluggish streams. Food predominantly minnows; fair amount of aquatic and surface insects.

Methods: Crappies are popularly still-fished, using
either worms or minnows for bait. Minnows of 1½
inches are by far the best bait. Drift fishing is one of the
best methods, letting the boat drift, with minnow over
the side on cane pole or fly rod, until a bite materializes.
Since these are school fish, a limit can usually be taken
where the first bite occurs. Near weed beds, around
stumps and logs, in channels and bayous, are the best
spots.

Crappies often stay during the day in water deeper
than for the True Sunfishes. Still-fishing must often be
done as deep as 15 to 25 feet. Toward evening, however, especially when insect hatches are on during spring
and early summer, they come up to the surface. At such
times two main methods of fishing with artificial lures
are most successful. One of these is fishing just beneath
the surface with the small plugs and spinners of the
spinning enthusiast. The other is fishing with a dry fly.
When dry-fly fishing, the strike should not be made too
quickly as the fish takes the fly. Crappies suck down a
fly peculiarly. A quick strike will take it away from
them. However they are caught, crappies must be
handled gingerly, for their mouths are very tender. The
hook tears free easily. But again, however they are
caught, they are good sport, and well deserve their
tremendous popularity.

Rock and Warmouth Bass: Both also called Goggle-
eye, Red-eye, many other names. Both have chunky
bodies, basslike but deep as the true sunfishes. Large
mouths. Both inhabit sluggish, often muddy, weed-filled
streams and lakes with submerged logs and stumps.

Iris of eye red. Rock Bass brassy colored with dark mottling and lengthwise rows of dark dots. Warmouth more mottled and without rows of even spots. Rock Bass has six spines in anal fin, Warmouth three. Both range throughout Great Lakes region south to the Gulf, but the Rock Bass only east as far as the Alleghenies. Warmouth more abundant southward. Food: crawfish, worms, minnows, insects. Not choosy.

Methods: These two species are not especially good fighters. Although they often strike viciously, they give up quickly when hooked. Rock Bass will often hit dry flies in the evening, but usually only the smaller ones are thus caught. The best method of fishing is to use bait, and the best all-round bait is the angleworm. Fine sport may be had with both these fishes, especially in places where other species are absent because of sluggish, muddy waters. A fly-rod outfit used to drift a worm under sunken logs, etc., in sluggish rivers gives good sport and makes a maneuverable rig for such fishing. Still-fishing with worms in ponds and weedy lakes, or in the cypress bayous of the South, either with cane pole or fly rod, is most effective. Keep bait near or on bottom, toss it against a stump and let it sink, or drop it at the mouths of hollow sunken logs. No. 4 to 6 hook can be used. These fellows run as high as 2 to 3 pounds, though the average is much smaller.

Sacramento Perch: A West Coast fish of the basin of the San Joaquin and Sacramento. Shape similar to Rock Bass but deeper in front of body. Color sometimes silvery, sometimes almost black. Scales have sawtoothed edges. Grows to 18 inches in length. No longer abundant. Mentioned here merely to identify it as a member of the sunfish family occasionally caught in the West. Its food and the methods of fishing for it do not differ from those of the True Sunfishes.

OTHER PAN FISHES come from several quite unrelated fish families. Three are extremely important over fairly wide ranges, two in restricted areas.

Yellow Perch: One of our most abundant and important pan fish. Delicious eating. Easy to catch. Called Striped, Ringed, Red Perch, etc. Chunky, elongated body. Yellow to greenish, with seven dark vertical stripes. Dorsal fin separated into spiny and soft portions. Great Lakes to Pennsylvania and Carolinas, west to Dakotas, widely planted, even to Pacific Coast. All manner of ponds, lakes, streams, except swift streams. Average one-half to one pound weight. Food mainly minnows, but not selective in feeding habits.

Methods: Can be taken at times on dry, wet, or streamer flies. Spinning enthusiasts will find small silvery spinners and spoons effective. For the most part, however, perch are still-fished, with worms or small minnows as bait. They bite well all through the season, but in spring during spawning runs, especially around the Great Lakes, where they enter small creeks, ditches, and large streams by countless thousands about mid-April, yellow perch fishing is sensational. Either fresh or salted minnows may be used, with a small split shot for sinker. Limits are quickly and easily taken in from one to six feet of water. During the summer, in lakes and ponds, fish minnows near weed beds in from five to fifteen feet of water. Tails of small crawfish also make excellent summer bait.

White Bass and Yellow Bass: Deep-bodied, fairly elongated fish, silvery, with rows of darker spots forming horizontal lines along the sides. Yellow bass more yellowish and greenish than silver, with the dotted lines broken and alternated along the lower sides. Dorsal spines long, very stiff and sharp. White bass range from the Great Lakes to Texas, widely planted. Yellow bass found mostly in Lower Mississippi Valley; important game fish only locally, for its abundance is spotty. It is a school fish mainly found in large rivers. The white bass likes very large, deep lakes, large streams, runs in large schools. Both species grow to several pounds, but average one or two. Minnows favorite food of both.

Methods: These fish are good scrappers, but are very erratic in their habits. They may be caught by the dozens one day, then "lost" for weeks at a time. The more important white bass feeds very deep, or very shallow, depending on his whim, is often extremely wary, especially on bright days, roams widely. Accepted way of fishing is to troll deep with minnows, with or without added silvery spinner. When a strike materializes, the boat is stopped and concentrated fishing is begun. The schools often move swiftly, however, and the alert fisherman must follow.

Wet flies and streamers often take white bass in streams. During stream spawning runs these lures or small plugs and spoons work well. During warm weather schools are easily spotted, morning and evening, surface feeding. A chugger-type plug, with a small weighted yellow or white "jig" tied behind it on 18 inches of monofilament, is deadly on these schools. Simply cast, "chug" the plug, and the fish strike the leaping jig. Large white (or yellow) bass fight well, are excellent eating. The big impounds such as TVA lakes are hot spots for them.

White Perch: A deep-bodied, greenish to silvery fish of salt and brackish water which runs up eastern coastal streams to spawn, and has become landlocked in certain New England and New York lakes. Weighs from one-half to two pounds. Food mainly minnows, also crustaceans and insects.

Methods: In coastal stream mouths, or in ponds and lakes where this fish is landlocked, spinner-and-bait combinations (either minnows or worms) cast around rocks in shallow water and retrieved slowly with fly rod or light plug rod will do the trick. Wet-fly fishing is sometimes effective, if the fly is cast upstream and allowed to tumble back. But this is difficult. Still-fishing is the most popular method. The fish takes the bait in a peculiar manner and is rather difficult to hook. A good eating fish, however, where found in numbers to make fishing it worth while.

Smelt: The fresh-water smelt of New England, where it long ago became landlocked, and of the Great Lakes, where it was inadvertently planted some years ago, was originally a salt-water species which ran up fresh-water streams in early spring to spawn. A slender, silvery fish, dark on the back. Maximum length about 10 inches, averages smaller. Food almost entirely small minnows.

Methods: Smelt are not usually thought of as hook-and-line fish except for ice-fishing. They stay very deep, as a rule, in summer and winter both, are sometimes caught by still-fishing deep in summer with small minnows. Mainly, however, the delicious smelt is taken by "dipping" during its fabulous spring spawning runs in streams, large and small, running into the Great Lakes. The "sport" is extremely popular, and consists of finding out when the run has started, choosing a location near the stream mouth, and dipping up the tiny fish in nets, buckets, or by whatever means are available. The runs are usually made at night. When they are heavy, it is easy to "dip" a bushel of fish in no more than an hour.

ROUGH FISH

THESE EMBRACE dozens of species both large and small. Many of them are almost worthless as food fish, although some are very good eating. Some are sensational battlers, but the majority are mediocre fighters. All are heavily fished in certain sections for lack of species more game. In general, the so-called rough fish should not be looked down upon. They are excellent substitutes for the better game fishes when and where necessary, and many an angler claims one or another of them as his top favorite, regardless of other, more game fishes.

THE CATFISHES are the most important rough fish. There are many species, running in size from the small black, brown, and yellow bullheads (called horned pouts in the East) to the very large blue and yellow "cats" of the Mississippi Basin and the South. All catfishes are delicious eating, even though spurned by many anglers. The small bullheads rank, in fact, as some of our very best "pan fishes" where the skillet is concerned. On the whole, the various catfishes are heavily fished and highly popular with and important to a great majority of fishermen.

There is little reason to identify the various species,

with the exception perhaps of the rather game channel cat. This trim fish, which sometimes hits an artificial lure, is pale silvery pinkish on its sides, with dark speckles scattered indiscriminately. All catfish have long chin "whiskers" or barbels, very strong spines in their pectoral and dorsal fins, and are scaleless. They have large, flattened heads, tough mouths, and all-inclusive appetites.

Catfish range almost everywhere over the U.S., up to the Rockies. They have also been introduced on the West Coast. All of them are bottom feeders, and though they will bite in the daytime, they feed most heavily at night, and are therefore much fished at night. Still-fishing is the method. Some fishermen run "trot lines"— long sunken lines with numerous hooks dangling— down a sluggish stream or across a lake. These are left set for weeks, looked at every day, and the catch taken in. Other anglers build a fire on the bank of a muddy river or lake at night, fish from shore, the pole laid in a crotched stick until a slow bite materializes. In large, slow midwestern rivers catfish enthusiasts drift slowly downstream, dropping bait into bank holes, under logs, etc.

Bait can be anything from dough balls made of flour, water, and absorbent cotton to hold them together, to liver, cheese, spoiled meat, partly decomposed chicken entrails and blood, to angleworms. Many catfishermen claim a bait must be sickeningly rotten and "high" in order to be successful. Whatever bait is used, the fishing should be done right on the bottom in muddy, weedy, or debris-strewn locations. Tackle should be matched to the size of the catfish species known to be abundant in the waters fished. Care should be taken in unhooking the catch, to avoid being badly gashed by the fin spines.

CARP, of which there are three rather similar species now in the U.S., are not native, but were introduced from Europe. They are fish of muddy, weedy waters, are today found in many U.S. waters where they root out vegetation and, by their bottom mud-rooting in search of small plant and animal food, muddy the waters dangerously for other, more desirable fish. Carp are dull brownish or greenish in color, with large scales, short barbels on the upper jaw, single strong, saw-edged spines in the dorsal and anal fins, toothless mouths. The back is highly arched, the body deep. Average size is one to five pounds, but much larger specimens are abundant.

Carp range nowadays, unfortunately, almost everywhere in quiet waters of the U.S. They are very prolific and drive out other fishes. In some sections where it is legal, they are speared in shallow, marshy waters at night, from a boat, using a jack light in its bow. As a rule, however, carp are still-fished, with dough balls used as bait as for catfish. They are exceedingly wary fish, timid biters. Stout tackle should be used, for carp are very strong, and hard battlers for a short period. Most successful still-fishing method requires a quill float (bobber). This is a bobber made of plastic or from a large feather quill. The slightest tug registers.

When taken in fairly clean waters, flesh of the carp makes good eating. But carp have acquired bad table reputations because of their abundance around sewer mouths and in other undesirable locations.

THE SUCKERS are elongated, large-scaled, brassy to greenish or silvery fish easily identifiable by their mouths, which are underneath, rounded, toothless, and thick-lipped for their job of sucking up bottom mud in which minute food organisms live. There are many species, all of them rather sluggish, soft-fleshed fish full of small forked bones. When they come from clear, cold water, they are fair eating, except for the nuisance of the many bones. They cannot, however, be considered either especially good sport or eating fish.

Some species, such as the northern Redhorse, which has reddish lower fins, the common sucker, a yellowish-silvery fish, and the white and black suckers (called mullet around the Great Lakes region), are popularly speared in spring when they run up streams and small creeks to spawn. Spearing is usually done at night, the spearman carrying a gasoline lantern with a reflector, the light of which shows the fish plainly if the water is reasonably clear.

Still-fishing is the only successful method of angling suckers. Worms or dough bait can be used. It should be fished on bottom. Most sucker species seldom run over a maximum weight of 5 pounds, averaging much smaller. Thus, almost any tackle will do. There is little reason to fish for suckers except in sections where other, better species are unavailable.

THE FRESH-WATER DRUM, or sheepshead, is the only fresh-water member of the large salt-water croaker family. It is a silvery to silvery-pinkish fish, back highly arched, dorsal fin partly spiny, partly soft, eyes large, toothless mouth set back under a blunt, rounded snout. It ranges widely, from Montana to Pennsylvania south to the Gulf, feeding mainly on fresh-water mussels (clams), which are pulverized by its heavy, flat throat teeth. The drum makes a croaking or grunting sound when caught, and also at times underwater. It is found in many large, sluggish rivers and lakes. In certain sections of the lower Mississippi Basin it is especially abundant. Average size is up to 5 pounds, but grows much larger, to 50 pounds or more.

The flesh of the drum is fairly good. It cannot be considered an especially game fish, although large specimens fight fairly well for short periods. Still-fishing, on bottom, near muddy shoals and banks, with mussels, worms, or fresh-water shrimp for bait, is the best method.

THE BOWFIN, dogfish, or mudfish, is one of the toughest and most ancient fish of fresh water. It is nearly worthless as an eating fish, but is mentioned here because of its awesome fighting qualities and because, though it is an undesirable species, it inhabits many muddy lakes and sluggish streams throughout most of the U.S. as far west as the Mississippi Basin. In the South it is especially abundant.

It is a long, heavy fish, with soft dorsal fin running from a few inches behind the head almost to the curiously rounded tail. Brownish-green in color, with a black spot often surrounded by orange at the upper base of the tail. Mouth large and very heavily toothed. A most tenacious fish which will put up with all kinds of discouraging habitats—ponds almost dried up, etc. Very difficult to kill.

The bowfin feeds on anything which is available, especially other fishes. It is often caught while casting plugs for bass, or while still-fishing with minnows or worms for other species, and battles far more wildly and strongly than any bass. Seldom does anyone purposely fish it. It should be handled carefully, for its teeth can inflict a bad wound.

THE BURBOT, cusk, fresh-water ling, or fresh-water cod, member of the cod family of salt water, ranges widely across the northern half of the U.S. Long, olive-and-black marbled, chin barbels, very long, low dorsal and anal fins. Appears scaleless, but has tiny scales embedded in the skin. Feeds on fishes and spawn, lurks in deep holes in large lakes and streams.

The burbot is fished primarily by ice-fishermen. It is caught incidentally in summer while still-fishing deep for other fish, such as lake trout. A fairly game fighter, but not an especially good eating fish, although quite popular for that purpose in the Northwest.

The burbot rounds out our survey of the fresh-water angler's targets. If there is any one thing which might be said regarding the setting apart of all these species or naming one as better than another, it is this: Remember that fishing is for fun, for *sport,* and for all kinds of anglers. What is great sport for one fisherman may be poor pickings for another, and thus, all in all, a broad view is necessary. No fisherman can be snobbish about his fish or his fishing and still get the most out of it. Learn how to catch all the different species and how to get the best out of each, tackle-wise, and you'll have good sport and good fishing, whether you wade the finest dry-fly streams for trout or doze on the bank of some sluggish river while a catfish nibbles at your still-fished bait.

Chapter Three

Ice-Fishing

*O*ne of the most surprising developments of recent years in the field of angling is the tremendous popularity accorded to fishing through the ice. This ancient endeavor practiced by Indians and Eskimos was for years merely a semi-sport followed by a few old-timers in rural areas. But with the advent of better outdoor winter clothing, and the high pressures of swarming anglers upon the resort sections, more and more people began to discover that winter is an excellent vacation time, and that fishing through the ice is an exciting, invigorating sport that fills a big lull in the outdoorsman's year.

The first thing to do if you intend to go ice-fishing is to check the laws of the state where the fishing will be done. Nowadays every ice-fishing state has regulations which apply, and in some few places ice-fishing is taboo. Once you are familiar with these widely differing laws, you'll have to get a license, just as for summer fishing. However, if you have a summer fishing license, it will generally be valid until the first of the year. Once that matter is taken care of, you can make your plans easily and quickly. Following, in brief, compact form, are sections covering the various facets of ice-fishing, from clothing to tackle to how to find and catch the fish. As you fish, you'll work out many tricks and kinks for yourself, but if you go armed with the information given here, you can't help coming back with a good catch the first time out, even if you've never fished before!

KEEPING WARM is of first importance. Only top-grade clothing combinations are here recommended. Outer garments: down filled; heavy virgin wool. They should eliminate drafts, i.e., parka instead of coat-and-cap, pants which tuck in boots. Under garments: long; loose-fitting woolen underwear; turtleneck wool sweater; *several* light wool shirts not one heavy one; several pairs of loose-fitting, long socks.

Never wear cotton or waterproof garments. The trick is to choose clothing that "breathes"—holds body *heat,* but lets moisture escape. Footwear: sheeplined aviator's boots; rubber-bottom, leather-top pacs; felts-and-rubbers. Mittens: soft oiled leather, fleece lined. Cheap work gloves and towel should be carried for handling tackle and drying hands.

On thick ice, a fire may be built, with fire bed of green sticks to ease melting. Where wood is unavailable, use folding grill and sack of oil briquettes, or pocket gasoline stove with small can of gas. Other small ice-fishing stoves are now available also. A gasoline lantern set in the sled box gives much heat, will dry gloves, etc. A tarpaulin folded beside the fishing hole keeps feet dry, and warmer.

Windbreaks can be made by stapling canvas six feet high by fifteen feet wide to several six-foot stakes. Set the stakes in a half circle, spudding holes and pouring water around them. Later they can be spudded loose. Or, to the side of your sled affix brackets into which poles of a miniature canvas windbreak are slipped. Sit on the sled, stove beside you.

Fishing shanties should be small if constantly moved, large only for permanent installation. The most sensible way to choose shanty type is to inspect several and incorporate the best features of each.

Plywood, tarpaper covered, makes a warm shanty. Small wood or coal stoves give superlative comfort. Runners are a must; so also are floor trap doors to keep holes from freezing overnight. See that the door and windows are weathertight. Wall seats should fold up to make room for extra ice holes. *Long* seats serve as bunks when you stay overnight. Shanties should have windows on every side, so tip-ups set anywhere outside may be watched. Build sliding covers, however. The shanty should be darkened when fishing or spearing inside.

SAFETY in ice-fishing is paramount. It requires only good sense, refusal to take chances, and a sound basic knowledge of ice. Here are the rules.

Start fishing *only* when *solid* ice has formed. Avoid: ice above fast-flowing water; protruding stumps, etc., where freezing pressures may cause melting; hummocks, which may be thinly crusted; snowy patches on early ice; sagging ice; discolored patches, which may mean mush from bottom springs; ridges, caused by buckling which often leaves open crevices.

Shallow lakes freeze quickly, deep lakes slowly. Leave the latter, and swift streams, for midseason.

Look out for: ganging up of too many fishermen when fish bite furiously; rural ice-cutting operations. Cut holes no larger than 7 to 12 inches in diameter, mark them with a stick when you're through. Don't expect everyone to do likewise. On a heavily fished lake, watch your feet.

Use boot calks. A fall, when you are carrying gear, can be serious. A sled and a coil of rope are indispensable. These may help save a foolhardy buddy. On big water, carry a compass to avoid trouble from blizzard or fog. If you're shantyless, get off the big lakes before dark. On bright days, wear sunglasses.

If you *must* use a car, use extreme caution with it. Lay out your season route beforehand, on foot.

Never continue ice-fishing toward breakup time. On large waters, a flow may trap you. Lastly, don't let everyday ice-fishing breed overconfidence. It leads to taking chances!

LOCATING THE FISH simply requires a solid knowledge of their cold-weather habits. These differ radically from summertime mainly because of food and oxygen restrictions. Since winter oxygen is limited, nature has arranged that fish slow down, thus requiring less food.

The food, happily, will always be where the most oxygen is; and thus, so will the fish. This means near weed beds, bottom springs, flowing inlets and outlets, deep holes where summer-stored oxygen may be abundant, open holes, cracks in the ice. But you have to know something else about the fish, too. Since they have slowed down in their metabolism for winter, many species will now need less food and thus will take only *very small baits. And,* at exact pinpoint locations of abundant oxygen.

The black bass bites well in early winter, slows down to hibernation at very low temperatures. Bluegills shun summer baits, bite best during mild temperatures, and only on miniature morsels. Crappies stay active, feeding on small minnows, until late winter. Then they switch diet to infinitesimal organisms, thus bite poorly. Yellow perch, walleyes, pike, pickerel, and deep-water fish such as smelt, lake trout, cusk, whitefish are least affected by cold. They are, therefore, the mainstay of winter fishing.

Bright days speed up the release of oxygen by underwater plants. Thus, bright days mean more oxygen, and lively fish. Therefore, weed beds where ice is snow covered won't draw fish as will those beneath clear ice. However, clear ice and active fish mean they're more wary. Thus, dark days, either clear or snowy ice, and your hole cut to let sun and oxygen through often mean good catches. Fish will swarm to the hole.

Deep lakes with ragged, weedy shorelines make good ice-fishing locations. Their oxygen storage space is greatest, and the minimum weed beds concentrate the fish. Fish in large, shallow, weedy lakes are difficult to locate. With oxygen abundant everywhere, they may be *anywhere.* Small, shallow, weed-choked lakes are seldom good except early in the season, for decomposition overbalances the release of oxygen. Fish become lethargic. If heavy snow covers such ice long, they die.

The best way to pinpoint good winter fishing spots on your chosen lake is to make close observation in summer of weed-bed locations, bottom contours, inlets and outlets. Also take depth measurements. If you haven't had an opportunity to do this, or if you are on a strange lake, surrounding shorelines will allow you to guess in winter with fair accuracy. For example, swampy shorelines usually mean a slow, muddy drop-off, plentiful weeds; steep, hardwood-covered shorelines usually indicate steep gravel or sand drop-off. Reeds thrusting through ice mean a shallow, sandy bottom.

DEPTH at which you fish is extremely important. After the hole is cut, take a sounding with sinker and line. Rough sinkers, or weighted hooks, will bring up weed samples if any are present. Such information is important to success. By lying flat, covering your head, and peering through the hole, you can often see surprisingly deep, even observe if fish are present.

Cut the first hole in fairly shallow water. If results are nil, keep moving deeper. If you still don't connect, try *extremely* shallow water. On a heavily fished lake, follow the experienced crowd; or look for signs of scales and blood where several holes have been chopped.

TACKLE, which becomes our next concern, is quite different from summer tackle, and if you're new at ice-fishing you'll be inclined to wonder what on earth such a conglomeration of apparently reasonless gadgets can be good for. But don't be fooled. Inexpensive, makeshift ice-fishing tackle will often be much more effective in terms of fish caught than a whole tacklebox full of shiny, sleek summertime gadgets. The fact that ice-fishing must be done on a *vertical* plane, without the opportunity to cast or fish on a semi-horizontal plane as in summer, forces it to look as it does and keeps it simplified. Following is a short discussion of everything you will need for various types of ice-fishing. Most of this tackle is now available in stores, thanks to the upswing in ice-fishing interest. If you don't find what you need, you can easily build your own.

A sled should come first, for easy transport of duffel. Build a removable box for it, with compartments for holding equipment. An ice spud is next. This is simply a chisel with a long handle. It can be purchased, or one can be made by welding a wide-bladed chisel to the end of five feet of three-quarter-inch steel pipe. A two-piece spud, the ends threaded and secured with a pipe fitting, is the easiest to carry. Attach a leather thong for the wrist—or a long rope—to the spud handle. Otherwise it may slip out of your cold hands and through the hole. Ice augers which cut seven-inch holes are also available in the stores. Whichever you use, clean up and bevel the sides of the fishing hole, so ragged ice won't cut your line. Companion implement to the spud is the skimmer, a regulation restaurant soup skimmer with a long handle, to dip bits of ice and slush out of the hole at intervals, so the line won't freeze in.

Rods and reels for ice-fishing are inexpensive and rather nondescript. The reel is used only to store extra line. The rod can be anything from a piece of brush, broom stick, chair leg, to a cheap plug-casting outfit. It should be no more than three feet long. Even a handline is perfectly adequate. For very deep fishing, as for smelt and whitefish, a tire-less bicycle wheel mounted beside the hole makes a clever "rod-and-reel." A spin lets line down, another brings the fish up, quickly. For pan fish an umbrella stay, the tip of an old fly rod, or part of an automobile antenna all make good, sporty rods. These are especially adaptable when ice flies are used for bluegills, etc. The "jigging stick" is another type of rod, used to jig metal spoons, for perch and walleyes. It is simply a short, stiff stick, with pegs attached as line winder so depth may be quickly and accurately adjusted. The jigging spoon is dropped to the proper level, then the stick is lifted and relaxed, causing the spoon to flutter up and down. When a fish strikes, it is quickly yanked out upon the ice.

Lines may be of the most inexpensive kinds. For very deep fishing, a heavy line, or a metal line, is best. No. 18 seine line is a good choice for average-depth fishing, as for pike. For the pan fishes, nylon leader material used as line will bring best results, for they are often wary in winter. When they are unusually disinclined, 3x or 4x trout leader tippets tied to such a line will often fool them. A wire leader should be used for pike, pickerel, and walleyes.

The tip-up is the most popular tackle for the larger, strong-biting winter fishes such as pike, walleyes, bass. There are numerous kinds. You can purchase them or make them. A crude one is made by cutting a forked stick, lopping off one prong, setting the butt in the ice, and looping the line over the remaining prong, which thrusts out over the hole. A bite will wiggle the stick, and you haul away.

Regulation tip-ups are of two general kinds: dry reel

(reel above the ice); wet reel (reel down in the hole below the water, so the line won't freeze). Either kind has a signal device fashioned from a foot-long piece of limber spring steel, bent over and hooked lightly to the trigger. A flag is attached to the end of the spring steel, the line is pulled from the reel and looped over the trigger. Dry reel tip-ups have the reel and signal device attached to a stake set beside the hole. Wet reel tip-ups are in the shape of a cross, one supporting stick lying across the hole, the other, with reel and signal attached, upright. When a strike comes, the trigger is yanked, the spring is released, the flag flies up. A black or red flag is most easily visible. The advantage of tip-ups is that several may be set and watched at one time. But only the strong biters will spring them. Very excellent tip-ups can be purchased. The wet reel type is preferable.

An adaptation of the tip-up is used in shanty fishing for deep, weak-biting species such as lake trout and whitefish. The spring steel is attached to the shanty wall, above the hole. The end is crimped, and bent down, the line being looped over the crimp. The weakest bite, unnoticeable when the line is held in the hand, jiggles the spring.

MISCELLANEOUS EQUIPMENT includes minnow bucket. Cut a hole and suspend the bucket through it by a stick across the hole under the bail. This will keep minnows fresh, and from freezing. A small tea strainer, fastened to bucket handle by cord, allows you to dip out bait without wetting your hands. A container of tallow should be carried for rubbing on the hands. This avoids chapping, or sticking to cold metal. Very light bobbers have a place in ice-fishing. By using them, weak bites which cannot be felt can be seen.

STANDARD BAITS of the winter fisherman are: minnows, large for pike, bass, and walleyes, small for crappies and perch; cut bait (from suckers or other fish) for lake trout, whitefish, cusk; salmon eggs; liver for bullheads (which sometimes bite during mild weather); live smelt for lake trout. Minnows can usually be purchased at bait ranches; or you can catch your own by sinking glass or plastic traps, baited with bread crumbs, beneath the ice in small streams.

The minnow rig should be made with sinker heavy enough to keep the minnow down. Use three-way swivels so minnow rig and sinker are at the same point, otherwise you may have a tangle. Fish minnows *near* weed beds but not close enough for the minnows to reach the weeds where they will become tangled. Chumming beforehand—cutting up suckers and scattering this chum down through the hole—is often effective in drawing fish.

It is when we come to the pan fishes such as the bluegill, etc., which make up a very substantial part of the winter catch, that we find many unorthodox baits doing the trick when ordinary summer baits fail. Some extremely successful baits are as follows: corn borer larvae, maggots, bee larvae, bits of angleworm, mealworm, "wigglers" (burrowing May-fly nymphs found in soft mud in shallows of weedy lakes), and even canned peas and corn. Wood grubs are also good, and another bait which is extremely popular is the tiny white grub found in the galls formed by this grub on goldenrod stalks. Most of these baits can easily be gathered by the angler, or they can be purchased from bait ranches. Also, there are several firms which advertise their wares in the outdoor magazines each season, and which specialize in various kinds of small white grubs. These can be sent through the mail, cost very little, and are top-notch bait for pan fish. When you once find out what sport it is to haul up big fat bluegills from the icy water, and what catches you can make of them at times, no bait-gathering chore will seem too difficult.

ARTIFICIAL LURES, it would seem, could not possibly have a place in ice-fishing. But they do. Centuries ago Eskimos had learned how to carve walrus-ivory lures, let them down through a hole in the ice on a sinew line, and, by dancing them up and down, or, as we say today, "jigging" them, set the fish into a frenzy of biting. Later a type of lure called a "jigging spoon" replaced the crude Eskimo lures among our old-time ice-fishermen. These were simply metal spoons with a hook soldered to them, shaped so that they would flutter enticingly when lifted and dropped in the water below the fishing hole. Today's jigging spoon is changed hardly at all from the early models and is one of the most effective methods and by far the easiest way of taking yellow perch and walleyes, and sometimes pike. Such spoons can be purchased in any tackle store, or you can make your own if you're handy at such things. Spoons about 2 inches long are best. Using them is easy. They are simply danced up and down at proper depth until fish are attracted into striking.

The most unique development in artificial lures for ice-fishing is the ice fly, which has gained great popularity over the last few years because of its effectiveness. These, too, can be purchased. Jigged very slowly, close to bottom, they are killers on bluegills and crappies especially. A fly baited with a grub or other tiny bait is also effective. In addition, there are currently several other artificial ice-fishing lures on the market—metal-and-feather bugs, minnow-like metal spoons with gang hooks. All are fluttered or jigged near bottom.

ICE-FISHING METHODS for the various standard winter biters are briefly as follows. (See Chapter Two for fish ranges and habitats.)

Lake Trout: handlines, 18-pound test, fished from shanties with spring-steel bite indicator; large hook, using cut bait or live smelt; strike at first indication of bite; fish deepest holes, sloping edges of sand bars. Whitefish: handlines, fished as for lake trout, very deep; large hook, light sinker, cut bait or small minnows; very often same locations as lake trout. Smelt: handlines, bicycle-wheel device, etc., fished very deep; small hook, small minnows; fish at night from shanty; light sinker, except in Atlantic coastal rivers where current requires heavy sinker.

Pike and Pickerel: seldom below 30 feet, usually shallower; minnow 2 to 10 inches, must be lively; large hook, heavy sinker, 18-pound test line; tip-ups; over or near weed beds; let fish run and stop before setting hook.

Yellow Perch: school fish, usually in from 3 to 18 feet of water; minnows 1½ inches, dead or alive; jigging spoons, small; nylon leader material line, 5-pound test; handline or short jigging stick, also try hair-trigger tip-ups; weed-bed edges preferably, but perch are rovers, may be anywhere. Walleyes: in winter very often in shallow water or over their spring spawning beds on shallow sand or gravel bars; school fish; minnows, medium size, lively; hook size No. 2 or large jigging spoons; seldom bite well after late February; handlines or tip-ups; often take bait and sulk so hook should be set quicker than for pike.

Bluegills: in small roving schools; timid in winter; seldom deeper than 1 to 18 feet, often over spawning localities in reedy shallows during winter, invariably near weed-bed drop-offs; baits as previously described, small portions only, and the bite weak; limber rods or handlines, with bobber when bites are extremely weak; ice flies excellent; small hook, even No. 10, with fine nylon leader material for line. Crappies: active in winter; school fish which cruise widely in bays, bayous, among stumps; often as deep as 30 feet, seldom deeper; minnows best, but cut bait, liver, raw beef will do, ice flies fairly productive, sometimes with spinner-and-fly combination; light rods or handlines, tip-ups possible but set triggers lightly; hook No. 4; set hook lightly and handle fish gingerly for crappie mouths are tender; precise fishing depth important.

Black Bass: depths in winter of 10 to 25 feet, near weeds, submerged stumps, logs; minnows preferable, and fish as for pike; will strike ice flies. *Trout and salmon:* very few places where they may be taken legally in winter, and best to fish them according to local practice as to baits and methods. *Bullheads, cusk:* fish on or near bottom in places where they are definitely known locally to be abundant; depth anywhere from 5 to 40 feet or more; particular baits seldom important.

SPEARING is fast becoming illegal over much of the U. S.

In sections where it still may be practiced, pike and yellow perch are the mainstays. For perch use a small spear, holding it in the right hand and luring them surfaceward by jigging a hookless spoon with the left. In this manner only the largest fish may be chosen, and fish may be taken at times when they refuse to bite. For pike spearing, live minnow decoys are used, threaded through gills or lips with leader material and allowed to swim below the hole. Artificial decoys are also available. A heavy spear and a fairly large hole are necessary. Spearing from a darkened shanty is most productive. Oyster shells previously poured through the hole form a white bottom backdrop against which fish are easily spotted.

Sturgeon spearing is practiced on certain Wisconsin and Michigan waters. This is no game for the amateur, for the fish run to 140 pounds. It requires a very large, heavy spear with rope attached and decoys made of large, red-painted, weighted wood blocks. It is fabulously exciting, but can be dangerous. No tyro should attempt it without advice from experienced local authorities.

There is plenty of sport to be had with all of our common fishes after the ice has closed the lakes to boats and casting rods. If you go out on the ice armed with adequate tackle and the facts given in this chapter, you'll quickly become enthused about a whole new field of outdoor endeavor which will fill what have perhaps previously been the dull months with excitement and thrills of a completely different kind.

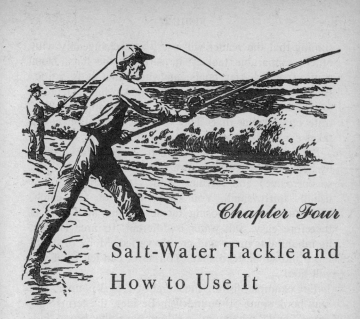

Chapter Four

Salt-Water Tackle and
How to Use It

Quite recently spinning has brought a drastic addition
to marine methods and tackle. Spinning tackle, described in Chapter One which deals with fresh water,
differs in salt water only in that marine spinning gear
is heavier. Rods are longer, two handed, stouter; reels
are stronger, of greater capacity, larger over all; lines
are of heavy monofilament nylon (or braided synthetics
impervious to salt water) in tests running from 15 to 50
or more pounds.

This *addition* of spinning tackle has not changed
regulation marine tackle and methods. Thus we will
make little mention from here on of spinning tackle, as-

suming that the reader will use it interchangeably with other comparable tackle—in surf, on the flats, from skiffs, from charter boats, anywhere that it is fitting. But because *regulation* salt-water tackle has a detailed terminology all its own, marine anglers must concentrate on learning that. The spinning innovation easily takes care of itself in all its fine simplicity.

Salt-water tackle differs from fresh-water tackle only by being fundamentally more rustproof (because salt is so corrosive) and sturdier. Bodies of fresh water are usually fairly small. You know what you will catch, maximum size. Choosing tackle on the light side is therefore easy. Salt water is different. Its area is vast, its inhabitants many and greatly varied. Many of them, large and small, feed alike. You never can tell what you will hook.

For example, fishing mackerel of 1 to 3 pounds, you may hook some 50-pound fish. Besides, the terms "average" and "maximum" seldom have the broad latitudes in fresh water one discovers in salt water. You may be catching channel bass of 3 pounds average, then suddenly snag one of 40 pounds!

It is thus easy to see why salt-water tackle must lean toward the heavy, sturdy side, with rods stiffer, lines stronger, and reels of larger capacity than for fresh-water fishing.

This does not mean that fresh-water bait-casting tackle, spinning, and fly-fishing tackle (Chapter One) are "out" in salt water. It means simply that the tyro should choose regulation salt-water tackle on the heavy side, and that as experience grows he may, to enhance the sport, cautiously try out what might be termed experimental "supersport" fishing in salt water, using the various fresh-water outfits. Chapter Five indicates, as each salt-water fish is described, which ones may be successfully and safely taken by experienced anglers on light tackle.

All regulation salt-water tackle is designed along the general lines of the *fresh-water bait-casting outfit*. Since terminology and description of bait-casting tackle have been given (Chapter One, Section "Bait Casting"), general terms and descriptions will not be repeated here. However, salt-water anglers and manufacturers of salt-water tackle have formulated certain terms, measurements, and practices peculiar to salt-water fishing. These the salty angler must know, and so the very first matter for us to take up as beginners in salt-water fishing is the description of the general tackle most in use, and the special terms attached to it. This we will do in the following brief accounts, and then we'll bring the various items together into balanced outfits.

RODS are extremely diverse, stiff as compared to fresh-water rods, made of tempered split bamboo, whole cane, solid tough woods, or glass. Most have two-handed grips or butts. (Most marine spinning rods are of glass.)

The stiff action is necessary to handle powerful fish and to work heavy baits, lures, and sinkers in swells, tides, currents, and at more than average depths. The materials (especially glass nowadays) solve the salt corrosion problem. The long butt section not only assists in casting heavy lures but gives leverage when a heavyweight battler needs to be subdued. When you consider that a great many salt-water game fish could rip ordinary fresh-water tackle apart in a split second on the

81

first run after being hooked, you have in a nutshell the reason for the general sturdiness of salt-water tackle. Such an occurrence might be the thrill of a lifetime— but a mighty expensive one! Indeed, the great spaces of "blue water" have inhabitants to match!

Salt-water rod weights are designated by weight of the rod (invariably one-piece) without the butt. The rod itself, then, is spoken of as the "tip." Thus, a 6-ounce tip is a rod which, without butt section, weighs 6 ounces.

Rod length (over-all, counting butt) may run anywhere from 4 feet (short, stiff rods often used for bait casting), to 9 feet with butt portion perhaps 30 inches (surf casting).

Very roughly, rods fall into four classes: still-fishing; surf casting; bait casting; trolling. This doesn't mean you *must* have four rods to fish in salt water. Most anglers use one all-round rod for all these purposes. Of course it must be a rod which will serve all purposes fairly well, as long as the angler doesn't go after fish too large, such as bluefin tuna and swordfish. Often such rods are called simply "boat rods." There is no standard for boat rods. They are usually around 6 to 7 feet over-all, with at least a 6-ounce tip.

LINES change swiftly nowadays, due to research in new and better materials. Nylon, Dacron, and other synthetics are much used. Monofilament is even used in somes areas for trolling. Synthetics have about replaced silk. Linen is still highly regarded for marine angling.

Linen is stronger when wet than when dry. Each thread has a tensile strength of 3 pounds, wet. Since linen line is braided, its strength is designated by number of threads. Thus, when salt-water anglers speak of "6-thread line," they mean an 18-pound test line. Seldom are salt-water lines designated by poundage test.

REELS are invariably of capacities from 150 or 200 or 300 yards on up. Some, special reels for salt-water bait (plug) casting, are simply oversized fresh-water reels. Such reels are equipped with level-wind, anti-backlash devices. Most standard salt-water reels do not have these devices. They do have in general a gear lever which allows "free-spooling" of the reel, or, when thrown into gear, winding in of the line. They also have a device called a star drag, which allows various pressures to be put upon the reel spool. This is necessary, when trolling, surf fishing, or when playing large fish, to keep the line from running off the spool too fast.

Most manufacturers use standard code numbers to designate reel sizes. Whether so numbered or not, tackle dealers always know what size reel you wish if you know the standard code. Obviously, these code numbers must be related to the size line you wish to use. For example, a size 1/0 reel holds 300 yards of 6-thread

REEL	LINE (THREADS)	CAPACITY (YARDS)
1/0	6	300
2/0	9	300
3/0	12	300
4/0	15	300
6/0	18-24	400-300
9/0	24	500
10/0	24	800
12/0	39	700
14/0	39	1000
16/0	39-54	1500-1100

line, but only 100 yards of 18-thread line. On page 83 is a chart which shows: (1) general capacities; (2) the line size, reel size, and capacity in most general usage. If heavier or lighter lines are to be put on the reel, capacities can be ascertained in any tackle store.

Now then, it is easy to see that with so many different rod sizes and weights, the same for reels, and for lines, and with these sizes all having very wide latitudes, as do the sizes and weights of the fish which are to be caught in salt water, it could very easily occur that the inexperienced briny angler might get together, a piece at a time, an outfit which, when set up, would be a most unwieldy affair indeed. This is exactly what used to happen years ago. In fact, many an angler spent money for various parts of his outfit and then found he couldn't fish comfortably with it after he had put it together. Thus, over the years, the better and more enthusiastic anglers kept trying to get some standardization of outfits which would be, as they said, *balanced*. The upshot was that several terms very confusing to anglers not familiar with them finally emerged to designate these outfits.

THE COMPLETE SALT-WATER OUTFIT which balanced best in a certain weight division might be called a 4/6 outfit, for example, or a 6/9, etc. These terms were simply a means, no matter how confusing to the tyro, of saying what the rod weighed and what size line was used on it. The line size then suggested the reel size. For example: A 4/6 outfit means a rod with a 4-ounce tip, on which a 6-thread line is used. The table opposite explains the meaning of the terms given to the most popular outfits. It is one of these that the average salt-water angler will want.

OUTFIT	ROD	REEL SIZE	LINE
3/6	6 oz. over-all, 5′ tip, 12″ butt	2/0	6-thread
4/6	4 oz. tip, 6-6½′ over-all	2/0-3/0	6-thread
6/9	6 oz. tip, of 5′ length, butt 14″-18″	3/0-4/0	9-thread

There are, of course, numerous other outfits—such as surf tackle and the outfits for big-game fish heavier than those in the above chart—but seldom are these designated by similar code numbers. When you hear someone speak of "heavy tackle," it usually means a rod of about 7 feet over-all, tip weighing from 16 ounces up, line of from 24-thread up, reel anywhere from 4/0 up. "Medium tackle" means a rod of at least 6½ feet over-all, tip around 9 ounces, 18-thread line, reel 4/0 to 6/0. But of course these categories apply to fishing for really big fish.

Going back to the chart, a 3/6 outfit is considered a very light outfit, a 4/6 light, and a 6/9 a medium-light outfit for general fishing from boat or bridge where fairly big fellows may be hooked and played out, but where no huge species such as big tuna or swordfish are to be tangled with. Naturally, the more expert the fisherman, and the more experienced in salt water, the lighter an outfit he will dare bring into use for big fish. But for the tyro, a light or medium-light outfit can be smashed in a hurry when he hangs a fish of great power. It might be high sport—but it likely wouldn't last long, and would be mighty expensive!

FISHING

LEADERS for salt-water fishing are invariably of wire, may be anywhere from 3 to 25 feet long, depending on type of fishing and fish. In some instances, wire cable is used, but it is not very popular. Wire leaders are either of stainless steel or tinned wire.

| | BREAKING STRENGTH, POUNDS | |
LEADER SIZES	STAINLESS STEEL	TINNED
2	27	30
3	32	35
4	38	40
5	44	48
6	58	64
7	69	80
8	86	100
9	105	115
10	124	138
11	140	160
12	174	200
13	195	230
14	218	265

There are still larger sizes for special purposes.

Leaders are usually purchased in coils of 25 feet, or in coils weighing 1 pound, from which the fisherman makes his own leaders as desired, attaching swivels to either end, and the hook to one of the swivels.

SWIVELS are invariably used in all kinds of salt-water fishing because of the tough currents and swells. There are many kinds. All are made in various numbered sizes. Most popular are the regulation barrel swivel and the three-way swivel. This last allows: line to be attached to one ring; sinker to the second; leader with hook to the third. For trolling and surf casting the three-way is usually essential.

SINKERS for salt water are quite different from fresh-water sinkers. They must be heavy, to take baits down quickly, often to great depths, and to hold against the roll of wave and surf. Some are barrel-shaped, with a hole through the center for the line. Another type is almond-shaped. The "bank sinker" is club-shaped and is used often for bottom fishing in deep water. The pyramid-type sinker, with sharp angles which will stick in the sand, is most popular for surf casting. Most salt-water sinkers may be had in weights of from ½ ounce to 1 pound.

HOOKS of the O'Shaughnessy type are as popular as any for salt water. A tinned finish is best, to resist corrosion. Very roughly, measurements of this type of hook run about as follows, measuring directly across the space separating point of hook from shank.

HOOK SIZE	DISTANCE IN INCHES	HOOK SIZE	DISTANCE IN INCHES
4	11/32	4/0	5/8
3	12/32	5/0	11/16
2	7/16	6/0	13/16
1	15/32	7/0	29/32
1/0	1/2	8/0	1
2/0	17/32	9/0	1 3/32
3/0	19/32	10/0	1 1/4

These are the most useful and popular hook sizes. There are still larger ones for special heavy duty.

SURF TACKLE AND ITS USE

IF THERE is one type of salt-water fishing which may be said to rate above all others in popularity, it is surf fishing. The reasons are obvious. Surf fishing requires practically nothing but a decent surf outfit. It is inexpensive, because one may simply go to any near-by beach and begin fishing. A great share of the time, bait may be found right along the beach, and, since few of our thousands of miles of beaches are private, or posted, this is a sport for everybody. It is the salt-water sport available to more anglers than any other. In addition, hundreds of different kinds of fish come in regularly and often in awesome abundance from deep water to feed at surf line or just outside it. Thus, a surf angler can often do just as well as the man who has a boat and goes far offshore, and he has a wide-open space in which to make the most of his gamy opponent. The exhilarating atmosphere of one's surroundings also adds zest to this fine sport.

Surf casting is, with the exception of regulation plug (or bait) casting, the only salt-water endeavor which differs quite radically from all other types of fishing. Therefore, its tackle and the know-how of its use deserve a special section. Following are descriptions of the various items of tackle and how to use them as a rig to bring to beach those fine eating and fighting fishes which lurk in the white water and foam along the surf line.

THE SURF ROD is made of the same materials as other salt-water rods, but it is heavy, long, and has a long butt. With the outfit it is necessary to cast heavy lures or heavy sinker-and-bait rigs long distances, often against high winds. The tip is from 6 to 7 feet long. Lightweight anglers should use the shorter lengths. The butt, on which the reel is seated, is usually 30 inches long.

THE SURF REEL should be fitted with star drag and should be of the free-spool type. It must be large enough to hold at least 200 yards of 9-thread (27-pound test) linen line. Lighter lines, perhaps 6-thread, are often used, but the heavier ones will stand up better.

SINKERS, for bait-fishing in the surf, must usually be heavy, up to eight ounces, in order to hold the bait against the wash of the waves. Pyramid-type sinkers are most popular, for they stick in the sand of the bottom.

THE BAIT-FISHING RIG of sinker-swivel-leader-hook for surf fishing can be made up in several ways. Two of the most popular are as follows. In the first, often called the "fish-finder rig," a heavy pyramid sinker is attached to a swivel. The line is now threaded free through the opposite swivel eye. To the end of the line another swivel is now attached. A wire leader of about three feet is then attached to the opposite end of that swivel, and the hook is attached to the leader. Thus, after the cast is made, the sinker will stick on bottom, but the bait can wash about, or a fish can pick it up and run with it without dragging the sinker, for the line will slip freely through the sinker swivel. The second rig is called the "three-way rig." For it, a three-way swivel is used. As previously noted, this is simply a ring to which three swivels are attached. The sinker is made fast to one, the line to another, the leader to the last. Thus, neither wave nor fish action can twist or foul the rig.

SURF CASTING is almost identical with fresh-water plug casting, except that with such heavy tackle both hands must be used in making the cast. The long rod makes this possible. The cast is begun with the angler standing either close to the water's edge or perhaps ankle-deep in the surf. He faces parallel to the shore-line, with rod tip pointing shoreward, the rod held about mid-chest high and at almost right angles to his body, the tip dipping slightly. The right hand grips the butt near the reel (which is placed near the top of the butt), thumb upon the reel spool. The left hand grips the far end of the rod butt. By keeping the hands widely spaced, greater power of swing, therefore greater distance of cast, is possible. The sinker and bait, or casting lure, is allowed to lie on the sand with a couple of feet of line between it and rod tip, until the cast is made.

Making the cast now requires nothing but a powerful up-and-over swing, thumb holding the reel spool firmly until the rod has reached almost a vertical position. The reel is then released, the lure travels high and swiftly out over the waves. Meanwhile, the caster follows through with the rod, swinging the right leg around so that, as the lure hits the water, he is facing the spot where it landed, his back to the shore.

A SURF BELT is a must for the surf fisherman. It is simply a leather belt, with a heavy leather cup in front, into which the end of the rod butt is dropped, to give support (and comfort to the angler) while reeling in, or while a fish is being played.

After completion of the cast, the butt is dropped into the belt cup. The left hand moves up to grip the rod just *above* the reel so that the thumb may be used to guide the line smoothly upon the reel during the retrieve. The right hand, obviously, moves up to the reel handle.

THE SPIKE, or rod holder—the item has numerous names among surf fishermen in various sections—is another *must* piece of equipment for the surf fisherman. It is used when you still-fish with bait in the surf—the most popular, easiest, and most effective method in general. The spike is a steel rod usually about three feet long, sharpened on one end so it may easily be shoved down into the sand. On the other end there is an aperture, or iron ring, or other device into which the rod butt may be slipped and solidly held. Thus, after the cast, the rod can be slipped into the spike top. This eases the work for the angler and serves to hold the rod tip high, which keeps the line out of the wash of the breakers. By watching the rod tip, the angler can tell the instant a strike materializes. He then simply slips the rod out of the holder, sets the hook, drops the butt into his belt cup, and begins the exciting business of wearing out his fish.

A pair of boots, or waders, is another piece of essential equipment for the surf enthusiast, especially when the water or weather is chilly. A long-visored cap and sunglasses should be worn. The newcomer to briny fishing should consider surf fishing perhaps before any other kind of salty angling, and get a surf outfit first. This outfit can be used as a "make-do" rig for other types of salt-water fishing, and most of the time the average angler will thus be outfitted well for the type of fishing at which he'll have the greatest opportunity.

SALT-WATER TROLLING

TROLLING IS the most important salt-water method for those anglers fortunate enough to have boats or financially able to rent, or charter, boats. It is done with small boats in the bays and from large cruisers which can operate offshore. Trolling is highly successful in salt water for the simple reason that it allows the fisherman to cover a larger amount of space in the vast ocean distances than he could otherwise cover. Many salt-water fish travel in schools and roam widely. By trolling, one of these huge schools can usually be located. Or, for those large salt-water prizes which are solitary travelers, trolling amounts to the same thing as big-game hunting. It is like *stalking* big-game fish.

Trolling near the surface is most popular, for it is easiest and eliminates the use of exceedingly heavy sinkers, which would otherwise be necessary to get a bait or lure down to great depth. And nearly all salt-water game fish which are commonly taken by trolling can be found at some time of day, or tide, near the surface.

Small-boat trolling in bays, lagoons, channels, etc., differs in no way from fresh-water trolling. The lure, or bait, is simply tossed overboard and allowed to run out some distance behind the boat. With artificials, such as plugs, etc., it is common in salt water, either in casting or trolling, to give the rod a long sweep, or jerk, every couple of seconds. (In casting, this is done by jerking the rod tip, then reeling in the slack caused, and continually repeating the process.) The motion thus imparted to a lure is peculiarly deadly for most salt-water fish.

For open-water trolling after the larger salt-water game fish, there are several differences from regulation trolling.

FLAT TROLLING is one method. It means you troll by the usual method, sitting at the stern of the boat, holding the rod, letting the line run straight back. This has many disadvantages. It means only one person at a time can successfully work a long line in open water. It is back-breaking work, when you must hold heavy tackle against the pull of the long, heavy line. It is difficult to fashion and hook up bait such as strips of fish or whole fish in such a way that flat trolling won't soon rip them from the hook or tear them to pieces.

OUTRIGGER TROLLING has therefore been developed to overcome the difficulties of deep-sea flat trolling. The outrigger is a long pole, several of which are placed at various angles sticking out and upward from the sides and stern of the trolling cruiser. Regular tackle is set up, but the line from each rod is held to the end of an outrigger by some such device as a clothespin. The line is thus held high in the air, and the bait, far behind, is made to skip enticingly along the surface by adjusting the speed of the boat. When a strike comes, the line is yanked from its outrigger holder, the angler grabs the rod, and takes over. Several trollers are thus enabled to fish simultaneously from the same boat without getting fouled. There is less water pull on the line, less wear and tear on the bait.

OTHER TYPES OF SALT-WATER FISHING

THERE IS perhaps more still-fishing done in salt water than in fresh. Along both coasts, every bridge, pier, high rock, or jetty has its quota of still-fishermen using all manner of tackle. In the bays, lagoons, bayous, salt-water marshes, etc., small boats by thousands anchor and drop various baits close to the bottom. Dozens of different salt-water species are successfully taken in this manner.

In general, in salt water, this is called bottom fishing, although bottom fishing is also done offshore in very deep water for some species. In any case, tackle should lean toward the heavy side, for it is impossible to predict exactly what species, or how large a fish, will take the bait. In deep-water bottom fishing, heavy tackle is essential, to stand the strain of pulling even a rather small fish up from great depths. Wire leaders and fairly heavy sinkers are usually used, so that waves or currents will not straighten out the line.

"Chumming" is in many sections a favorite help to still-fishing success. It means feeding the fish bits of chopped fish or small shrimp, etc., in order to attract them to the vicinity of the baited hook, and also to *keep* a school in that vicinity for as long as possible. Where there are currents, chumming is done by tossing bits of bait overboard so that they float down with the current. Presently the baited hook is also floated along with the chum. Or, small fish called "mossbunkers" are chopped up and thrown in, creating an oily "slick" on the water. Fish are attracted, held in compact schools, and easily caught. The "chum pot" is also popular in some sections. This is a wire-screen container, filled with chopped fish or other bait and sunk on the bottom, let down over the side of a boat, or from a bridge or pier. Fish gather around it. Then the baited hook is lowered.

For certain species, such as weakfish, a common and most successful method is to fish with no sinker and with a float set only a couple of feet from the hook. Live shrimp are most often used for bait. A leader as invisible as possible is used. The bait is dropped in, or cast a short distance, sometimes used with chum. It sinks naturally, dangles just below the surface, where it is moved slowly and with short jerks by the angler.

BAIT, OR PLUG, CASTING around salt-water channels, bays, etc., is another extremely popular method nowadays. It differs in no way from regulation fresh-water plug casting, except that as a rule a nylon line of at least 20-pound test and a reel of somewhat larger capacity than for fresh-water casting are used. Rods may be of a type made especially for salt-water use, or they may be regular fresh-water plug rods. If you use one of metal, it must always be thoroughly washed in fresh water after use. Lures are in general identical with those used in fresh water.

SALT-WATER FLY CASTING is becoming more and more popular also. On the whole it is not a sport for the tyro. But it is a fabulously thrilling one for the finished fly-fisherman. Although a regular fresh-water fly rod of bass weight may be used, it is best to get a rod of salmon weight or a special extra-sturdy fly rod made especially for salt-water use.

As a general rule, surface flies are not as successful in salt water as in fresh. However, tarpon, striped bass, etc., may be taken at times and in certain sections by the use of "bugs" like the popping bugs used for fresh-water bass fishing. Streamer flies in whites, yellows, reds, bucktails in the same patterns, or small metal spinners and spoons are the standard lures of the salt-water fly-fisherman.

The reel should always be of large capacity and should have plenty of backing line. For most of the larger fly-rod lures the line will give best results if it is of the "forward taper" (torpedohead) type, of a size and weight, of course, to match rod action and length It should be of nylon.

SPINNING is also just as deadly in salt water as in fresh. There are special, heavier, more sturdy spinning outfits now on the market for use in salt water. This tackle, and its use, differs in no way from use of the same type of tackle in fresh water.

SALT-WATER BAITS

THE ANGLER who lives near salt water always knows every kind of bait which is available along his shores. But the inlander, stranger to salt water, is often puzzled as to what he should use for bait. Since nowadays thousands of fresh-water fishermen get their first chance at salt-water fishing each year on vacation trips to the seacoasts, the more common salt-water baits deserve special mention.

In fresh water, there are many species of fish whose diets are made up to a great extent of insect life. This is almost unknown among salt-water species. Fish always feed upon those items most abundant and most easily available in their habitats. In salt water, this means: other fish; crustaceans; mollusks; various sea worms.

"Cut bait" is very popular for salt-water fishing. This means simply chunks of fish, cut from side or tail of a large bait fish, in sizes which fit the hook. "Strip bait" is a strip of bait fish sliced in a manner so that it will wriggle and flash when it is trolled. Menhaden and mullet are popular bait fish. Minnows, or often quite large fish used whole, are also among the popular salt-water baits.

Fish with crusher teeth eat many varieties of crabs in salt water, from the large blue crabs of restaurant fame, to the small fiddler crabs which any angler may find burrowing in swarms under vegetation along certain portions of the bay and lagoon beaches. These make excellent bait for those fish capable of eating them. So do red-clawed hermit crabs, which live in the cast-off shells of mollusks, have soft bodies, and may be pulled from the shells they inhabit and cut up for bait. Sand fleas, small crustaceans of pale color similar in form to large beetles, may be dug from the sand at surf line. They are a top-notch bait. Clams, mussels, and other mollusks, removed from the shell and attached to the hook, are taken avidly by many salt-water fish.

Shrimp, small eels, and squids (or strips cut from white squids) are among the most popular of the standard salt-water baits. So also are blood worms, or sand worms, which may be dug from salt-water mud flats at low tide. Any of the above may be purchased at docks which rent boats for salt-water fishing, or from "bait ranchers" near the beaches. Or, with ambition and a little experience in the vicinity of salt water, the angler can quickly learn to locate, and gather, his own.

PLAYING SALT-WATER FISH

ONE FACET of salty angling seldom understood by fresh-water anglers about to be initiated, or by sportsmen who are introduced to fishing via the beaches, is that on the whole salt-water fish are much more swift and powerful than those of fresh water. They may not be any better fighters from the point of view of pure sport, but the fight for survival in salt water is an extremely vicious cycle. In addition, the great spaces and the necessity to run down other swift fishes for food, fishes which may have no hiding places into which to dart, make the top salt-water game fishes near-frightening battlers to fishermen new at the game.

It is well, therefore, to know what to expect, and to be prepared. Though a salt-water fish may wear himself out as quickly as any other, his first runs are often powerhouse affairs which can smash too-light tackle, rip it from an angler's hands, or at least give him badly skinned knuckles. Exciting, to be sure, and even at times a bit frightening, but no one wants to buy new tackle every day or so!

The first prime requisite is to be certain the tackle is sturdy enough to hold rather large fish, and heavy enough to allow the angler to work on his fish. The dainty handling accorded fresh-water trout by dry-fly fishermen, for example, has little place in average salt-water fishing.

The second rule is to match the tackle to the habits of the fish. If the fish sought are fish of the rocks or reefs, species which habitually run among rocks or other hiding places to avoid danger, then tackle must be heavier than just for the weight of the fish. It must allow the angler to lean back and *stop* the powerful dash of the fish to its hiding place. Otherwise the line will be cut.

Likewise, for fish which rely upon their speed and power in open water, *plenty of line* is always essential. Such fish should not be stopped on their first mad runs. Attempting to do so is inviting smashed tackle. They should be allowed to run, but with solid pressure put upon them by the rod and the reel drag. These species will not attempt to run under rocks, etc. They must be allowed to wear themselves out.

The third rule is never to attempt to boat or beach a large salt-water fish too quickly. Always be prepared, when he is on his side, apparently worn out, for at least one more terrific dash for freedom. When the line is short, tightly held, and the fish brought close to boat or beach, the angler must be at his most alert. Many a salt-water prize is lost at the second when it appears beaten. The short line gives it an opportunity to tear free. In addition, bringing a large fish within sight of boat or gaff often frightens it so that a tremendous last spurt of energy materializes.

Hooked fish are said to "sound" when they head for deep water and sulk at the end of a long line. The standard method of bringing them up is known to salt-water anglers as "pumping." The fisherman leans his weight into a mighty upward heave, then reels, lowering the rod tip to take up the line he has gained. This process, repeated over and over, serves to bring the game up—but the tackle must be able to take it.

The main salt-water rule is: Always be ready to be surprised, and never underestimate the tremendous speed and power of the quarry.

SALT-WATER FISHING SERVICES

FOR THE inland angler who may have opportunity to fish only for short and uncertain periods in salt water, it is well to know that the purchase of salt-water tackle is not absolutely necessary. Almost all charter boats for deep-sea party fishing furnish tackle if the angler desires it. Such boats charge from $20 to $100 per day (usually about 7 hours) for boat, tackle, and guide service. For those who cannot afford such stiff tariffs, a good thing to do is to get up a party of several persons, and split the expense.

Many popular sport-fishing ports have at least one large boat in operation which makes daily trips to off-shore or bay fishing grounds on a come one come all basis. Such boats have anywhere from ten to fifty or more fishermen aboard, often with their families. The charge is nominal, from $1 to $5, as a rule. Tackle is furnished, for a small fee, on such boats. Bait, of course, is always furnished on all charter marine fishing boats. All nominal-fee fishing is of the bottom (still-fishing) type.

In some ports, boats are available which can be boarded at night. On these you rent a bunk and sleep while the boat runs out to the fishing grounds. A steward wakes you; you get breakfast and other meals aboard; tackle is available. The cost, all told, is seldom prohibitive for the average angler. Certain of these boats furnish both trolling and bottom fishing, with a rotation system for passengers so that each gets his chance at the best, or stern, position.

In other ports, offshore anchored barges are available. A speed boat leaves the dock and returns at regular intervals, taking you out and bringing you back. This "floating island" type of fishing usually gives excellent results, too, for the barge, on which food and tackle can be had, is anchored where the best fishing occurs. This service seldom costs, all told, more than $3 to $7, plus whatever is spent aboard.

For the angler who may get but a few days each year on the coast, and wants to have his own tackle, the best bet is to get together a nominally priced surf outfit. A regulation fresh-water bait-casting outfit can be used, of course, but it may be ruined. The surf rig can be used for surf fishing anywhere along the beach, or for bridge, pier, or jetty fishing (although it is a bit unwieldy), or it will serve as a reasonable outfit for whatever boating opportunities arise. The cost of such an outfit will be well worth the investment, when those few days of opportunity for salty sport materialize.

SPINNING IN SALT WATER has made such fabulous recent growth that numerous anglers are forsaking all other tackle. They use, for example, fairly heavy fresh-water gear for catching weakfish and channel bass on the so-called grass flats. They fish school tuna and yellowtail off California on charter boats with heavy marine spinning outfits of the two-handed kind. Many even surf fish with extra-heavy rigs. It is quite possible that one day standard salt-water tackle will be replaced to a great extent by the newer gear. Because it is new, little has been done about setting up rigid standards for it. But the newcomer who will learn fundamentals can relate his spinning tackle purchases to other standard tackle, as far as the job it must do.

In the following chapter concerning marine fish and methods of catching them, specifications for standard tackle are given. All but the very largest of the species can be—are being—taken on spinning rigs nowadays. It is a very sporting activity. Readers should consider for what they may be fishing most and perhaps take up spinning rather than other methods. The standard-tackle specifications, however, give one a basic measuring stick by which to judge which spinning outfit will be best in relation to the fish to be caught.

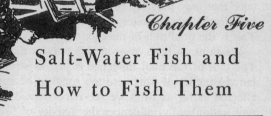

Chapter Five

Salt-Water Fish and
How to Fish Them

Almost always, when a fisherman experienced in the ways of fresh water and its denizens makes his first contact with salt water he goes about it timidly, for even the water itself doesn't seem to look, or *act,* the same as it does inland. In addition, with such awesome expanses to look upon, the proposition becomes more than a little confusing. Where should a fellow put down his line? Where are the fish going to be?

In truth, salt water *is* different in the way it "acts." But at the same time many of the complex influences which have important bearing upon the catching of fish in fresh water will also apply in the oceans. For example, if water temperature is either too high or too low, fish become listless, no matter which kind of water they inhabit. Wind direction which may muddy or cool the water will also inhibit fish. A falling barometer generally causes fish to lie close to bottom and bite poorly, while a rising barometer will usually accentuate activity. Again, low or high oxygen content makes fish listless or active respectively.

It is all of these complex influences acting together, and many more thrown in, that make fishing the wonderfully exciting game it is. But there is another influence that may possibly be stronger than all of these, in both fresh and salt water, and especially so in the latter. This is the tidal pull of the moon.

We think of tides as occurring only at the seacoasts. The pull of the tidal influence is just as strong inland, but the bodies of water are too small to be appreciably affected as far as what we see is concerned. This tidal pull undoubtedly influences the activity of fish. In salt water, however, the tides, which we can actually *see,* govern *directly* much of the activity of all marine life, not alone by the mysterious moon pull, but far more by the formation of currents and by lowering and raising the water levels several times each full day.

Thus, to be a successful salt-water angler, one must understand this great influence. It is as important as the tackle one chooses. It is an interesting subject in itself, and, related to angling, it will actually govern the size of the catch, almost without fail. In other words, the salty angler must plan his fishing in relation to the tides.

TIDE TERMINOLOGY and explanation are as follows:

> incoming tide........toward shore
> high tide..........crest of incoming tide

outgoing tide........away from shore

low tide..........minimum low water level
of outgoing tide

The varying water levels caused by tides radically shift and change feeding conditions for fish, closing off or opening up new feeding grounds, covering and uncovering food, forcing forage fish to move, changing shallow-water and beach contours. There are two low, two high tides each full day, roughly six hours apart.

Tides are caused by the pull of both sun and moon. The moon pull is strongest. A "moon (lunar or tidal) day" is almost an hour longer than a "sun (solar) day." Thus, each day every tide is a little later, and some days therefore do not have four tides.

Newspapers in coastal towns print tide times daily. The wise salt-water angler will follow them.

Tides obviously cause currents. "Flood tide" means a shoreward current, "ebb tide" an offshore current. "Slack tide" means maximum high, or low, thus no current. "Tide rips" are caused where opposing currents, fashioned by quick depth changes, or shore contours, battle each other.

RULE OF THUMB: Fish swim with the tides, feeding most avidly on an incoming tide, retiring to deeper water on an outgoing tide. From an hour before high tide to an hour after is generally the peak feeding period. Currents and tide rips stir up food along shoals, bars, inlets, passes, and are therefore hot spots for shore or near-shore anglers. Also, the half-hour to hour immediately following slack tide, either low or high, usually sets the fish feeding, for the new water movement, whether inshore or offshore, stirs up food and causes small forage fish to move. Knowing these facets of salt-water fishing, an angler will have won the first battle in filling his fish sack and assuring himself of hair-raising sport. It is time enough for the tyro at the seacoast to learn about the different kinds of fish he may catch *after* he understands the tides and their dominating influences.

There are literally thousands of fish species in our oceans. Used to great, unobstructed spaces, many of them range widely and certain ones are migratory, appearing along each portion of our coasts only at certain times of year. As in fresh water, most of the species serve as forage for the fewer large species.

It would be impossible to cover all salt-water species. But happily, since certain unusual or rare or unpopular kinds bite now and then when fishing is directed at some specific game or food fish, methods given in the following pages successfully cover the entire field. Only those species most popular with anglers are described.

Very loosely, the more popular salt-water species may be put in the following classes: Big-Game Fish; General Game Fish; Bottom Fish. These groups greatly overlap, and, even more than in fresh-water angling, methods greatly overlap also. Commonly, numerous species are caught while the fisherman is directing his endeavors toward his special favorite.

BIG-GAME FISH

OUR SEVERAL species which are considered as marine "big game" are fish of the open oceans. They require considerable expense in tackle and guide service to take them successfully, but to those who have the opportunity and like to pit themselves in battle against the most powerful of hook-and-line fishes, they are the thrill of a lifetime.

These big-game fish are not abundant species-wise, but the few of them with which the sport fisherman does big business are the very best of what the world's marine heavyweight class has to offer. Brief descriptions of them, and the most popular methods of fishing them, follow.

Bluefin Tuna: Ranges along both our coasts. Most famous fishing grounds: Bimini, West Indies, winter and spring; New Jersey to Nova Scotia, summer and fall; Catalina Island vicinity, California. Color: gray-blue above, silvery below; iridescent. Elongated "tear-drop" shape, tail portion of body proportionately slender, with deep-arched, powerful tail. Food: menhaden, mackerel, flying fish, etc. Runs in large schools. The schools of smaller fish, called "school tuna" by anglers, average 20 to 100 pounds. Really big fish weigh from 200 to over 1,000 pounds.

Methods: Trolling is standard, from charter boats, along offshore banks and at tide rips. "Chumming"— dropping overboard chunked herring or other "chum" —is the usual procedure, with the hook, baited with a whole herring or mackerel, drifting along with the chum each time it is thrown over. In certain areas, still-fishing and chumming get results. Feathered jigs trolled deep are the usual tuna artificials. Outriggers, set to skip bait over the water to imitate flying fish, are often used also.

Tackle: A leather shoulder harness, a rod butt holder, and work gloves are musts for heavy tuna fishing, to assist you in wearing out the fish, which fights deep, "sounding" as anglers say, and making long runs. Rod, usually of solid hickory, should have tip weighing from 23 to 36 ounces. Reel should be size 10/0 to 16/0. Line 39- to 54-thread for very heavy rods, 36-thread for lighter rods. Ten to twenty feet of line next to the leader should be doubled. Leader: about No. 12 wire, 15 feet long; or 500-pound test cable-type. Hook: 10/0 to 14/0, with 12/0 standard.

For small school tuna, a 6/9 outfit is adequate. For medium school tuna use a 12-ounce tip, 400 yards of 24-thread line.

Swordfish, or "Broadbill": Pacific, coast of California; Atlantic, north to Labrador. Color: dark above, dirty white below. The bill, or "sword," long, flat, broad. Tremendously powerful tail. Feeds on squids and fish. Abundant in Pacific location in fall, in southern Atlantic fishing ground in early spring, farther north during summer and fall. Average weight 250 pounds. Maximum over 1,000. Usually solitary; often located while sunning at surface.

Blue Marlin: Ranges along East coast, usually in the Gulf Stream, from Florida to New York. Also in the Gulf, off Texas. Back fin extends almost full length of back, as opposed to the more narrow upright fin at back of head of swordfish. Color: dark blue above, brilliant silver below. Bill round, shorter than swordfish. Weighs from 200 to over 700 pounds.

Striped Marlin: The marlin of the Pacific, coming north off California to about Balboa. Color: lighter, with stripes from back down across sides. Weighs about the same as the blue marlin.

Methods: These three species are among the world's

greatest game fish, spectacular leapers, vicious fighters. They rarely take artificial lures. All are fished from charter boats, with guides, by trolling, using outriggers to skip the bait along the surface. Bait may be a whole bonito, mullet, squid, dolphin, etc.

These billed fishes hit their prey with the spear to kill it, then turn and grasp it in their mouth. Thus, when trolling, this "tap" is felt first. The bait is then allowed quickly to drop back some distance on a slack line, so it will appear dead or injured. As the fish finally seizes it, the fisherman rams the hook home, *hard*.

Tackle for all three species must be heavy, approximately the same as for the heaviest tuna fishing (see Bluefin Tuna). Some marlin and swordfish anglers favor cable leader because the leaps of the fish are not so likely to kink it. Leaders for marlin are usually 25 feet long.

White Marlin: Although this fish, and the two sailfishes which follow, average much smaller than the foregoing, they are included under Big-Game Fish because they are members of the Marlin family. The white marlin ranges in our waters from Florida to Massachusetts, occasionally in the Gulf off Texas. Color: black, blue-green with grayish vertical stripes; belly silver. A small edition of the blue marlin. Off Florida about March, farther north during summer. Averages to 100 pounds. Sometimes travels in small schools.

Methods: As for other marlin, except that feathered jigs sometimes work well, and strip bait (strips cut from mullet or other fish) skipped along the surface from outriggers do as well as whole fish for bait. In all marlin fishing, if the tap is felt, then the bait dropped back slack without results, it should be put into action again immediately. Sometimes a second bill tap occurs, thus making sure of a fish which would otherwise have been missed. Tackle for white marlin can be as light as a 6/9 outfit, with 15 feet of No. 8 wire leader, hook of size 9/0. The tyro, however, should use a rod with 12-ounce tip, 400 yards of 18-thread line, 6/0 reel.

Sailfish: Two species, Atlantic and Pacific, the first from Florida and Texas to New York, the second to about Monterey, California. Size: 30 to 100 pounds, with Pacific species averaging the larger. Color: brilliant dark blue above, silver below. The spear very slender. Differs distinctly in appearance from marlin because of the very high, long back fin with peculiarly scalloped edge.

Methods: Usually sailfish are caught some miles offshore, most of them along the Texas and Atlantic-Florida coasts, largely in the Gulf Stream. Best months are from first of the year to midsummer. Trolling from charter boats, with bait used as for marlin and handled in the same manner, is the ticket. Tackle should be of weight about as for White Marlin.

GENERAL GAME FISH

THIS GROUP encompasses the real prizes for average anglers. Some of these species require charter boats and guides, but most can be caught inshore, from small boats, shore, bridges, piers, in surf, with average tackle. It is this group that will most appeal to the new crop of spinning enthusiasts. Most of the species are beautifully tailored to this newer tackle. In this group are some of the best fighters that swim. This is the fish group, then, with which the angler who spends either a lot of time or an occasional session on salt water will be most concerned, and in which he will find every variation of sport to suit his every whim.

No attempt is made here to classify the various species into their numerous families. Instead, for easy reference, they are described alphabetically.

Albacore: Atlantic, off Florida coast, not common farther north; Pacific, abundant off southern portion of California. Unmistakable because it looks like a small tuna except that the pectoral fins (back of gill) are extremely long, almost half as long as the entire fish. Color: dark blue above, yellow to silvery below. Weight: average, 15 pounds; maximum, about 50. Food: small fishes. Runs in schools, near surface. Excellent eating.

Methods: For the most part, this is a Pacific game fish, taken ten miles or more offshore, from charter boats. Trolling at rather fast speed is the method. Either strip bait or feathered jigs are effective. Tackle: a 6/9 outfit, with leader of about 6 to 8 feet, No. 9 wire.

Amberjack: Atlantic, north to Carolinas. Most abundant about Florida. Long, deep-bodied, of the general "mackerel" outline. Powerful. Color: pale bluish-silver, fins yellowish. Solitary, or in small, loose groups. Feeds on small fish, around offshore reefs and rocks. Weight: average, 15 pounds; maximum, 100.

Methods: Trolling from charter boats around the reefs, using strip bait, or feathered jigs, large spoons, etc. This fish is noted for its slashing runs into coral or other rocky hiding places when hooked. Heavy tackle must therefore be used to stop these runs; otherwise the line is quickly cut. Tackle should be approximately as

111

follows: 12-ounce rod tip; 6/0 reel; 300 yards 18-thread line; 8-foot, No. 8 wire leader; No. 8/0 hook.

Barracuda: Several species, all very much alike. Very long, pikelike fish, with dangerous teeth and large mouths. Vicious temperament. Most abundant off Florida and California. Bluish or dark above, silvery below, with some indistinct dark spots. Food: fishes. Awesomely swift, fearless, usually solitary. Pacific species usually averages somewhat smaller than Atlantic. Weight: average, 5 to 12 pounds; maximum (Atlantic), 100. Found both offshore, and, in certain areas, around inlets and other protected waters.

Methods: The vicious, fearless nature of the barracuda makes good catches possible. Offshore trolling is standard, around the reefs, keeping either strip bait or a feathered jig, or spoon, down near bottom. Tackle should be about as for amberjacks (see Amberjack). For inshore fishing, where the fish usually run smaller, the 6/9 outfit will do. At times, in bays and around near-shore shoals, small barracuda may be taken with plugs or spoons, using a regulation salt-water plug-casting outfit. Or try a heavy fly rod, large streamer, fished slowly. Heavy wire leader is essential.

Striped Bass: Called "Striper," Rockfish. Atlantic, entire length U. S. coast; Pacific, northern California to Oregon coast. Long, deep-bodied, "basslike" fish, silvery with dark longitudinal stripes. Food: shrimp, small fish, eels, crabs. A school fish of surf, shore line rocks. Also runs in fabulous numbers up fresh-water rivers to spawn in spring. Weight: average to 10 pounds in bays, etc., to 25 in surf or rocky shore lines; maximum above 50.

Methods: This is one of the most popular surf-fishing targets. An excellent fighter, good eating. Late years fly-rod addicts have been very successful, using both streamer and other wet flies, and "popping bugs" similar to those used for fresh-water black bass. May also be taken with bait-casting tackle, on plugs, feathered jigs, spoons, either in surf or inside waters. Most popular method is surf casting, using either chunk bait or fish, shrimp, crab, bloodworms, etc., or an eelskin lure. Feathered jigs and plugs are good for surf casting also. Trolling near shore, around river mouths, etc., with eelskin rig, spoon, spinner, or jig is likewise effective. During summer, night fishing is usually best. At all times of year, the incoming tide furnishes best results as a rule. Tackle: For trolling, etc., the 4/6 outfit is adequate, unless the fish are running very large. For surf casting, tackle about as follows: 7-foot, 12-ounce tip, 30-inch butt; 3/0 reel; 200-300 yards 9-12 thread line; pyramid sinker up to 8 ounces; hook from 4/0 to 9/0.

California White Sea Bass: Most abundant along California coast, but some farther north. Light powder-blue above, silvery below. Long, heavy but slender, with squared tail. Dorsal fin in two sections, spiny and soft. An inshore fish of the kelp beds, where it feeds on crabs, small fish, etc. Weight: averages to 30 pounds; maximum 75 at least.

Methods: Although still-fishing from boats with squid, herring, etc., as bait, and casting with spoons, feathered jigs, metal "squids," etc., are successful methods, this fish is most popular as a trolling gamester. Most sure-fire is the method of trolling the edges of the large kelp beds, in and under which the white sea bass lives and feeds. Either bait or spoons, or spoon and bait combination, trolled deep around the beds is the ticket. Tackle: rod tip around 10 ounces; 4/0 reel; about 300 yards of 15-thread line. Lighter tackle (as the 6/9 outfit) can be used by experienced anglers.

Channel Bass: Also called "redfish," or "red," or "red drum." Texas Gulf Coast to New Jersey. A long, heavy fish, silvery with reddish hue, unmistakable because of black spot at upper base of tail. School fish of surf, sandy inlets, channels, and bars. Food: small fish, shrimps, crabs. Weight: average, 3 to 5 pounds small, 10 to 15 large; maximum, to 75.

Methods: This fish is the ace of the surf fisherman. Though often taken from bridges and jetties by still-fishermen, and by bait casters using spoons, plugs, etc., on regulation salt-water bait-casting equipment, surf fishing accounts for by far the largest number of "reds." Regulation surf tackle, with bait of cut mullet, shrimp, crab, or clam. Wire leader not necessary (channel bass are nearly toothless), but a good idea because of possible strikes from other fish.

Bluefish: Maine to Florida, including the Gulf. Small ones in bays, sounds, brackish river mouths, often called "snapper blues." A trim, elongated, blue-gray and silvery fish with deeply notched tail, distinct dark lateral line along side, large, sharply toothed mouth. Awesomely voracious, feeding on menhaden, squids, etc. Runs in schools; unpredictable as to where they'll turn up, and when. Weight: anywhere from 1 to 25 pounds.

Methods: This fine battler is so greedy that he'll hit practically any moving lure, from squid, shrimp, bait fish such as mullet or menhaden, to spoons, tin squids, plugs, feathered jigs. Many are taken surf fishing, using regulation surf tackle. Plug casting with regulation bait-casting tackle is also effective in inside waters. The fly rod, with small metal spoons and spinners, a streamer fly, or minnow bait, is great sport when schools of "snapper blues" can be located. For trolling or still-fishing a 3/6 or 4/6 outfit is excellent. Hook sizes should be from 3/0 to 6/0. In all bluefish angling, wire leader must be used. It need not be extremely heavy, nor long. In the South, midwinter to late spring is best; farther north, spring through summer. Chumming with chopped menhaden is commonly done, until an oily "slick" forms on the water. The baited hook is then drifted or cast into the slick.

Bonefish: Pacific, casually to northern California; Atlantic, to lower New England. Most abundant about the Florida Keys. Brownish and bright silvery, chunky but elongated, with mouth set far under, and an odd, overlapping, humped snout. Feeds over mud flats, on bottom, in extremely shallow water during high tide, taking crabs, mollusks, crustaceans predominantly. Very wary, very swift, powerful. Often located when "tailing" —feeding snout down with tail breaking water. Weight: average, 2 to 6 pounds; maximum, 15.

Methods: This is a real thrill fish, the last word in excitement for those who can get to his mud-flats hangouts around the Keys during spring and summer and early fall. Wariness of the fish and the shallow water make "bonefishing" an exacting sport. It is done either wading, or from a double-anchored skiff. The angler, having located bonefish feeding grounds, places himself and awaits the tide, watching for signs of swirling or "tailing" fish. Sometimes chum or shrimp or hermit crab is thrown out, the baited hook, with light sinker, or with no sinker, following. The bite is a slight tug as the fish mouths the bait. The angler must strike immediately.

Tackle: a 4/6 outfit; reel about 1/0; 250-300 yards line; hook generally 4/0; leader short, of very fine wire, or twisted gut. Fly-rod fishing, with a fairly heavy outfit, and size 1/0 trout flies is terrific sport. The fly is quietly cast very close to a feeding fish. Have plenty of backing line on a large single-action reel. These fish are awesomely swift, strong, never-say-die battlers. Occasionally they will hit surface plugs cast past where they're feeding and retrieved near them. Bonefish are fished for sport only and should be released. They are too bony to make good eating.

The Bonitos: At least four species in our waters. All are "tuna-shaped" fishes, closely related to the tunas, extremely powerful and swift, with narrow, forked tails. Colors: blue above, silvery and yellow below. All have dark stripes running the long way of the body, but usually on an upward angle, each stripe beginning at the lateral line and running back and up toward the back. Common Bonito: from the Gulf and Florida to Massachusetts; average weight 2 to 5 pounds, maximum about 15. Striped Bonito: range about the same in our waters; seldom over 5 or 6 pounds. California Bonito: most of U. S. Pacific Coast, most abundant along mid-California; weight about as for Striped Bonito. Oceanic Bonito: both coasts, most abundant in southern portions; averages 15 or 20 pounds; has dark stripes along belly. All are predominantly open-sea fish, running in schools near surface as a rule, feeding on small fish.

Methods: The bonitos are fabulously game, sensational swimmers and battlers. It is difficult to fish just for bonito, for usually they are taken while fishing for larger species, and the angler can never be certain a larger fish won't strike. Thus, though light tackle, such as a 4/6 outfit, makes for great sport with the bonito, heavier tackle, at least a 6/9 rig, is practically a must. The accepted method is trolling, using strip bait, squid, or feathered jigs and metal spoons. Wire leader is necessary.

Cero, or Kingfish: This is the king mackerel, largest of the mackerel tribe, ranging from Florida and the Gulf to the Carolinas. A close relative ranges along the lower portion of the California coast. Very long, slender, swift, powerful, a high jumper when hooked. Color: blue-green above, silvery below, extremely iridescent. Runs in large schools, offshore, feeding predominantly upon small fish. Weight: average, anywhere to 15 pounds; maximum, 75.

Methods: This is one of the most important winter targets for Florida charter-boat anglers. Huge catches are the rule when the "kings" are in. Trolling with bright metal spoons, or with strip bait is sure-fire. Tackle: for experienced anglers a 4/6 outfit; for beginners at least a 6/9. Wire leader.

Cobia, or "Crab-Eater": Florida to the Carolinas. A long, dark brown to cream-colored fish, heavy, powerful, the lateral line dark and jagged along its forward portion. Mouth large, head flat. Usually solitary. Frequents open water, but most often caught on bottom around bays, bayous, inlets, along mangrove shores, etc., where it feeds largely on crabs. Weight: average, 3 to 15 pounds; maximum, upwards of 100.

Methods: Seldom is it possible to fish strictly for cobia. The fish is a fine fighter, but, being mostly a lone wolf, is usually taken only incidentally while trolling, or bottom fishing for other species. Mentioned here for purposes of identification.

Dolphin: Gulf to Carolinas; California to Oregon. Most beautiful of salt-water game fish; colors change rapidly, from green to blue to yellow to purple, or combinations, always with dark speckles scattered over body. Unmistakable because of blunt snout with underset mouth, extremely high "forehead," body tapering, streamlined, to forked tail, dorsal fin high and tapering likewise, full length of back. An open-ocean fish, very swift, spectacular swimmer which runs down small fish. May be alone, or in schools. Weight: average, 2 to 7 pounds; maximum, upwards of 70.

Methods: Trolling, with strip bait, whole mullet or flying fish, or with metal spoons or feathered jigs. The school fish are usually of average weight. For them, a 4/6 rig, or even a bait-casting rod, makes for terrific sport. Solitary dolphin are usually large, and usually taken on heavier tackle while trolling for other open-ocean fish. Trick of successful school-dolphin fishing is to tire out the first fish hooked, then keep him near the boat without landing him. These fellows have the curious habit of tagging after a hooked brother. Spoons, jigs, or bait cast near the one held struggling in the water invariably brings strike after strike from the remainder of the school.

The Jacks: Several species, in both Atlantic and Pacific, but the Pacific ones are not common far enough north to be important in U. S. waters. Most common, in the Gulf and about Florida: Common Jack, or Jack Crevalle. Steep, blunt forehead, deep body, forked tail. Lateral line deeply curved down, toward tail, and with bony plates along it on tail. Color: iridescent gray-blue and yellowish. Food: shrimp, small fish, crabs. Weight: average, 1 to 5 pounds; maximum, to 25.

Methods: Jacks are not especially good eating fish, but are swift, powerful, stubborn battlers. They will hit almost any lure, or take bait. Offshore, large ones are taken trolling, with large spoon, plugs, feathered jigs, or strip bait. Rig for these should be 6/9. Many are also taken surf fishing. In addition, the jack is a standard sport fish for plug casters fishing bays, inlets, channels, either from shore or boat. They show preference for yellow plugs or jigs.

Ladyfish, or "Ten-Pounder": Most abundant around Florida's coasts. Too bony to eat. Long, very slender, silvery, pale greenish above. Large eye. Close relative of tarpon, but runs small, from 1 to 3 feet.

Methods: Ladyfish, which run in schools and battle beautifully, with many high leaps, are great sport, but should be released. Taken usually on plugs or feathered jigs, by bait casters fishing from shore or bridges for other species. For anglers who want pure sport, a school of ladyfish supplies it in top grade.

The Mackerels: Several species, along both coasts. Long, forked-tailed fish, silvery below, dark mottled on back. Run in large schools, both in open sea and near shore, feeding predominantly on small fish. The Spanish Mackerel, abundant in the Gulf and north to the Carolinas, is an iridescent gray-blue to aluminum-colored species, with bronze spots. It weighs from 2 to 20 pounds. Other common mackerels average around 2 pounds.

Methods: Trolling is standard, with 4/6 outfit and metal spoons or feathered jigs. Still-fishing from bridges or piers, in some locations, using minnows for bait, is also effective. Near-shore schools can be taken by bait casters, with small plugs, spoons, jigs. Fly-rod fishing, with streamer flies or small spinners, is great inshore sport. Backing line is needed, for the fish are powerful, making long runs. Locate a feeding school, circle it with a boat, cast into the school, work fly (or plug) *swiftly*.

Pompano: Common Pompano, from Carolinas south into Gulf. Round Pompano, range about the same. Permit, around Florida Keys. Pacific Pompanos do not come north into our waters. Compressed, deep-bodied fork-tailed fishes, blunt nosed, with mouth set almost underneath. Large eye. Color iridescent gray-blue, with silver and gold overtones. Swift, tough, bottom and surf feeders. Food mostly sand fleas, shrimp, small crustaceans and mollusks. Delicious eating. Weight, Common and Round Pompanos, 1 to 5 pounds; permit, up to 8.

Methods: Fished in surf with sand fleas, shrimp, or hermit crab for bait, using small sinker, and hook about 3/0. Around Florida most commonly taken on a small, yellow feathered jig, cast from bridges or channel shores with regulation bait-casting tackle. Sinker and swivel are placed at end of line, then two feet of wire leader, another swivel, and weighted jig. Cast, let the lure sink to bottom, retrieve by giving quick jerk, reeling up slack, quick jerk, repeat. An extremely sporty fish.

Snook: Around Florida and the Gulf Coast. A relative in Pacific almost at bottom of our range. Long, silvery fish with humped back, undershot jaw. Unmistakable because of black lateral line which dips sharply from behind head, then runs clear on along body and extends into tail. Food: mostly small fish. Brackish rivers and inlets, mud flats, mangrove shores, sandy channels. Weight: average, 2 to 5 pounds; maximum, 50.

Methods: This fish is the plug caster's delight. Will smash almost any plug—surface, diving, or sinking—as well as jigs, spoons, etc. Can also be taken on streamer flies in canals and over mud flats. Often hits best at night. Taken from piers and bridges on bait such as shrimp, cut bait, etc. Also taken trolling, slowly with spoons, jigs, or bait. For trolling or still-fishing, 3/6 outfit is adequate. Fly and bait casters should use fairly heavy tackle. The snook is a tough guy. Excellent eating.

Tarpon: Most abundant about the Gulf and the Atlantic coast of Florida. Large-scaled, silvery fish, iridescent, bluish along back. Dorsal fin with long "streamer" behind. Large, bony mouth. Food: crabs, pinfish, mullet. Tarpon from 3 to 20 pounds abundant in bayous, brackish river mouths, canals. Larger ones, 50 to 250 pounds, feeding in large schools near surface, abundant from early spring throughout summer in open water from near shore to a mile offshore.

Methods: This is one of our greatest game fishes, a hard battler, spectacular leaper. Bony mouth makes the tarpon hard to hook. Leaps make him difficult to *keep* hooked. Standard methods are: locating a school by watching for them rolling and feeding near surface, then trolling slowly, with live, or strip bait, or metal spoon, around edges of school, or following school and still-fishing. This is done mostly with whole blue crabs, or pinfish, using a float to keep bait about three feet from surface, throwing bait out into or near the school. Hooks should be 9/0 to 11/0. Tackle: trolling and still-fishing, either 6/9 rig or outfit somewhat heavier, about 12- to 16-ounce rod tip. No. 9 wire leader, at least 6 feet.

Plug casting and streamer-fly and "popping bug" fishing for small tarpon in bayous and canals are very sporty methods also. For plug casting, either a 4/6 outfit or sturdy salt-water bait-casting rod. For fly-fishing, a heavy fly rod, plenty of backing line.

Wahoo: In our waters only about south Florida and the Keys. Color: blue or green above, silvery below, with yellowish bars running indistinctly around its very long, heavy, rounded body. Powerful, one of the swiftest, most vicious of fish. Large, heavily toothed mouth. Solitary in deep water of open sea and along deep offshore reefs. Weight: average, 15 pounds; maximum, over 100.

Methods: Since the wahoo is not especially abundant, it is usually caught incidentally while trolling with whole or strip bait, or spoons and feathered jigs, for other species. An awesome battler. A 6/9 outfit will do, but heavier tackle—9-ounce tip and equipment to match —is preferable. Wire leader essential.

The Weakfishes: Several species. Most common are the Weakfish, the Spotted Weakfish (Sea Trout, Speckled Trout). The first most abundant from Massachusetts to the Carolinas, the second from the Carolinas to the Texas Gulf Coast. Fish of the surf, inlets, channels, tide rips, bayous, sand and mud shallows. The weakfish is brownish yellow with indistinct spots; the spotted weakfish dark above, silvery below, with distinct dark speckles and spots. Weights: average, 1 to 5 pounds; maximum, upwards of 20. Food: mainly small fish, shrimp.

Methods: Weakfish are among the most important

targets of surf fishermen, trollers in inside waters, bridge and bayou fishermen. Commonly fished with bait-casting tackle, using underwater plugs, small yellow feathered jigs, etc., with the jerk, reel, jerk, reel technique. Around Florida, live-shrimp fishing in "trout holes" in the bays is common. A float is used, holding the shrimp a foot or two under. Cast is made, retrieved very slowly, with short jerks. Still-fishing from small boats, using chum, is also extremely effective. These "sea trout" have tender mouths, must be handled gingerly when hooked. Can also be taken on fly rod with streamer flies.

Pacific Yellowtail (sometimes called "amberjack"): California coast. Another fish (see "Bottom Fish") of Florida is also called yellowtail, but it is an altogether different fish. Shaped much like the amberjack, its relative. A yellow band running full length of body. Runs in schools fairly close inshore, around rocks, feeding upon small school fish. Weight: average, to 15 pounds; maximum, about 75.

Methods: This is one of California's top game fish. Can be taken surf casting at proper locations, but is most often fished by trolling, using herring or sardines, or metal spoons and feathered jigs. For this method, a 6/9 rig, or something a bit heavier, is required.

BOTTOM FISH

As HAS been stated, the groups as given here greatly overlap and are only for convenience. In this group fall all manner of salt-water fish, all of them good eating, some very good fighters, but on the whole most of them somewhat more sluggish than those species already covered. In this group, too, are included the numerous salt-water "pan fish." They are legion, and thus cannot be described in detail. They range all the way from the zebra-striped spade fish and the bright-colored angel fishes to the sluggish and delicious blowfish, and the catfishes. Many of these numerous kinds are taken by still-fishermen and surf fishermen who are after other species. Thus, methods seldom differ for any particular one. Only the more important bottom fish are described here.

Sea Bass: Blackfish, Rockfish. Maine to Gulf, most abundant Massachusetts to New Jersey. General "bass" shape, long dorsal fin spines. Color: grayish to black, with indistinct mottlings or stripes. Food: clams, crabs, small fish, etc. Around rocky places, both deep offshore banks and inshore waters. Average size, 1 to 3 pounds.

Methods: Either handline or bait-casting rod, hook about 2/0, baited with cut bait, clams, etc., fished on bottom. For deep offshore fishing, sometimes down to over 200 feet, heavier tackle is needed because of strain of reeling fish up from such depths.

Jewfish: One called California Black Sea Bass; another, around Florida, called Spotted Jewfish. Dark, mottled, huge-mouthed fish. Feed on bottom around rocks, near jetties, wharves, pilings, in inlets, channels. Weight: 50 to 600-700 pounds.

Methods: Usually taken with very large hook, often a rope for line, with whole fish of several pounds, or several crabs, fished on bottom, either still or from drifting boat. These fish are good eating, but fishing them is more labor than sport. Smaller ones occasionally strike slowly trolled spoons and jigs.

Groupers: Many species, in both oceans, but in our

range only in Atlantic, and most abundant around both Florida coasts, the Gulf Coast, and thinning out north to the Carolinas. Shape quite like fresh-water black bass. Species: Black, Red, Yellow, Nassau, Rock Groupers, Red Hind, Rock Hind, Tripletail, etc. Groupers change colors quickly when hooked, but all species are spotted or mottled, usually somberly. Food: small fish, crabs, shrimp. Weight: average, 5 to 25 pounds; maximum, over 100.

Methods: Groupers are very popular charter-boat fish around Florida, taken offshore by trolling with strips of mullet attached to a spoon, or by still-fishing over deep rocky reefs. Inshore, in bays, inlets, etc., they are taken either trolling with spoons, plugs, or feathered jigs, or by still-fishing near bottom, using cut bait, shrimp, etc. Tackle for offshore fishing should match at least a 9-ounce rod tip, with hooks about 8/0, for the fish run heavy, fight hard and deep, and must be turned if they try to dive into deep rock holes. Inshore trolling does not require heavy tackle, for the fish usually run lighter. All groupers are excellent eating fish.

Snappers: Numerous species, in our ranges only in Atlantic. Red Snapper very important along Gulf Coast. Gray, Mangrove, Lane Snappers, Schoolmaster, Muttonfish, Dog Snapper—all are basslike fishes, but with somewhat deeper bodies, and underjaw jutting a little. Colors run from red to gray, purplish, greenish, etc., some with stripes or mottlings. All feed on or near bottom, often most avidly at night, taking all manner of food. They frequent both deep and shallow water. Example: Mangrove snappers can be caught by dozens in three feet of water along mangrove-bordered shore lines around the Florida Keys; red snappers are often taken out in the open Gulf, in very deep water.

Methods: Handlines, or light bait-casting tackle, still-fishing with cut bait, shrimp, etc. None of the snappers ever weigh much above 2 to 4 pounds. Good eating fish. The "Yellowtail" (of Florida) belongs to this family, but looks quite different. It has a forked tail; color grayish-blue, silvery and pink, with yellow swath down the side and tail yellow. Runs small. An important bottom fish around the Florida Keys.

The Grunts: Many species, in our range all in the Atlantic except a relative, the Sargo, along the southern California coast. Gray Grunt, White Grunt, Yellow Grunt, Pigfish, the last-named north to New York, the others most abundant about Florida and the Gulf. Small bottom fishes, their shape reminiscent of the fresh-water sunfishes. Many have red mouth lining. Good eating fish.

The Porgies: Quite similar to the Grunts. Most abundant and most heavily fished species, the Northern Porgy, ranging from the Carolinas to Maine. Seldom run over 2 pounds.

The Surf Perches: Pacific fish; Striped Perch, Barred Perch, Surf Perch, etc. Shaped like fresh-water sunfishes, colors varied, from silvery to quite brilliant red and yellow stripes. Weight from ½ to about 2 pounds. Found over sandy bottoms, in the surf, in bays, etc. The inshore pan fish of the Pacific.

Methods: The above three groups are taken for the most part still-fishing, from bridges, jetties, small boats. The Surf Perches are often caught by surf fishermen. Cut bait, shrimp, bits of the clam, crab, bloodworms, sand fleas—any natural bait is productive.

Cod: From North Carolina north. Long, deep-bodied. Color: somber, browns to grays, with scattered dots; pale below; lateral line light. A chin "whisker," or barbel. Inhabits both very deep and shallow water, depending upon season. Food: eats practically anything. Weight: average, to 15 pounds; maximum, upwards of 250.

Methods: Mainly fished offshore, deep, around rocks, by handline, from live-bait boats. Best to use hook size at least 2/0, to keep other small fish from getting hooked. In shallow water, any bait-casting or boat rod will do. Line should test about 20 pounds.

Pollock: Most abundant from New Jersey north. Quite similar to the cod, but greenish in color. Runs in large schools, usually in deep, cold offshore waters. Often feeds on the surface, however, making forays into bays. Weight: average, to 15 pounds; maximum, 40.

Methods: In deep water, pollock are taken by deep, slow trolling, using either spoons, jigs, etc., or spinner-and-bait combinations, usually strip bait. Tackle for this deep work should be fairly heavy: rod tip at least 9 ounces, line up to 24 thread, hook size around 9/0. When a surface-feeding school can be located, trolling around the edges of it, then swinging to bring the lure into the school, gets excellent results. In bays, pollock are caught by still-fishing from boats, or casting with surf tackle from shore.

Black Drum: Massachusetts to Texas. Deep-bodied, large-scaled. Chin "whiskers." Silvery gray with blurred black vertical stripes, or, when very large, almost entirely dark silvery. Makes a croaking sound. Large, tough spines in fore portion of dorsal. Feeds on mollusks and crustaceans, crushing the shells with large throat teeth. Surf, bay, and inlet feeders. Weight: average, 2 to 5 pounds; maximum, over 75.

Methods: Still-fishing from piers, bridges, jetties, or small boats in bays, etc.; surf fishing. Clams, shrimp, etc., make good bait. Drum seldom hit artificials. Sluggish fighters but fairly good eating.

Croaker: Several species. Most important ones are the Yellowfin and Spotfin Croakers of the Pacific; north to about San Francisco. Related to the drums. Make croaking sounds. Colors: yellowish and silvery, or steel-blue and silvery, with scattered dark dots. Feed along the surf outside the breakers, and generally inshore in bays and lagoons. The Common Croaker of the Atlantic Coast has the same habits. Weight: seldom over 5 pounds.

Methods: Still-fishing in the bays, down around 10 feet or a bit more. Surf casting, using cut bait and leaving it inert on bottom after a long cast past the breakers. Croakers are top surf-fishing prizes especially along the California coast. Fair fighters. Good eating.

Tautog or Blackfish: From the Carolinas north. A chunky, steep-headed, dark-mottled fish of rocky bottoms around bays, coves, etc., where they feed on various shellfish. Weight: 2 to 5 pounds, up to 20.

Methods: This is an important New England fish. Taken most generally either by still-fishing from small boats just offshore in about 5 fathoms of water or by using a surf-casting outfit and fishing around the deep holes along rocky shore lines. Clams, crabs, etc., make good bait. Hook size should be about 4/0. Good scrappers. Good eating.

Sheepshead: Cape Cod to Gulf. A steep-headed, very deep-bodied fish with large scales and wide vertical zebra stripes. Very sharp, long dorsal spines. Extremely strong "buck" teeth for cutting up shellfish and crabs. Hangs around piers, bridge pilings, reefs, etc. Weight: average, 1 to 5 pounds; maximum, over 20.

Methods: Still-fishing, usually with small fiddler crabs as bait, although almost any bait will take them. Wire leader and good hooks are needed. Their mouths are comparatively small but exceedingly hard. Sheepshead bite very gingerly and are also rather wary. Learning how to hook them consistently requires some experience.

Flounders: Several species, all unmistakable because of their extremely compressed bodies, the fact that both eyes are on one side of the head, and that they lie on bottom, flat on one side. Underside white, upperside dark, mottled, or spotted depending on species. Winter Flounder, Summer Flounder, Halibut, California Halibut, etc. The flounders run from 1 to 20 pounds, the halibuts much larger, especially the Atlantic species, which go to several hundred pounds. Fishes of sandy bottoms, in both very shallow and very deep waters. Food: shellfish, crustaceans, crabs, small fish.

Methods: Still-fishing in bays, etc., from small boats or piers and jetties, using small hooks (these fish have rather small mouths) and keeping the bait on bottom. Surf fishing. Slow drift fishing, either with live minnows or cut bait, or slow trolling with small spinners, is also effective and helps locate the fish. Reasonably good fighters, excellent eating.

There are innumerable other salt-water fish which make good catching and good eating—the huge schools of Silver Hake of the northern Atlantic Coast, the surf-loving Whiting, the various Rockfish of the Pacific, the California Sand and Kelp Basses, and many others. If, however, you master the exciting art of successful fishing for those covered here which best suit your location and opportunities, you will easily be able to catch any of the others you desire. In fact, you'll often catch them when you aren't even fishing for them!

Part 2.

HUNTING

Chapter One

Hunting Equipment
and How to Use It

Outdoorsmen in the U.S. may well be thankful that hunting, one of man's oldest sports, is still in America an activity for *everyone,* not, as for so many centuries in the Old World, entirely or partly restricted to the wealthy. No country in the world had a greater variety of game, a greater abundance of game, or species better suited to the widely divergent sporting tastes of tens of thousands of hunters, than the U.S. had in its early days.

But, from the beginning, we have been wasteful of these extremely valuable natural resources. In many instances we still are today. Luckily, we have hundreds of career scientists who have gone into game and forestry work with our conservation departments. It is possible, game men know, to keep reasonably abundant game in most areas, IF money enough is forthcoming to pay for the tremendous amount of work and research involved. But the game men cannot do the work alone. Today, every man who shoulders a gun each fall must first be a conservationist, second a hunter. He must train himself to think more and more in terms of *enjoyment* rather than the numbers of his kill. And he *must* nurture a more friendly and helpful relationship with the landowner. Otherwise, hunting in the U.S. is doomed eventually to become a private preserve sport!

We do have excellent hunting still today in much of our territory, and fair hunting over most of it. Obviously therefore, the picture is far from hopeless. Thus, we should enjoy to the utmost the wonderful sport our game furnishes us. But our foremost aim should be to instruct new generations so thoroughly in wise conservation—that the future of U.S. hunting may be as bright as its past.

One of the small ways in which we can each help in keeping that important future of the grand sport of hunting bright is by knowing as much as we can about hunting equipment, the most important parts of which, naturally, are our weapons. A thorough basic knowledge of these weapons, and their ammunition as related to various kinds of game, is a prime requisite in being a successful hunter. But beyond that, such knowledge contributes a great deal to good conservation practices, assuring less game crippled and lost. Clean kills must always be the paramount interest of the good sportsman. And, as our hunters' legions grow, absolute safety at all times becomes more and more important. Otherwise, we may wake up one day to find so many of us acting carelessly, with such deplorable results, that the law will be tempted to outlaw hunting entirely.

The whole point to be made here is that probably nine out of ten hunters are persons who get out in the woods and fields only a few days each season. Though they enjoy the high exhilaration of the chase and the surroundings just as much as anyone else, many such hunters know very little about the weapons they carry. The study of weapons is not the simple matter that the study of proper fishing tackle is. All its knowledge must be based upon very exacting science. It cannot even be made entirely simple in these pages. It requires some study, some thought and concentration on the part of the person who wishes to use the information to the best advantage of everyone concerned in the field. But it is not an insurmountable problem, and its compensations are large, both in the size of the bag and the satisfaction of assurance while afield. Those who know most enjoy most.

As has been said, the main equipment of the hunter is his weapon, and the proper ammunition to go with it. This can be, in the U.S., a rifle or a shotgun, depending upon the game sought, and upon the state laws where the weapon is to be used.

With the exception of some sections of the South, where deer are traditionally hunted with shotguns, and some heavily populated sections where rifles are excessively dangerous and therefore locally outlawed, the rifle is almost always used for all kinds of big-game animals. It is also used in what has come to be known as "varmint hunting." This is the sport of using a light rifle to shoot animals ranging from woodchucks and prairie dogs to coyotes. The shotgun, on the other hand, is traditionally the gun in universal use for shooting birds on the wing and for shooting small running game animals, such as rabbits.

RIFLES

THE RIFLE is a gun intended to shoot at long ranges, a gun with thick, heavy barrel, whose cartridge is loaded with a single large shot, or pellet, as opposed to the numerous small short-range pellets of the shotgun, or "scattergun." In order that this single shot may travel long distances and still have killing power and accuracy—which it would lose if its velocity were too quickly dissipated and the action both of its slowing down and of gravity caused it to drop too far—it is necessary that it leave the barrel at high speed. Therefore, a rather heavy charge of fairly fast-burning powder must be used to give it a tremendous push.

This, in turn, requires that a metal case be used to house the charge and hold the base of the bullet. It also requires that rifles be built extremely strong, therefore quite heavy, so that they will not be blown apart by the discharge. The thick barrel is necessary to absorb the heat of friction caused by the single high-speed ball passing through it so swiftly. In addition, the recoil shock of the explosion and of a bullet given such a tremendous push would cause a too-light gun to "jump" so that little accuracy would be possible.

In order to keep a bullet true on its course, gunsmiths long ago discovered that the bullet must not only travel straight ahead but must rotate as it travels. This was accomplished by cutting spiral grooves inside the barrel, throughout its length. The discharged bullet expands against these grooves, thus follows their exact spiral, and its spinning motion is begun.

RIFLING is the name given to these grooves of the barrel. In a barrel of given length, several complete turns are possible in the rifling. There may be a complete turn, for example, in 10 inches, or in 14 inches. Upon the "speed" of the rifling depends the rotation speed of the bullet. Too fast a spin of a high-velocity bullet may harm rather than help its accuracy. All standard-make rifles are rifled by the manufacturer to give the best average results in accordance with the ammunition intended in that gun.

CALIBER of a rifle is, in simple language, the diameter measurement of the hole in its barrel, stated in fractions of an inch. It is, therefore, the *bore diameter*. Remember, however, that the rifling, which consists usually of four grooves, each cut approximately .004 inch deep, would change this measurement if it were taken from groove to groove. The measurement therefore is taken across the actual barrel, as if the grooves weren't there. When you look down the barrel, the barrel portions between grooves appear to (and do) thrust up higher than the grooves. These are spoken of as the "lands." True caliber is thus measured from land to land. A .30-caliber rifle measures, bore diameter, .3000 inch.

In the U.S., we drop the extra ciphers. However, a true caliber of .2570 would be called a .257. Also, under the British system, three digits are always retained. Europeans use metric measurements.

Unhappily for beginners, and old hands also, there

is no standard calibration system among gun makers. Examples: caliber .250/3000—the "3000" means muzzle velocity of the bullet; .30/06—the "06" indicates the year the cartridge became standard; .30/30—no one is sure *what* the last "30" stands for; .25/20—the "20" indicates powder charge weight. In addition, many popular "calibers" are not true calibers at all. Examples: the .220 Swift is actually .219; the .303 Savage is actually .300; etc. The inexperienced prospective rifle buyer, therefore, should know all details of the caliber designation of a gun to be sure it is what he wants, before buying it.

THE ACTION of a rifle, as the term is generally used, means the type of device it has for reloading. For hunting, a single-shot gun is very nearly worthless. One or more extra shots may be needed more quickly than the gun could be reloaded by hand. Repeating rifles, with magazines holding extra shells, are therefore most useful and popular.

Action types are as follows: *lever action* (back of the trigger guard there is a lever, into the grip of which the three last fingers of the right hand fit; after the shot, these fingers push the lever down and ahead, then back and up, ejecting the spent shell case and throwing another shell from the magazine into the barrel); *bolt action* (a knob, placed at the right side of the gun near the trigger, is grasped, shoved upward to unlock the gun breech, pulled backward, which ejects the spent shell, thrust forward carrying the new shell from the magazine, pulled down to lock the breech again); *pump action* (a handgrip below the barrel rests in the left hand as the gun is fired, then is pulled back, and pushed

138

forward, ejecting the spent shell and shoving the new one into the magazine); *autoloading* (varied mechanisms utilize recoil power of the shot to eject the spent shell and throw another into the barrel; the trigger may then be pulled again and the second shot fired without any manual action of the hunter).

Pump action rifles have never gained much popularity. Autoloading rifles built for hunting purposes are few, and their use illegal in certain states. The lever action is, for the tyro, perhaps faster than the bolt action. Bolt action is, however, much stronger and more simple. Though rifle action is a personal choice, the bolt type is undoubtedly the all-round best and most popular. Before action is chosen, however, the rifle buyer must decide what caliber gun he wants. Manufacturers make only certain actions in certain calibers.

CHOICE OF CALIBER is a complicated matter, dependent upon: (1) state laws (some states have outlawed rifles entirely in certain sections, and some have laws stating that certain game must be hunted with rifles no lighter than a specified caliber); (2) the kind of game for which the rifle will be used (obviously a light rifle, easy to carry and capable of killing coyotes would be an illogical choice for deer or bear); (3) the type of country where most of the hunting will be done (in open or mountain country, very long-range shots may be the rule, and these require a different gun from one used in brushy country where the average range will be short); (4) the amount of money the buyer has to invest.

Thus, in actual practice, since it is the *bullet* that does the killing, the rifle enthusiast, to make a logical choice of gun, must first decide upon *exactly* what it is he wants the *bullet to do.* Once he knows that, in a sense he chooses first his ammunition; then, from among the various rifles chambered to shoot that type of ammunition, he chooses his gun.

RIFLE AMMUNITION is as confusing a matter as is caliber. It is without recognizable system of nomenclature. Many a cartridge *name* does not match the true caliber either of its bullet or of the gun which will shoot it. Example: the .218 Bee cartridge and the .220 Swift are both .22 caliber, or so called, yet actually neither is *true* .22 caliber, but rather .217 and .219 respectively. Experimental development aimed constantly toward better loads has been partly responsible for the confusion; so has the lack of a standard naming system. The average hunter will, therefore, find it advantageous to consider in the beginning only the basically different *types* of ammunition, built for specific purposes, and only those few calibers most popular for various kinds of game, and terrain.

There are light calibers (example: the .22, with its various loads—.22 short, .22 long, .22 long rifle, etc.), medium calibers (example: .250 Savage), heavy calibers (examples: .30/06, .270 and .348 Winchester), and super-heavy or "magnum" loads (examples: .375 H. & H. Magnum, .401 and 405 Winchester).

There are, among these and the many others, cartridges of high and super-high muzzle velocity, and cartridges of relatively low muzzle velocity. High muzzle velocity gives a "flat trajectory." Trajectory is the arc described by a bullet between muzzle and target at a given range. As it travels, a bullet first rises slightly, then loses some of its original velocity, and gravity pulls it downward. The faster it travels its course, the less it will drop. Flat trajectory means, therefore, that the point of actual aim can be nearer to exactly "on" the target at long ranges than with a low-velocity bullet. This is obviously advantageous. The .220 Swift, for example, leaves the muzzle at over 4000 feet per second. It drops hardly at all in 100 yards. A .22 short leaves the muzzle at less than 1000 feet per second, drops well over a yard at 100-yard range.

High muzzle velocity does not necessarily always mean a better load (or gun). Fast, light bullets are easily disintegrated, or thrown off course, by hitting even a small twig. Since a hunter must center his interest on both *accuracy* and *shocking power* as well as flat trajectory, a low velocity load may be to his advantage. For instance, in deer shooting at short ranges in brushy country, a low-velocity bullet (which can be designed with soft, rounded point so that it will mushroom upon impact) would be sure to get to the deer intact, give necessary accuracy, and *more* shocking power than a high-speed bullet, which, having to be built pointed and steel jacketed, might pass right through the deer with little damage—if it reached him without being deflected. The high-speed bullet would be requisite, however, for shooting bears or mountain sheep at long ranges in the mountains, or for shooting distant groundhogs, etc.

There are innumerable bullet designs: soft point, hollow point, blunt nosed, sharp pointed, boat-tailed, etc. All have their special purposes, related to velocity, range, weight, etc., and to the powder charges behind them. Bullets are measured by weight in grains. Certain caliber guns also have ammunition available in different weight sizes. Example: the .270 Winchester may use loads the bullets of which are of 130 and 150 grains, each with a different type of powder (slow-burning or fast-burning) and amount of powder behind it, depending upon the job it is required to do.

It may be seen, therefore, that choice of a rifle, and the load to be shot in it, is not a simple matter, but one which requires real study and consideration on the part of the individual. No one can tell you which is the best rifle to use. The choice depends entirely upon the job it is required to do, and upon personal likes and dislikes of the hunter. In Chapters Five and Six, various calibers and loads are suggested as examples of good choices for various game animals. Rule of thumb: Choose a gun not for "trick" shots at extreme ranges, but one *heavy* enough and chambered for ammunition of the right type to put down for keeps the animal in question at normal ranges in the country where it is to be hunted, with the *least* number of shots.

It is easy to see, opposite, how bullet *weight* is related

Table of Representative Popular Modern Calibers

Among the cartridges indicated there are various makes, various bullet styles—that is, shapes—various bullet materials, various powder loads, etc. The ones chosen therefore indicate *very roughly* the ballistics of that *class* of load (and gun). Most .22 caliber rifles, for example, are chambered to shoot short, long, and long-rifle shells. And there are many different load *types* of each of these, all differing slightly. The table intends to show only by comparison what general caliber *classes*—light, medium, heavy—are capable of. Once a rifle is chosen, the shooter must make a study of its various loads to determine which is best for his purposes. Ammunition companies can furnish complete ballistics tables for all their products.

CARTRIDGE CALIBER	BULLET WT. GRAINS	FT. PER SEC. VEL. MUZZLE	FT. PER SEC. VEL. 100 YDS.	ENERGY, FT. LBS. 100 YDS.
.22 short	29	1030	860	48
.22 long	29	1375	1020	67
.22 long-rifle	40	1375	1080	104
.218 Bee	46	2860	2260	520
.219 Zipper	56	3050	2530	795
.22 Hornet	45	2650	2080	430
.220 Swift	48	4140	3490	1300
.22 Savage	70	2780	2480	955
.250 Savage	100	2810	2490	1375
.257 Roberts	117	2630	2330	1410
.270 Winchester	130	3140	2820	2295
.270 Winchester	150	2770	2490	2065
.30/30 Win.	170	2200	1930	1405
.30/06 Springfield	180	2710	2420	2340
.300 H. & H. Magnum	220	2610	2380	2770
.303 Savage	190	1960	1740	1280
.32 Win. Special	170	2260	1960	1450
.348 Win.	150	2880	2380	1890
.35 Win.	250	2160	1910	2025
.375 H. & H. Magnum	270	2720	2460	3630
.405 Win.	300	2220	1940	2510

Table is based on random choices from Western Cartridge Company ballistics chart.

to velocity, loss of velocity, and shocking power delivered. A light bullet with high muzzle velocity plus low loss in velocity at 100 yards will mean flatter trajectory and greater long-range killing power. If game is to be shot mostly at 100 yards or less, the low velocity calibers and loads with soft, heavy bullet will be best. If average shots will be 200 yards or more, flat trajectory becomes extremely important. Bullet *style*—soft nosed, steel jacketed, etc.—must always be considered in relation to the job it must do.

NEW CALIBERS are constantly being researched by arms companies. Some prove excellent. New powders make possible shorter cartridge cases to gain the same power. These new cartridges, often with newly designed bullets, in combination with new calibers occasionally give brilliant results and are out on the market. Lately there has been much activity in this field, with major arms companies offering whole new "families" of rifles.

Examples: From Winchester, the new .243 with 80-grain bullet leaving the muzzle at 3500 feet per second, an extremely flat-shooting gun for long-range varmints and light big game such as antelope; the .308, with bullets of various weight, a gun comparable in performance to the old 30/06; the new .358, to replace somewhat the older .348; the caliber .458, the first U. S. attempt at a reliable gun for African big game. Other arms companies are also offering new calibers comparable to the above, and even as you read this, new ones will be reaching the market. It behooves the beginner buying his first rifle to consider carefully these newer guns, whose advantages for specific, and sometimes general, purposes are impressive.

RIFLE SIGHTS are of several kinds. It is important to have good ones. The front sight is usually some sort of "bead," often enclosed in a metal ring or cylinder. Rear sights are "open"—that is, simply a V-shaped piece of metal into the bottom of which the front sight is aligned—or "peep" type, the latter being preferable. Roughly, it is a disk with a small hole in the center, through which the shooter looks, aligning the front bead in the center of the hole. The above is merely a basic description of general sight types. There are many variations. A rifleman must try various types, make a point of studying their functions and differences, until he finds what suits him best.

The rear sight has a mechanism calibrated in "minutes of angle," enabling the gunner to: (1) move it left or right to adjust for cross-wind velocity which would push the bullet off course, or for eccentricities of his shooting which cause him to hold slightly right or left; (2) move it up or down to adjust for various ranges.

SIGHTING IN A RIFLE is the process of adjusting the rear sight to make the bullet strike at the point of aim at a certain known range. In hunting, remember, the gunner must *estimate* the range of the game. With high-velocity loads to be shot at long ranges, the rifle is usually sighted in to hit the point of aim exactly at 200 yards. For low-velocity loads sighting in is usually done for 100 yards, or under, especially if most actual shots will be at about those distances.

The hunter must know the exact trajectory of the ammunition he is shooting. These figures can be learned from ballistics tables. One "minute of angle" on the rear sight calibration will equal approximately ½ inch at 50 yards, 1 inch at 100 yards, 2 inches at 200 yards, etc. If trajectory of a specific load is a drop of, say, 8 inches at 100 yards, the sight is moved *in the direction the shooter wishes the bullet to go*—in this case up—8 minutes of angle. Thus, if he is shooting from his best position and shoots accurately, his *point of aim* will be exactly on the target 100 yards away, and he will hit it. Actually, he will be aiming 8 inches high, movement of the rear sight having made the "invisible" compensation of angle.

Sighting in requires a number of shots at this known range. Once the sights are adjusted properly to hit dead center at that range, if the gunner judges range accurately in the field and shoots straight, he will hit his point of aim at the sighted-in distance, or, assuming that he thoroughly knows the trajectory path of his bullet, he will hold his point of aim low or high, as the case may be, for less or greater distance. Flat trajectory now may be seen to be extremely advantageous. If a certain hypothetical type of load shoves its bullet along so that it drops only, say, 1 inch at 100 yards, 2½ inches at 200 yards, 5 inches at 300 yards, the gunner could be a poor judge of range and still bring down his game. By aiming a bit high on the shoulder of a deer which he *supposed* to be 200 yards away, but which was actually 250 yards distant, he would still hit squarely.

THE TELESCOPE SIGHT is, fundamentally, a rear sight made in the form of a telescope. Inside, there is some device such as a forward post and rear cross hairs which are aligned as are regulation gun sights. Telescope sights are never standard equipment. They must be purchased, in the magnification power the shooter desires, and with a type of mounting which will fit his particular rifle. There are "top-mounted" scopes and "side-mounted" scopes for use relative to the action type of the rifle. Some scopes are made to swing aside, so the regular sights may be used. There are also scopes of variable power. One new one, for example, may be switched simply by turning a ring to any power or half power from 2½x to 8x. The field of view in any scope diminishes in direct proportion to its "x" rating. Example: A 2x scope may have a 30-foot field at 100 yards, an 8x scope only 16.

The purpose of scopes in hunting is of course to give a better, clearer view of the game, therefore making possible more accurate sighting. For long-range shooting, either of big game or varmints, scopes are highly advantageous—in fact, at extreme ranges they are requisite. The sight adjustment mechanism with the telescope sight is quite similar to regular sight adjustments —each minute of angle on it equals roughly 1 inch at 100 yards.

Scopes are rather complicated, delicate mechanisms. They require expert mounting. Be absolutely certain of what you are getting when you purchase one; have a good gunsmith mount it properly; study its purpose and its mechanics thoroughly.

THE BINOCULAR is one of the rifleman's most important pieces of equipment if he is after big game at long ranges. Only dependable ones should be considered, preferably those made small and light. Their sizes are indicated as 6x30, 9x35, etc. The first number refers to the magnification power, the second to the front lens diameter. The larger this diameter, the better the light-gathering power.

Hunting Binocular Suggestions	
TYPE OF HUNTING	BINOCULAR
Open country (plains or mountains)	9x35
Moose, grizzlies, etc.	8x30
Deer, varmints	7x35
Thick woods	6x30

SHOOTING A RIFLE properly and accurately is not difficult. It is often made difficult, however, because the shooter *tries* too hard. The first principles of accurate rifle shooting are to relax as many muscles as possible, avoid all tenseness, and *squeeze,* not pull, the trigger.

Once sights are correctly adjusted, aiming a rifle is a simple process of lining up the sights and the target. The rear sight should never be *seen.* If it blurs, forget it. Line the front bead in its center, or V, depending on the type of rear sight, *then* line the two on the target. In aiming, the cheek is rested firmly, but not pressed tensely, against the stock.

In long-range shooting at game unaware of the hunter, time should be taken for the hunter to get his breath controlled, so that he may *hold* steadily. Holding is difficult only because of tenseness. The rifle can then be rested across a log, padded by the hunting coat, perhaps, to hold it easily and lightly. The hunter then places his arm well up near armpit through the loop in the gun sling—if he uses a sling, which is advantageous to good holding—and may shoot from the easiest of all positions—prone, left elbow on the ground slightly left of directly under the gun, right elbow planted at an outward angle, body at about a 45-degree angle to the target, legs spread.

The breath must always be held while aiming and holding—*not* with lungs full, but only normal.

Sitting position for rifle shooting is done with legs fairly wide apart, knees up, elbows rested on knees, body at a 45-degree angle to target as in prone position.

In a standing position, a good balance is paramount. The shooter stands almost at right angles to his target, left elbow well under the gun, cheek pressed more firmly against stock. Each shooter must find the position which will balance him best on his feet and allow him to relax the most.

Squeezing the trigger without spoiling good aim and good holding is the most difficult, and most important. The difficulty generally comes from the shooter anticipating the recoil of the gun, and therefore tightening up and flinching. To avoid this, the squeeze should be so light and *gradual* that the shooter cannot even *guess* when the gun will fire. Thus, with practice, since he never knows when to anticipate recoil muscularly, he is continuously relaxed—and he hits the target.

Throughout this brief rifle discussion, the tyro may become somewhat discouraged because everything may seem to be immensely complicated and exacting. To be sure, it is exacting, for that is the very essence of the science of rifles, their ammunition, and their handling. But the subject will seem much more complicated than it is. Once the facts given here are understood reasonably well, then surely anyone can take heart and set about the job of choosing a rifle and load, and learning to shoot well, with little difficulty.

To put that encouraging statement into practice, let us say that you are new to rifles, although you may have done some bird hunting with a shotgun. You "bone up" on the subject of rifles, as we have done here, so that you realize what an entirely different weapon the rifle is from the shotgun. In your section of the country there is little game which you would ordinarily shoot with a rifle except white-tailed deer, and possibly an occasional black bear. The country is not mountainous, but it is brushy. Thus, you immediately realize that your shots will seldom, if ever, be more than a hundred yards.

They can't be, because you won't be able to see your deer or bear farther than that in the terrain where you'll hunt.

You don't want to become a rifle "bug." You just want to have a fling at deer hunting each fall. So now, you can forget the guns which will give you exceptional muzzle velocity and extremely flat trajectories. You can simply buy a gun which you are sure has killing power enough at your maximum 100 yards to do the job you want it to do. And then you will use in it a load for which it was intended—one which won't travel especially fast to be deflected by brush, one which will have solid killing and shocking power at the ranges at which you'll shoot it. Chances are that you won't need a scope at such ranges, and for your purpose. Once you learn to shoot the gun accurately and adjust your sights accurately, you don't need to experiment with other loads or other guns unless you want to. Today's guns are well built. You'll be set, with a weapon to do adequately what you require of it.

If your hunting problem is more complicated than that, or if you will be needing a gun for both long and moderate ranges to be used on trips both to the West and for deer hunting in the East, then you will simply, step by step, go over the most important items relative to *all* your needs, and form a compromise, in case you cannot afford more than one gun. Perhaps this might turn out to be a .270, loaded with different bullet weights and styles for the various kinds of shooting.

That's just about all there is to it. You don't have to be a ballistics wizard to be a rifle hunter. But, as with all things, the more you know about your tools, the better you'll be at using them, and the more accurate because of greater confidence through knowledge. You can be assured, however, that any problem which may come up regarding the purchase of either guns or loads will be answered in detail for you by any of the weapons and ammunition firms. These firms are, in fact, excellent headquarters to which to take your troubles, via mail. They are interested in how well you shoot and how much enjoyment you get from your rifle. Otherwise they couldn't stay in business! So, simply go at the job of owning and shooting a rifle patiently and systematically, one step at a time—and you'll be a crack big-game or varmint shot before you know it!

SHOTGUNS

IN THE U.S., rifle shooters are somewhat in a class by themselves, because of their enthusiasm for the single-ball cartridge. But even they, when the general hunting seasons roll around, put aside their long-range weapons and pick up the old shotgun from the corner. As a nation of hunters, we are in the majority shotgun shooters, for our wealth of game-bird species has dictated over the years what guns should be most used. The shotgun is tied up indestructibly with visions of fall leaves turning, of frosty mornings when the birds lie tight, of bird dogs crisscrossing the fields and woodlands, and of the explosion of various favorite feathered bombshells from their coverts. The shotgun, in other words, is everyman's gun. It is the one piece of equipment above all others which identifies the American hunter, in his duck blind, on the southern dove field, in the pine woods where grouse whir, and in the farm fields where pheasants consort. It is the means and the basis to one of the grandest sports known to man, and one which has centuries of tradition behind it.

Thus, there are by far more shotgunners than riflemen, for the shotgun is used for hunting all kinds of birds and small game. The basic principle of the shotgun, of course, is that its large shell—made of tough paper products with metal base—carries a powder charge above which are packed numerous small pellets. These spread out after leaving the muzzle, the circular "pattern" becoming larger (and "thinner") in direct proportion to the length of the range. Obviously, this makes "wing-shooting"—that is, shooting flying birds —possible.

The shotgun is an extremely deadly weapon at short ranges. But the numerous pellets quite logically lose velocity quickly. The average shotgun's maximum effective killing range is about 50 yards.

GAUGE is the term applied to shotgun size, as opposed to rifle caliber. Originally the gauge of a shotgun was designated by making a round lead ball which would just fit the barrel, then determining how many of these there were in one pound. Example: A 12-gauge shotgun had a bore diameter (hole in the barrel) equal to the diameter of a 1/12th pound lead ball. Later, the term "gauge" was kept, but the various sizes were standardized in inch measurements. In addition, the huge early gauges (4, 8, etc.) were completely discontinued and became illegal for hunting. The 10-gauge hung on for some time, and is still in casual use, but most manufacturers today do not even build it. There is no practical need today for anything larger than a 12-gauge.

Gauge Measurements	
GAUGE	BORE DIAMETER, INCHES
12	.729
16	.662
20	.615
.410	.410

The .410, smallest of our shotguns, was an exception, named for its bore diameter. There is also the 28-gauge, intermediate between the .410 and the 20. It is manufactured, and used, very little. Best, and most popular, gauges are the 12, 16, and 20.

SHOTGUN ACTIONS are much like rifle actions in terminology: single shot, bolt action (these two not very popular); pump, automatic (these two very popular). There is also in shotguns the double barrel, this being a two-shot gun with twin barrels, the barrels either side-by-side or over-and-under, and with either twin or single triggers. The side-by-side double, twin-trigger model is perhaps the most popular of all shotguns, with pumps and automatics following, in that order. (See "Rifle Actions" earlier in this chapter for description of action mechanisms.)

CHOICE OF ACTION depends upon the use to which the gun will be put and upon personal likes and dislikes. The automatic is heavier than the pump as a rule. Each holds from 3 to 5 shots, but for much hunting in the U.S. no more than 3 shots are legal, which requires plugging a portion of the magazine in a 5-shot gun. As a general rule, the double or pump is most popular for upland birds, the automatic as a duck gun. Actually, the arguments pro and con for any style are academic. The man who points the gun is far more important.

CHOICE OF GAUGE depends entirely upon the game to be shot. But this, too, hinges largely upon the capabilities of the shooter. For fairly long ranges, the 12-gauge gives a few yards additional killing power, more pellets in the pattern. For very swift birds where shots must be fast, the lighter gauges handle better. Rule of thumb: If your hunting is to include much waterfowl, stick to the 12-gauge, which can also be used (with small shot) for any shooting; for all-round use, including some waterfowl, the 16 is excellent. If you can judge range accurately, are willing to pass up extreme long-range shots, like a light, fast gun to carry and handle, will be hunting upland birds mostly, and can shoot well, settle on a 20. All told, however, the 12 is the most popular shotgun.

CHOKE of a shotgun signifies the taper in the forward portion of its barrel. By tapering this portion of the barrel slightly, the shot are crowded together compactly as they leave the muzzle, and thus do not spread out so rapidly over various ranges. A "cylinder bore" gun means it has no choke. A list of the various standard chokes, showing roughly the percentage of shot they will put in a 30-inch circle at 40 yards, follows. List based on chart of shells of Western Cartridge Company.

Thus, the longer the average range will be, the more the choke should be. Heavily choked guns, for example, are best for duck hunting, but for brush hunting such as for woodcock, or for quail hunting over dogs where

CHOKE	PATTERN, IN PER CENT
Cylinder	25 to 35
Improved cylinder	35 to 45
Modified	45 to 55
Improved modified	55 to 65
Full	65 to 75

shots will be fairly close, the more open bores are best. At short ranges, open bores cover more territory with their patterns. This is an advantage when shooting must be done quickly. They also avoid "shooting up" game badly. In a double gun, it is advantageous to have the first barrel bored either cylinder or improved cylinder, the second barrel choked down more. Thus, in quail hunting, if the first shot misses, the second one at longer range has more punch behind it, with a thicker pattern. Or, if the first shot connects, the chance at a second bird at lengthened range is better.

The larger the gauge, generally speaking, the worse the gun "kicks" (recoil). That is a point to consider if gun kick annoys you.

The average shot at upland game such as quail, grouse, pheasants, etc., will be 25 to 35 yards for the sensible gunner. The average shot at ducks will be usually a bit more. Choke should therefore be carefully considered in relation to exactly what you want the gun to do in an over-all way, unless of course you can own several guns.

MULTIPLE CHOKE ATTACHMENTS are available to make possible a variety of chokes on single-barrel magazine guns such as the pump and automatic. They are excellent for the hunter who may hunt quail today, high-flying doves tomorrow, pheasants the next day.

Choke thus can be quickly adjusted to fit the situation. There are even choke devices nowadays that adjust the choke for longer range after the bird has flushed and you have missed with the first shot. This automatic tightening down is a unique invention. The same device can, of course, be manually set, too.

SHOTGUN LOADS differ basically in only two ways: the amount of powder; the size of the shot. Regarding the powder charge, there are in general two types of load: high-speed loads, and what are usually called "field loads." The last has a lighter powder charge, thus kicks less, has a little less effective killing-power range, but for most shotgun work is perfectly adequate, regardless of opinions to the contrary—IF the shooter can judge range, and shoot accurately. For waterfowl, undoubtedly high-speed loads are advantageous. For other birds and small game, standard field loads are in general best, except in cases of pheasant flushing wild at long ranges, doves flying very high, etc. In such instances, the load won't be half so important anyway as the accuracy of the gun pointer!

Shot size is a different matter. Sizes run from No. 12, with over 2000 to the ounce, to 00 Buck (buckshot), with 135 to the pound. Buckshot is used mainly for deer, where shotguns are so used. For birds and small game, No. 8 to No. 4 are most popular. Smaller sizes are seldom marketed.

The larger the shot, the more wound damage each individual pellet will do; BUT, likewise, the less shot in the pattern at any given range. In addition, *shocking power* is the most important consideration. This, curiously, increases in direct ratio to the square of the number of pellets which hit, regardless of size. Thus, 3 striking pellets equal 9 times the shocking power of 1, etc. However, penetration is also necessary. Therefore, for ducks or for tough-skinned squirrels, a large shot size gives the penetration power not needed for birds such as grouse or quail. General rule: For small birds at short range, use size 7½ or 8, field load; any birds except waterfowl, longer range, 7½ or 6, heavy load; pheasants, large birds, general ranges, same; waterfowl, squirrel, 6 to 4, heavy load.

SLUG LOADS are also made for shotguns. These contain a single slug, rifled (spirally grooved) to make it spin. They are used for deer hunting by many hunters who do not own rifles. They are fairly accurate and very deadly *at short ranges*.

SHOTGUN SHOOTING, fundamentally, is much more difficult than rifle shooting. Now that may sound like a very strange statement, and one with which you may be inclined to disagree. "Why," you say, "anybody can pick up a shotgun and have a fair chance of bringing down a bird, but it takes a real rifle shot to bag big game consistently."

The trouble is that most gunners think just that. And, instead of really learning to shoot a shotgun, they shoot it on a blind hit-and-miss basis, and, with reasonable luck, are able now and again to bring down enough game to make them feel that it is all very easy. This comes about because the spread of a shotgun pattern makes it possible to point the gun in the general direction of a flying bird and *sometimes* score, without knowing exactly how it was done. The rifle shooter, on the other hand, *must* learn to shoot his weapon accurately, or his chances of ever hitting anything would be mighty slim. When you begin to understand what must happen in shotgun shooting each time you fire at a moving target in order for you to make *consistent* kills, you realize that shotgun shooting is a very complicated affair indeed.

A shotgun must not be *aimed,* it must be *pointed.* Since it is almost always shot at swiftly moving game, and since its load leaves the muzzle at comparatively low velocity, a certain split-second of time will elapse between the pointing and shooting operation and the instant at which the shot reaches its target. Meanwhile, the target will have moved. Thus, a proper "lead" is required. In other words, the gunner must shoot where he estimates the game will be when the charge reaches it. Obviously this lead must increase proportionately to range increase.

Woodcock fly slowly when flushed, probably about 20 m.p.h.; quail average probably 35 m.p.h.; pheasants in full flight anywhere up to 50 to 60 m.p.h.; doves from 35 to 70, ducks 35 to 90, depending upon species. Tail winds step up speeds of full-flight, high-flying birds.

Thus, a shotgunner must first learn his game, and then *judge range.* No one can accurately tell him how. He can only practice it by learning patterns of known distances. Range of low-flying birds is most easily judged by comparison to ground objects. High-flying birds limned against open sky are deceptive.

Once range judgment is fairly accurate, amount of lead to use must be learned. No one can tell the gunner how to do this, either. Each shooter will have different lead ideas, dependent upon the way he handles his gun.

Very generally, shooting at 35 yards at birds moving at 35 to 40 m.p.h., the gun will be pointed, at the instant it is fired, from 1 to 2 feet ahead of a bird flying at right angles to the hunter. Lead, logically, must decrease in proportion to any decrease in angle.

In order to hit a bird flying straight away, directly level with the gun, obviously a direct-point shot is necessary, with no angle compensation of any kind. A rising bird going directly away requires shooting *above it;* a lowering bird directly away, shooting below. Likewise, rising birds crossing at right angles or any portion of a right angle require *two* lead computations, above and in front; lowering, in the same manner, below and in front. For incoming birds, the hunter must raise his gun until bird is blotted from sight in order to compensate for angle.

No shotgunner can hope to be a successful wingshot if he merely shoots blindly and entirely by guess, trusting to the number and spread of his pellets to compensate for his mental laziness. He must practice, know exactly what his gun does at various ranges with any given load, know exactly where he is shooting and *why,* evaluate *why he hit or missed* under each separate set of shooting conditions.

There are three main methods of shotgun shooting, covering all conceivable field situations. They are: full snap shooting; half-snap shooting; swing shooting.

Snap shooting is necessarily used at extremely close ranges. The gunner simply throws up his gun, points instantly at the spot in mid-air where he judges the bird will be—or directly at the bird if it is *very* close—and fires. He cannot do otherwise. To follow the bird with his pointing gun, attempt to get ahead of it with his point, and fire, he would have to move the gun practically as fast as the game moved—an impossibility.

At intermediate distances (25 yards or more), snap shooting loses much of its accuracy. Here the *half-snap* is properly used. The gunner would have difficulty swinging his gun fast enough to overtake, pass, and lead his bird. He thus points quickly, directly below it, swings the gun swiftly for a very short distance along the line of flight, and fires. Thus, the shot is partly a snap shot, partly a swing shot.

Swing shooting is the most reliable method of scoring at average ranges (30 to 40 yards). The gunner points his gun behind the bird, swings swiftly along its exact line of flight, passes the bird with his muzzle point, moves the point on ahead until the lead he judges proper is established, and fires. But he *must* learn *not* to pause in the gun swing at the moment he fires. If he does, his proper lead will be ruined and he will shoot *behind*. For this reason, swing shooting requires that he learn to keep the speed of gun swing constant as he squeezes off the shot, and that he "follow through"— that is, keep swinging momentarily *after* the shot is fired. His timing is ruined if he shoots and then abruptly stops the swing. He will unconsciously slow the swing at the time of firing.

When first practice is begun in learning the trick of wingshooting, it seems that the shooter hasn't time to make all the necessary computations and then score. After he has begun to score a little, however, he also begins to realize what he *did* in order to score. And suddenly, when a bird flushes, he is doing the proper thing, complicated as it is, with absolutely no thought as to what he should do under these particular circumstances.

SAFETY WITH GUNS

THERE IS one facet of hunting today that puts an uneasy edge to the grand sport of it: with the number of hunters always increasing so swiftly, the number of careless hunters also increases in proportion. Hunting conditions, becoming more crowded constantly, make the careless hunter ever a greater liability and danger. It is for this very reason that one should learn thoroughly how to shoot a gun accurately. The person who knows the most about guns and how to shoot them usually best realizes their potential danger, and is better equipped to handle them with safety both for himself and those around him. Knowing how to use a gun safely is far more important, and will always be so, than any other facet of hunting! Thus, this brief section should be thoroughly studied and all but memorized, not alone by the beginner but by the old hand as well—the old hand who has become so used to his guns that he has forgotten caution!

Guns are neither toys nor playthings. They are DEADLY weapons. The gun owner who goes afield with a gun that needs repair, or who shoots little and goes afield not knowing all he should about his gun and how it works and why, is guilty of plain and simple criminal negligence. The careless gunner is a potential murderer, gravely guilty even though he may never have an accident!

There is *never* legitimate excuse for shooting accidents. No gun should ever be loaded except during the time in the field when actual hunting is taking place. This means no loaded guns in houses, camps, automobiles. Even when you pause to rest, unload your gun. Your gun should never be loaded when it is out of your hands.

Do not assume that other hunters are observing safety rules. Assume every gun to be loaded, no matter *where* it is, even your own, until it has been definitely *proved* otherwise. Make it a practice to leave the breech open when handling your own or other guns. Be absolutely *positive* no extra shells are in the magazine. Be more than sure. Look twice, three times—always be suspicious!

Do not climb fences, trees, brush piles, etc., with a loaded gun. Always carry your gun so that the muzzle is in a position which will render it harmless to yourself and others, and so you positively can avert an accident even if you should fall.

If you *must* drink, don't go gunning. If you must go gunning, don't drink. This means even *one* drink. Knowing better, you are a common criminal if you do!

Never shoot at vaguely seen or imagined targets, at a "movement" or sound. See your target *plainly*. Game and men do NOT look alike! Know positively what is behind your target, in line of fire. Don't be trigger happy. Shoot calmly. Hold fire and give up a shot rather than shoot *anywhere near* another hunter, a building, or livestock.

Watch that barrel constantly! A minor obstruction—snow, dirt, leaves, mud—in the end of the barrel can blow it up as you fire and kill you!

Never slip off the safety with which all guns are equipped until you are actually raising the gun to make the shot!

Never shoot at water, flat rocks, etc., from which shot

may ricochet. Learn how far your load is dangerous. For some rifles it is a mile. High-speed rifle bullets disintegrate easily on slight impact; low-speed bullets may ricochet.

Never try in your gun ammunition other than it calls for. A load may fit, but blow up the gun and kill you or, at the least, ruin the gun. Center fire and rim fire ammunition, incidentally, are not interchangeable. Most rim fire cartridges, except low-power .22's, are now obsolete.

Last, but most important, *never* point a gun at anything you do not intend to KILL!

Hunting is a wonderful sport, basically safe. Only careless, dull-witted persons make it dangerous. Don't be one!

Chapter Two

Dogs and Their Training

*W*hen we make a quick review of all the breeds of dogs in the world, we find that, after several thousand years of association with man, almost all of our dog breeds have either had their origin in the sport of the chase or are still today at the same exciting game. It is no more possible to write about hunting or think about hunting, either past or present, without considering dogs than it would be to eliminate guns from this pastime.

For centuries dogs have been used in all kinds of hunting, to do what the hunter cannot do for himself. Today in the U.S. they are used for everything except big game. And even in that field they are used in some sections for bear and deer. Indeed, hunting with a dog is half of the thrill of the sport, whether or not any game is brought to bag. No hunter can realize to the full the grand thrills of gunning, without the companionship of a dog, his teamwork, and the exciting drama of watching him at his job.

It is not absolutely necessary, of course, to have a hunting dog, but it is purely from a practical standpoint alone highly advantageous. The dog can locate much more game than the hunter; he can often maneuver it into position where a shot will be afforded, while a hunter working alone could not. Conservation-wise, dogs are highly valuable, in finding downed game, locating cripples which the hunter would surely lose, and retrieving fallen game from spots the gunner cannot reach.

Above all, it is not necessary, as many gunners seem to believe, to have an expensive, highly bred dog in order to fill the game bag. There are thousands of such dogs which turn out worthless, and thousands of mongrels which are excellent hunters. A well-bred dog, well trained, is a great satisfaction to its owner, and usually works with greater efficiency and *style* than the mongrel. The important matter, however, in order to get the most in enjoyment out of hunting, is to have a good dog of *some* breed or mixture which will *hunt*—and then to train it properly.

Obviously, the hunter must choose his breed, or type of dog, according to the use to which he expects to put it. And sometimes—often, in fact—if he desires several kinds of hunting of a dog, he can strike a happy compromise by training the same dog to do several kinds of work reasonably well.

In the matter of dog choices, we are exceedingly lucky, for breeders have so meticulously worked on various breeds that no type of dog work can be found for which there is not an excellent working breed available. All told, hunting dogs fall into three broad general divisions: hounds (rabbit hounds; "fur" hounds for raccoon, opossum, etc.; fox hounds; "cat" hounds for wildcats, mountain lion, etc.); bird hunting dogs (setters and pointers for pointing birds, spaniels for finding and flushing birds); retrievers (generally used only in waterfowling for retrieving ducks and geese).

If the gunner can afford but one dog and expects to do several kinds of hunting, then he should choose a breed which will give him amiable companionship afield and still be adaptable to varied hunting. For example, the little beagle hound makes a fine pet, is a top rabbit dog, yet will usually hunt pheasants or other birds. Again, the springer spaniel will hunt pheasants and other birds (flushing only, not pointing), yet can double as a duck retriever if properly trained and used in water not too frigid. In southern states, where quail and doves are the only upland game birds, obviously the setter or pointer who hunts only quail will give the hunter the most pleasure and service, and he may be used to retrieve a few ducks now and then, if necessary.

GENERAL TRAINING

SOMEHOW THE average hunter has been brought to believe that training a dog to hunt is an awesomely difficult task. Nothing is farther from the truth. Any intelligent person can do the job, *if* he has patience, good sense, and will refrain from venting ill temper from lost patience upon his charge. No matter what breed of dog he may choose, several rules of basic training will apply. These we should look at first.

Dogs procured at about nine months of age will be found best. They will be pliable, somewhat over their puppy foolishness, and not yet harmed in habits by kennel or former-owner experiences.

Keep the dog in a kennel, not in your house. He will be more healthy, more easily managed. Don't believe advice that making a pet of a dog will ruin it for hunting. The dog should have discipline, but he will work *better* for you if you and he fully understand each other and are fast friends.

Any punishment of a dog should be firm, brief, and *for good reason,* but never seriously painful. Constant punishment will give you a ruined dog. For example, if your dog barks in his kennel, he must learn—by the "rolled-up newspaper" or leafy switch method—to be quiet. If he barks at a passing dog, he is not to be blamed. You cannot expect a well-trained dog unless you show at least as much logic in reasoning as he does.

All commands should be firm, and in few words. The first things he must learn are to come when you call him and to lead well. Every dog is an individual, with personality to match, just as are humans. No would-be trainer should forget that. Some are stubborn, some tractable. The stubborn dog takes more *firmness,* not, necessarily, more lickings!

Never shout or rant at your dog. *Patience trains dogs.* You didn't learn to shoot your gun in a day. All lessons in obedience should be brief. A dog, just as a youngster, gets bored or loses interest. Tell him to "Come." If he has other ideas, use a long lead rope and pull him toward you. Don't *jerk* him. If, when first leashed, he sits or lies down, refusing to lead, pull him to his feet, force him to follow. But always reward with a pat and kind word his every obedient act, even though obedience was forced. Treat him as you would want to be treated.

Don't give up easily on these first lessons. Some dogs learn such things slowly. Yours will learn, if you keep your temper, speak quietly but firmly, repeat lessons often enough, and always end training lessons with something he does *well,* so he may be patted at the lesson's end rather than punished.

His next general lessons are: "Down," meaning he must sit or lie until you command him to "Come" (and he should stay put when commanded "down," even though you go out of his sight); "Heel," meaning that either leashed or free he must not run in front of you but *walk* obediently at your heels, or, usually, at your left, with the head close beside your leg.

The "Down" lesson is taught by gently forcing the dog down with your hand upon his haunches, back, or shoulders, then walking away, cautioning him. Again, repetition, short lessons, and patted rewards—*not* a beating—will do the trick. He is taught to "heel" by being led on short leash, pulled back firmly but gently each time he tries to run out ahead. Later, when off leash, a rolled newspaper or other harmless "switch" held down before his nose will keep him reminded as you walk. *Never* strike him in the face with it. Merely tap his nose, calling "Heel" as you do so.

A dog that has thoroughly learned these few simple lessons—and any others you wish to teach him according to your special uses for him—is ready for field training. Although it is a job requiring patience, it's as easy as that! Now let's have a quick look at the various hunting breeds, so that choice of dog for special purposes may be easily made.

HUNTING-DOG BREEDS

BIRD DOGS—as the term is generally used—mean the setters and pointers. Their most important use is for quail, the various grouses, pheasants, woodcock. These birds they locate mostly by air, or body, scent, not by keeping nose to ground for foot scent. When a bird is located, they point, and then retrieve it after the gunner has made a killing shot. The several most popular kinds of birds are described below.

Setters are long-haired dogs. There are three main breeds: English (ground color white, with black, brown, lemon, or "blue" in ticks or splotches; average weight 60 pounds); Irish (color red; weight as for English); Gordon (color black, trimmed with tan; weight about the same as above).

The Gordon is today almost unknown. It is an excellent hunting dog, least high-strung of the setters, but hard to see in cover. The Irish setter is quite often high-strung, hard to manage, but an excellent working dog, though also somewhat difficult to see in cover. English setters are by far the most popular and best all-purpose setters as the breeds stand today, congenial to management, easy to spot in heavy cover, hard working, and intelligent.

Pointers are short-haired dogs, of two main kinds— the one called simply "pointer" or "English pointer," the other the German short-haired pointer. The first, heavier than the setter as a rule, with white ground color and splotches of ticks of various shades of brown, is the most popular. The German short-hair is a rather slow, heavy but trim dog, liver or brown-grizzled in color.

Pointers are less affectionate than setters, their sole interest usually being in hunting. In that all-important function they are determined and tireless.

Choice among the above breeds is purely a matter of the owner's likes and dislikes. For hot-weather hunting in the South and Southwest, the pointer has the advantage of short hair. For briar covers and colder climates, the setters stand the hunt better. Either breed is keen of nose and highly intelligent. As a pet, and one-man dog hunter, the setter may perhaps be considered before the pointer. As a kennel dog, where hunting is all-important and affection secondary, the pointer is mildly advantageous.

SPANIELS are long-haired dogs, smaller than setters and pointers. They have shorter legs, therefore do not range as far from the hunter or work as fast. Their job, in fact, is to stay within killing gunshot of the hunter, find birds either by foot or body scent, flush them, and retrieve them. They do not point as a rule. For dog owners who have limited space in which to keep a dog, and want it both as a household pet and hunter, they make excellent dogs. Many of them, however, do not stand hard hunting as well as the larger, more rangy bird dogs. But they are excellent all-round dogs, hunting rabbits and squirrels as enthusiastically as birds, retrieving ducks eagerly when the water and weather are not too cold.

Cocker Spaniels may be brown, buff, black, black-

and-white, or ticked. They weigh from 20 to 30 pounds. They are extremely affectionate, easy to handle, and highly intelligent, although some individuals tire quickly in heavy cover.

Springer Spaniels are black-and-white or brown-and-white, weigh up to 50-odd pounds. They are strong, as affectionate and intelligent as the cocker, stand hard hunting better. There is perhaps no better dog for the casual hunter, or for the hunter who wants his dog to do all kinds of hunting reasonably well.

The Brittany Spaniel and the *Clumber Spaniel* are also good little hunters, the first being something of a pointing as well as a flushing dog. Neither, however, has so far gained any great popularity in America. Hunters who want a "different" breed, however, would do well to look these over.

RETRIEVERS are generally used only by those hunters whose main activity is waterfowling. They are excellent dogs, all of them most intelligent and affectionate. They have dense oily coats fashioned to stand cold weather and water and constant immersion. Their job is to stay quietly, but ever alert, in the marsh blind or boat, or follow at the heels of the waterfowler who wades a marsh. When a duck or goose is shot, they fetch it upon command. They swim down cripples or follow them into cattails or reeds and bring them out. The top-notch retriever will "mark down" several ducks as they fall to the guns and bring them back one at a time unerringly.

Chesapeake Bay Retriever: Color, brown to faded brown-gray; weight to 75 pounds. One of the best breeds. Stands weather to zero and water with high, icy waves and seems to enjoy it.

Irish Water Spaniel: Color, solid liver; weight to 65-70 pounds. Long, curly coat, top-knot on head, smooth-haired tail. A laughable appearing but most affectionate and keen dog, ever eager to get into the water.

Labrador Retriever: Color, generally solid black; weight upwards of 60 pounds. Smooth, dense coat. One of the very best, and probably nowadays the most popular, of all retrievers.

Curly-coated Retriever: Color, liver or black; weight to 60 pounds. Coat mass of tight ringlets. An excellent dog in every respect, but not especially popular in the U.S., and for no good reason.

Golden Retriever: Color, gold; weight average 60 pounds. Smooth, long, silky coat. Very affectionate, easily handled. Extremely popular in the western states. A fine choice of dog.

Choosing a retriever is again a matter of personal opinion, and latitude—the tougher breeds for colder climates. Although their main job is waterfowling, they can be used to retrieve, and even hunt, all manner of upland game. This should be kept in mind by the general hunter. In addition, no better dog can be had for companionship.

HOUNDS are in general long-eared, heavy-boned, smooth-haired dogs which trail game by foot (trail) scent, nose to ground, and give tongue as they run the trail. The excitement in their voices increases as the trail grows "hotter"—that is, as they get closer to the game. They are almost invariably used to run mammals, from rabbits to mountain lions, so that the hunter may get a shot. The smaller hounds work very well in locating and flushing birds, much like a spaniel.

"Fur" Hounds are those dogs used to run raccoons, possums, skunks, etc., at night. Some are even used to run mink along rivers in daytime. Others, of course, are used strictly to run foxes, either day or night, and to work either singly or in packs.

Hound colors are usually mixtures of black, white, and tan. The Walker Foxhound bears these colors in splotches. The Black-and-Tan, now a recognized breed, is colored mostly black, with tan trimmings. Some other hounds of mixed breeds are known as redbones, blue-flags, blueticks, roans, etc.

Hounds used for wildcats in the northern states may be any of the above or mongrel hound mixtures. Southwestern and western mountain-lion and bear dogs are hounds carefully bred for stamina and courageousness from some certain blood lines, even sometimes with Airedale blood mixed in. Bloodhounds, though excellent dogs, are not used very much for general hunting. True strains are difficult to raise.

All of the "fur" hounds are large dogs. Most are not only exceedingly tough, strong stubborn trailers, and courageous in regard to discomfort of terrain and danger in actual battle with large animals, but very intelligent and affectionate dogs as well.

Basset Hound: Color, black, white, and tan mixed; weight, 20 to 50 pounds. Very long ears and very short legs. An excellent dog for rabbits and pheasants for those who like a slow worker.

Beagle Hound: Color the same as the Basset, or nearly all black with tan trim; weighs 20 to 40 pounds. The most popular hunting dog in the U.S., numerically. Fine on both rabbits and birds. Highly intelligent, affectionate, keen nose. Works fast and with thoroughness, easy to handle, a fine pet.

FIELD TRAINING

GENERAL FIELD TRAINING includes several points which pertain to *all* hunting dogs. They must be broken not to chase domestic stock or fowl. Thorough obedience training usually accomplishes this automatically. But young dogs should be watched for any sign of interest especially in sheep or chickens, and most severely reprimanded. In addition, with the few exceptions where deer are hunted with dogs, all hunting dogs should be harshly, even somewhat painfully, reprimanded for chasing deer.

The next point pertains to the trainer. All young dogs having their first field experiences may still be inclined to some playfulness or foolishness. They may also be puzzled by the game, its escape tactics, etc. Some may learn very slowly, showing little improvement even for a couple of full seasons. But these same dogs often suddenly blossom forth as amazingly good hunters as they grow older and settle down. Therefore, *patience* to the fullest is required of the owner, and reprimands for things the dog does not understand should be few. He should simply be allowed free rein, even in forming rather bad habits, until he is no longer a pup. Too-anxious trainers spoil many a dog.

The third point also is a caution for the trainer. No dog is gun-shy unless made so by its owner. The very best way to avoid it is never to subject the dog to gunfire until he actually has opportunity to connect the gun with his fun in hunting. Be sure the first shots are when the dog is some distance from the gun, yet while he is actually working and close enough to see the game fall. Thus, under excitement, seeing what the gun does and connecting the two, he quickly learns not to be startled, but rather to be eager for the sound.

All dogs should be "started" on the game they are to hunt most. Example: A coon hound should be started out on a coon trail; a quail dog on quail, not on pheasants. Later, the bird dog will be just as willing to hunt other birds, and the coon dog to run possums.

Meanwhile, since the "fur" dog must not chase rabbits, nor the bird dog point them or chase them, and since rabbits are the most common game which will get in the way of their duties, they must be taught that rabbits are taboo. Properly started on the game they are to hunt, many dogs will not even care about rabbits and will pay no attention if one jumps up before them. If a dog (either fur hound or bird dog) persists in showing rabbit interest, and vocal reprimands fail, a rabbit should be shot in front of him and used as a "whip" to beat him soundly. He won't be hurt, but will find the experience decidedly unpleasant.

Hounds need little actual hunting "training." The owner has but to give them plenty of opportunity to hunt and plenty of time to learn the tricks of the game, and they will, so to speak, train themselves. Of course, the owner's help or steadying influence will be needed at times, and he will have to reprimand them for bad habits which show up, such as leaving one trail for another.

Bird dogs and retrievers, on the other hand, need a lot of help from their owners if they are to become

175

good, steady workers. Some of them, of course, seem to have natural talents and ability and inclinations, just as youngsters do. They may begin retrieving without any training whatever, or they may point game perfectly the first time out. These are the exceptions, again as with human youngsters. The retriever as a rule will have to be taught something about the refinements of his job of bringing in downed birds from water, but in general the job of retrieving will be almost the same for the bird dog as for the waterfowl retriever, and thus a more or less standard procedure of training any dog to retrieve can be followed, no matter what the breed and special purpose.

The straight upland bird dog, however, has another tough job in addition to retrieving, and that is in learning to point accurately and steadily. This he must learn long before he learns that it is also his job to bring back a dead bird. Thus, before we take up the matter of retrieving, let us get in mind first a few of the basic principles of assisting an upland bird dog to learn proper pointing.

TRAINING YOUR DOG TO POINT, it must be remembered, is basically a matter of merely assisting him to bring out a natural inclination which is sunk deep in the consciousness of his breed. It is like helping him to remember, or discover, a talent which lies buried in his brain. And then, once he has discovered that he has this talent, the trainer's job is simply to help him to use it smoothly and efficiently, to the hunter's best advantage.

Nothing is of so much value in bird-dog training as simply taking the dog out, as a pup, in places where upland game birds are sure to be found, and letting him romp and hunt. Think of this pup as a human youngster. He won't be very serious about any real work, but he will undoubtedly begin to look for birds, to point them unsteadily, and probably to chase them. Don't reprimand him for his faults. Just let him go. Let him form bad habits if he wants, for first he has to learn to hunt and want to hunt. Until he gets mature sense, reprimands will only confuse him, for he doesn't know yet that this is serious business.

It may even be that he won't care a bit about hunting, and if he thus shows little interest in finding birds and pointing them, it is likely that he never will amount to much, although you should not give up on him right away. Some dogs which appear to be worthless suddenly snap into shape at as much as two or three years old. If the dog continues from puppyhood onward, however, to lack interest, or to insist constantly upon trailing by ground scent—that is, putting his nose to trails —better get rid of him and start over with a better pup. Remember, if you once get a *good* dog trained well, you are going to have him, with luck, for years. So, it's worth starting with good material, no matter how much patience in selection and trial this requires.

Incidentally, curing the young bird dog of chasing rabbits should not be begun too early or too severely. He must learn to *like* to hunt, remember, and at first he won't care what he hunts. Caution him, but don't punish him severely until he gets sense enough to realize what his job is to be.

Some trainers use vocal commands in the field, some use a whistle. Whichever you use (he'll be able to hear the whistle better, and farther), begin your signals or commands when you first take him out. One signal, usually two short whistle blasts as you unleash him, signifies that he is to strike out and begin hunting. Later, when you wish to take him up, one long blast signifies that he is to come in. Keep at such signals until you are certain he realizes what they mean. Then later, for example, if he is hunting and suddenly begins fooling around not tending strictly to business, the "start hunting" signal will remind him that this is work. Don't expect any sudden results. Repetition until full understanding is reached is what will make a good dog for you.

Almost any worth-while bird dog will begin pointing a little from puppyhood onward. This does not mean he should *hold* a point. It means simply that once he scents a bird he will make a momentary pause. Don't be alarmed, however, if he doesn't do so immediately. Perhaps he'll stumble upon birds and flush and chase them. That's all right—at first. When the scent is right, he'll wind them and pause. After he has done this a few times, you must watch for an opportunity to be near him when one of these embryo points occurs. Now it will be your job to steady him, encourage him to hold, speak soothingly to him, make him see that this is what you want him to do—to *hold*. If you can get close enough, get your hands on him, so that they steady him along with your voice.

But one major caution. Don't try to *hold him steady*. That's the quickest way to unnerve him. The opposite procedure is much better. As you stroke him and talk to him, exert pressure from behind to edge him toward the lying bird. His reaction will be to shove back against this pressure, for as badly as he may want to rush in, he won't want to be off balance. Don't overdo this, of course. These first points are important and take delicate handling.

Some trainers like their dogs to flush the birds. But this is not a good idea. It excites and unnerves a dog and may cause him to keep on chasing birds after they are flushed. You should do the flushing, while he still holds the point. But in the beginning don't make him hold too long. A full minute will be excellent for the first few times, after which you can hold him longer. And, when you step in and flush the birds, don't try to keep him from chasing. That will come later.

In fact, once he has learned to hold staunchly, his next lesson is what is known as steadiness to wing—meaning staunchness and no chasing when the game flushes. Some dogs can be taught this vocally, and seemingly have little desire to chase. Most have to have the checkrope. You simply attach a fairly long stout rope to his collar, or put it around his neck. Grip it tightly, step in and flush the bird as he points. When he chases, command him to stop, and continue to command him until he hits the end of the rope and swaps ends. True, this isn't very pleasant for the dog, and of course you don't want to harm him seriously. But usually a very few lessons with the checkrope will have him standing prettily. Use patience. He just has to understand, that's all, that he is not to chase.

From then on, the worst of the training is over. If you've made friends with the dog and he really likes you and likes to hunt, all the little refinements can be worked out as the two of you work together. Unless he has been frightened by a gun without knowing its meaning, chances are he won't be gun-shy, especially since he will be excited over the game when the gun is shot. But you should make sure that his first shooting experience does not occur too close to him, and also you should do your very best to bring down that first bird. He will then understand what the gun is for and what it can do.

You can train him to wait until your command before retrieving if you wish. It is usually best, however, to let him race for the bird the instant it falls. That way there's not so much of a chance of a crippled bird getting away. In addition, you should have a command that the dog understands, such as "Dead bird," which indicates to him that you want him to look for a bird. Then, in cases where a bird may have fallen when he was not aware of it, you can easily send him in to look for and find it. Training for this maneuver should be obvious. You can plant a dead bird somewhere when he isn't looking, and keep encouraging him to find it. By assisting him, you'll soon have him catching on to what the command means.

Once your dog is working well, a whistle or vocal command to get his attention, plus a wave of your arm to right or left, will soon teach a dog that you wish him to range more widely, to come closer in, to work right, or left. All of these little refinements are simply a matter of getting a dog's confidence and having him want to please you and rely on your judgment.

If you use a spaniel such as a springer instead of a pointer or setter, his training will be identical to that of the pointing breeds, except that he can't be expected to point. He must learn to stay within gun range—that is, no more than 30 yards from you—at all times, and to work back and forth in that area. Sometimes a long checkrope must be used to teach this. He must also learn to be steady after he makes the flush. This again usually requires the checkrope. But his training will be much more simple than that of the pointing breeds, and there is no reason why it should cause the slightest trouble.

TEACHING A DOG TO RETRIEVE is sometimes difficult, and sometimes easy. Some dogs will retrieve immediately with no training whatever, but professional trainers consider it best to use a system of training called force training, to offset any possibility that the dog may later in life begin to shirk his retrieving duties. The idea here is that force training makes retrieving so much a part of a dog's working existence that it never occurs to him that he might get away without doing it.

Briefly, the force method is to teach a dog, by use of a training collar which applies pressure to his neck, a short piece of training rope, and some object such as a piece of wood, to associate with your command, such as "Fetch," or "Dead bird," or some brief command which you will always use when you want him to retrieve, the idea of picking up this object. First you will merely hold it before him, apply collar pressure, give the command, and thus get him to open his mouth as if to receive the object. These lessons should be given slowly and patiently. When he has learned to open his mouth and accept the object, you proceed to hold his mouth shut upon it, not roughly, but with encouragement.

Next you teach him to carry the object, but also to give it up when you extend your hand. If he does not want to, fearing the collar pressure, apply the pressure so that he understands this is really necessary. Don't try to make a game, or fun, of these lessons. The dog must know that this is real discipline. Now he must learn to pick up the object at your command. This may require pulling him toward it with the cord, or even forcing his head down. From here he progresses to picking it up and giving it to you, then going a few steps after it, picking it up and bringing it to you. Always he should be rewarded with a pat and encouraging words, and never should a lesson continue until he gets tired or nervous.

The main point in all of this rather tedious training is that he must consider it *work,* and therefore must be absolutely obedient, and that you must never accept a halfway job on his part. If he inclines toward biting the object, nails driven into it and bent over, or a strip of tin tacked to it—not so he will be hurt but so his teeth will strike this hard, unpleasant material—will soon have him carrying easily and lightly, as he must do with a bird.

Once he has been "forced," so to speak, to retrieve the training object, he can be tried on a dead bird and taught to handle it carefully by your attaching nails to it if necessary. From here he will get some lessons in finding a dead bird in the grass where you have tossed it and bringing it to you. From here on he can progress to actual work in the field, either on waterfowl or upland birds, and he will never think of refusing to retrieve, for it will be part of his work, drilled into his consciousness. But you must never allow him to bring a bird halfway and spit it out. He must know that always his work must be completed, and that you will not accept halfway measures.

If you will train yourself to be patient and to follow the basic instructions set down here, there is no reason why you cannot train your dog as well as any professional trainer can. Meanwhile, keep in mind that three important rules must always be followed: you must like the dog and get him to like you so much that he is willing to do anything for you; no amount of hunting will be too much, nor can any amount of formal training at home replace actual field work; never expect something of your dog that you would not expect of yourself. A good hunting dog is half of the fun of hunting. There's no reason why you cannot have one!

Chapter Three

Hunting Upland
Game Birds

*U*nquestionably *the great majority of U.S. hunters* think of the game birds first when they think of hunting. And, of these, since the lowland game birds, such as ducks and geese, require highly specialized habitats around water, the upland game birds, of which the ring-necked pheasant and the quail and grouse are examples, are the first love of nearly all hunters.

Of all shooting endeavors, this upland wingshooting is probably the most tricky and varied, and possesses the maximum number of thrills while requiring, undoubtedly, the minimum amount of equipment and expense. What but a gun, a box of shells, and a hunting coat must such a hunter take along? Nothing, indeed, unless it be a canine companion. Yet the hunt is by no means over when the bag is full, for among our upland game birds are some of the finest of gourmets' feasts!

Most of our upland game birds, curiously, belong to the same scientific group as that from which the barnyard chicken originated. These are called gallinaceous birds, and include several species of grouse, several of quail, the ring-necked pheasant, the wild turkey. One other bird, usually classed as an uplander, but actually an in-between, may be lumped for all practical purposes with these birds, although scientifically he is closer to the lowland shore birds. This is the delightful and intriguing woodcock, a famous and unusual woodland personality. The remaining upland birds are found in the pigeon tribe. They are the mourning dove, the band-tailed pigeon, and the white-winged dove. These complete the true "upland birds"—that is, those which do not require marsh or swamp surroundings, as opposed to the "lowland birds" which do.

In actual practice, there is not a great deal which must be known, technically, about the hunting of each individual species of game bird. If you know how to shoot your gun, are able to identify the various game birds, know their ranges, their general habitats, and their special habits, you have only to go to their covers and begin hunting. If you have a dog, he'll do the actual locating of the game. If you don't, you simply keep walking, spying out those spots which will surely be favorite haunts of the species in question, covering these thoroughly in the hope of flushing the target.

The reason it is necessary to mention this is that many inexperienced hunters become confused about just how to go about hunting a bird strange to them. The whole secret, besides being able to shoot well after a bird is up, is simply to acquaint yourself with the kind of bird *personality* with which you are dealing in each case. In other words, if you know what sort of daily life the species in question leads during the time of year when you are after him, then you will know precisely what kind of cover to search, depending upon the weather and the time of day.

All game, birds or otherwise—all wild creatures, in fact—have three driving urges which are more important as far as the hunter is concerned than any others. These are: food, shelter, safety. If you get so you think, in your hunting, in terms of these three items as related to the game in question, nature will hold far fewer mysteries. For example, if you were hunting ruffed grouse in the fall, you would expect them ordinarily to be on oak ridges or in other such places where feed is good. But suppose that an unseasonal snow greets you on opening day. What would you do if you were a grouse? Stay on the open-woods ridges in bitter weather? Indeed not! You would go a little hungry in order to get down into the thick cedars or alders. Shelter would become more important than food.

The above is a simple example, but it tells in a nutshell how you can become a successful hunter, no matter what the game; and since upland birds are the most important game to a majority of hunters, it is especially important in this chapter.

THE QUAILS

FROM YEAR TO YEAR, more states have open season on quail than on any other game birds. Roughly forty states each year allow hunting for them. Although quail are small targets, they travel in sizable coveys of from six to twenty or more birds, are inclined to feed in open farm fields over much of their range, have a rather straight flight and one not especially swift, lie exceptionally well to a dog, and therefore are extremely popular. The joys of quail hunting as compared with other hunting are hard to argue down when you are among quail enthusiasts, and anyone who has followed these immeasurably sporty little feathered buzz bombs afield will remember them with utmost pleasure, and be after them again and again as long as he lives.

There are several quail species in the U.S. Brief descriptions of them and methods for hunting them follow.

Bobwhite Quail: A bird weighing about 6 ounces. Several subspecies varying slightly in color. General colors mottled brown, and black, with throat white or yellowish, breast striped and speckled with brown and white of varying shades, some white around and behind the eye, the cock usually more distinctly marked than the hen. A very plump little bird, often heard using the "bob-white" call from which its name derives. Range, counting the subspecies, includes all of the eastern U.S., west throughout the Great Lakes states, south to New Mexico and Texas. A bird of the fields and the woods' edges, which roosts on the ground, seldom alights in trees. Gregarious, traveling in sizable coveys. A strong flyer, but will run for cover unless pressed, when it will freeze until flushed. The flight not usually long, always to the nearest dense cover.

Methods: Of all our upland game birds, the bobwhite quail is one of the most popular. It is a kind of measuring stick of upland sport, perhaps more so than any other upland game bird. Although nowadays the bobwhite is predominantly a southern game bird, there is still fair shooting to be had in some of the middle states.

When you are in quail country, you may find the birds almost anywhere, either close to dwellings or far from human habitations. But always they will be found in country that is not entirely dense forest or second growth, for they are seed eaters and not wilderness birds.

The only way to know if quail are in a territory is if you live there and have heard them calling during the summer. Otherwise, in strange country, you must rely on the word of landowners and others in the vicinity. Even then, if opportunity affords, the best spots may be found by taking your dog out and going over the hunting territory some days before season to locate coveys. Bobwhite quail do not range far, and you may be certain that each covey thus located will be in the general section when the gunning season opens.

Although bobwhite can be hunted without a dog, he is best hunted with one. This little fellow lies better to a dog than any other game bird. And, even in very thin cover, since he will run or lie tight rather than fly, the dogless hunter is up against a big gamble, for surely he will not be able to see birds on the ground, and only by chance will he flush them. Thus, perhaps more than of any other game bird it may be said that a good quail dog—setters and pointers are best—is a necessity for the hunter who wants real sport with bobwhite. In addition, the work of the dogs in the fairly open cover where these quail are found is half the fun of the hunt.

Like most birds, the bobwhite, given decent weather, leaves his roost and begins his feeding early in the morning. Thus, early in the day, fields such as corn fields, where abundant feed is available will be the best bets. Toward noon and for some time after, the coveys will usually seek a place of dense cover to rest. Now it may be necessary to go into the edges of the pine roughs or other cover surrounding the fields. But the covey will be difficult to locate. The shooting is exceptionally sporty, however, for obstacles get in the gunner's way. Toward midafternoon the coveys will begin moving about once more, and will continue feeding until toward dusk, making their way back to their roosting places as it grows later, but almost always *walking* and feeding, not flying. During inclement weather, however, the birds will stay closer to cover, and won't be inclined to be out quite as early, nor will they be as easy to locate.

Once you have learned a little about quail habits, you next have to learn several items about the actual shooting. The flush of a covey is a very noisy and confusing affair. Often several birds flush, then just as you are aiming your gun several more flush from underfoot, throwing you off. Tyro quail shooters are inclined to shoot blindly at a flushing covey, for it always looks as if several birds could be dropped by such a blind shot. But usually not a bird is put down thus. Also, many hunters habitually shoot quickly, and miss because the birds are still rising. The confusion and noise of the flush make you think they are moving much faster than they actually are. Thirty to forty miles per hour is roughly top quail speed.

In quail hunting, the thing to do is train yourself first not to be disturbed unduly by the flush. Next, as a covey flushes, immediately pick one bird, forget the rest, and keep your eye *only* on this one, even if another seems suddenly to be an easier shot. Shoot calmly and deliberately, yet with dispatch and efficiency, and you will usually discover there is still time to take a second bird before the remainder of the covey is out of range. Train yourself, too, to have a kind of "second sight" in marking down where the scattered escaping birds drop while you are shooting at your birds. Hunting down singles is one of the most exciting and enjoyable sides of quail hunting. Never, however, should a covey be hunted down too closely. Three or four birds taken out of a dozen-bird covey should be the limit. Leave the singles, then, and go after another covey.

You must know, too, that bobwhite will always have planned, before he flushes, exactly where he is going to head. It will always be straight for the closest dense cover. In this determination, nothing will turn him. Thus, when the dogs pin a covey, the wise gunner will approach so the birds are between him and the closest cover. That way he will get straight-away shots. Otherwise, the birds will invariably fly straight at him and over his head, giving well-nigh impossible shots.

Gun and load: Gun gauge is not important, but whatever gauge you use it should not be close-choked. Shots are seldom at long range. A fairly open gun means a higher percentage of kills and fewer birds badly shot up at close range. Shells should be, preferably, loaded with a light powder charge. Shot size should be no larger than No. 8.

Gambel's Quail: One of at least two subspecies of a fairly large quail of the desert ranging from southern Colorado and California through New Mexico and Arizona. The male is blue-gray above, has chestnut on the sides, with gray breast, sides striped with white, a black and white lower belly, black throat encircled by white, a chestnut crown, and a fine crest formed of several upright and forward-curving black feathers. A gorgeous bird of the mesquite and cholla thickets of the desert.

Valley, or California, Quail: A large quail quite similar in general appearance to the Gambel's quail, including the plumed head. Chestnut coloring lacking on the sides, less plain white and black on the belly, and more of a "scaled" appearance on the belly, due to white feathers edged with black. Ranges along the Pacific Coast, with some overlapping into Idaho, Nevada, Utah.

Scaled, or Blue, Quail: Two subspecies, distinguished by the chestnut belly of the one as against the gray-blue belly of the other. Sometimes called "cottontop quail" due to the little white-tipped crest. A rather somberly colored bird, easily identified by the scaled appearance of cape, breast, and belly, the feathers being edged with black. Range: western Texas, New Mexico, southern Colorado to central Arizona.

Mountain Quail: The largest of our quails. A beautiful bird predominantly of the high mountain slopes of the Pacific Coast. Crest consists of several long, straight, upright black feathers. Throat deep chestnut outlined in white, breast blue-gray, sides marked with white on brown, black, and chestnut.

With the exception of the Valley (California) Quail, none of these quails lies well to a dog. They are runners, and a real experience in leg work for the hunter. A springer or cocker may be used on them, and all are worth hunting because of the different kind of sport they turn up, but they mean a real workout. They run swiftly, are hard to flush at all times, and, when flushed, run again after alighting. The mountain quail usually requires hunting in rugged, high terrain. For him a close-choked gun is necessary, for shots are usually long. For the others some choke in the gun is a good idea.

The exception, the Valley Quail, is a very popular bird, and the westerner's counterpart of the bobwhite. They cannot be pinned down in coveys, like the bobwhite, but first must be chased—they're runners—and flushed. After that, if the hunter has been careful to mark them down, they will lie perfectly as singles. Use of a dog is therefore most important to success. Gun and load as for bobwhite.

All told, though all of the beautiful and delicious western quails are fine sport, none of them quite comes up to the much more widely distributed bobwhite in the category of perfect all-round game bird. But wherever you find them, of whatever species, quail are exciting targets dear to the hearts of all wingshooters.

THE PHEASANT

AFTER THE bobwhite, judged by numbers annually killed, comes the ring-neck pheasant—a bird imported and stocked years ago in the U.S.—as our next most popular upland game bird. It is doubtful if nowadays there is anyone in the country not familiar with the big, gorgeously colored, long-tailed male of this species. He has had far more publicity than any game bird native to our hunting territory, mostly because of the astounding manner in which he has adapted himself so abundantly to our habitats. Though the ringneck has not so far been able to establish itself in the South, clear across the northern and central tiers of states he has bloomed mightily, in a heavily agricultural habitat where every hunter has been able to know him intimately even in the outskirts of our large cities, from New York State clear across to Washington. Only the mountainous districts of the western states are without the ringneck, and he ranges southward through Pennsylvania, Ohio, Missouri, Kansas, etc.

In appearance the pheasant could not be misidentified. The female is a uniform buff mottled with darker brown, and with tail somewhat shorter than the cock. The iridescent cock has a black-green head, red wattles, a white collar, red-bronze breast scaled with black, much pale green, gray, chestnut, and brown here and there. The tail is very long. The average full-grown cock will weigh from two to three pounds. The only confusion the term "pheasant" might possibly have is that in some southeastern states where a small ruffed grouse population is found in the mountains, the grouse is locally called "mountain pheasant."

The ringneck is a bird not of woodlands or mountainous country, but of agricultural districts, his food predominantly grains and seeds. Brushy fence rows along corn, bean, and wheat fields, or other crop fields form good cover. Swales grown up to goldenrod, sumac, willow, and scrub poplar, with marsh grass deep underneath, make excellent roosting and hiding places. However, in the best portions of pheasant range, which is almost without fail in heavily settled sections, the pheasant may be found almost anywhere. Though this is a large bird, it is one shrewdly adept at utilizing the most meager cover. For example, alfalfa fields with second or third growth, which would appear to be far too low to hide a pheasant, are often found to contain many. They skulk close to the ground, and can run nearly as swiftly as a horse without their presence being made known.

Methods: Pheasant hunting is a rip-roaring gun sport for all comers. The shooting is almost always open, or reasonably so, and the target large. Though the pheasant is swift (top speed close to 60 m.p.h.) when once in full flight, his weight and his plumage make him a slow starter. He usually flushes by bounding straight up, and must continue beating his way upward for a few feet in order to gain altitude before setting his course.

Most misses on the flush are made because the hunter shoots too quickly. Wait out a flushing cock, fire as he tops his rise and begins to straighten out, and you will catch him practically standing still in the air. The course flight is seldom very high, and often skims the cover. Once the bird alights, which may not be for a long distance, he will not stay put, but may run a quarter of a mile before stopping.

Though many a cock is bagged without a dog, it is a very good idea to use one. The pheasant is a past master at hiding when crippled, and because of his long tail and abundant plumage many crippled birds are dropped. The hunter, firing at so large-appearing a target, forgets that he can draw a lot of feathers without killing his bird. Many cripples can never be run down, or located, without a dog. The pointing breeds, if *trained* on pheasants, often can work them so that they will lie perfectly. But very often the pheasant will lie, then get up and run again. This unnerves a dog trained on close-lying quail or grouse. A good cocker or springer, schooled in pheasant ways and in working fence rows, briar patches, ditch banks, etc., yet one which will stay close to the hunter even when the scent is hot and the bird moving, is, as a rule, a better pheasant dog than the pointing breeds. Curiously, the beagle or basset hound trained to run pheasants makes an excellent dog for these race-horse birds.

The hunter working alone has merely to stalk quietly into those covers (such as the ones noted above) where the wise old cocks will usually hide as soon as gunning season has started. And he should work into the wind. Otherwise, his birds will run ahead of him and he'll never get a shot. When hunting either with dogs or without, it is general practice to "drive" pheasants, with several hunters working together. In a standing field of corn, for example, several hunters are posted at one end of the field, the others enter from the other end and walk through. Running birds will be flushed, some on the way, the rest when the end of the field is reached. The same technique is used in swales and along ditch banks.

Like the quail, and most other game birds, pheasants are out feeding at dawn, given reasonably good weather. By midmorning most of them will have retired to heavy cover, even into wood lots if undergrowth is available. At about three to four P.M. they sally forth again to feed up until dusk. These feeding periods are the best hunting times, especially if by quiet hunting you can come on the birds unawares. As with all wild creatures, inclement weather keeps them closer to the heavy cover. In rainy weather pheasants are sometimes extremely determined not to be flushed.

One important trick of pheasant hunting, especially when your hunting territory is restricted, is to keep making the rounds of it. The birds will keep moving, especially if a lot of hunters are out and hunting conditions crowded, as often happens nowadays. A grass field or stubble field which was combed without result may pay off with a brace of fine cocks an hour or two later.

Gun and load: Pheasants take a goodly amount of killing. Though some top-notch shots even pride themselves on killing ringnecks with a .410, this is no pheasant gun. A 12, 16, or, if you're a good shot, a 20 gauge, is needed. The first two are most popular. At least some choke is essential, for many long shots will be in order, as well as quite a number of close ones. The close ones, however, can be waited out. Loads used are usually those with heavy powder charge, shot size of either No. 6 or No. 7½.

PARTRIDGES

SEVERAL BIRDS, such as the ruffed grouse, are often locally called "partridge." But there are two game bird species, both imported and stocked over the past few decades in various parts of the U.S., which really come under this heading everywhere.

Hungarian Partridge, or European Gray Partridge: A European native first introduced here almost half a century ago. Half again as large as the bobwhite. A plump bird predominantly gray on the back, lighter below with red-brown markings, throat light buff. Often called "Hun" by hunters. Has taken best to plains habitat, with much open country, little woodland. Consorts in coveys, which lie fairly well to a dog, but these birds are very wary, scatter widely when flushed, and often fly far.

Though many states have tried them, and in some sections they have now caught on well enough to be a standard game bird like the ringneck, their ranges are inclined to be spotty. The plains provinces of Canada furnish good hunting for them. Open seasons in the U.S. occur in a number of states, from the Great Lakes area on across the plains. When selecting a state to hunt in, it is best to make sure which sections of it hold the high "Hun" populations.

These fellows are wonderful game, but masters at skulking and running. A good dog is called for, especially because of the wide-open-spaces habitat of the bird. Shots are likely to be at fairly long ranges; therefore a choked-down gun and loads as for pheasants are not out of place. Stubble fields in the more settled districts, the same type of cover or grass plains in the prairie states and provinces, are the best locations. Certainly this swift, canny bird, a table delicacy as well as a real sporting proposition before the gun, should not be overlooked by those fortunate enough to hunt his scattered territories.

Chukar Partridge: Introduced from Asia. A fine game bird about the same size as the "Hun." During recent years the chukar (sometimes called red-legged partridge) has, after a slow start, become well established, especially in a number of western states. At present there are annual open seasons in several areas, with birds plentiful enough so that a substantial amount of hunting can be done. Color of the bird is blue-gray above; throat white outlined with black; belly white; lower sides beautifully marked with black and chestnut; legs, feet, and bill red.

The chukar is a covey bird, a master runner and skulker, always moving uphill when pursued. It has taken to the roughest of canyons, and is thus difficult to hunt, making gunners climb swiftly in tough going. Chukars usually "talk" among themselves when running, giving hunters a clue. Guns and loads should be about as for pheasant. Both "Hun" and chukar are reminiscent, in habits and actions before the gun, of the impetuous and unpredictable western quails.

THE GROUSES

ORIGINALLY, THE grouse family had representatives in practically every kind of U.S. habitat with the exception of the damp and swampy Deep South, to which these birds never were adaptable. The heath hen, which was the eastern race of the big grouses of prairie chicken lineage, became extinct some years ago. The prairie chicken, once fabulously abundant from Illinois to the Rockies and south into Texas, is a bird of the open fields and grasslands. Today it is so near to extinction in most areas, or completely extinct in others, that only in a few places are there open seasons on it. The sage hen, our largest grouse (old cocks sometimes weigh up to eight pounds!) has a paltry few representatives left, in the sage plains of the West. Now and then seasons of a single day to a week are set on this bird, but it is not an especially good game bird, and often hardly edible because of the bitterness imparted to its flesh by its sage diet. The several species of spruce grouse, birds of the northern coniferous forests, though still to be found spottily in some numbers, are not hunted to any great extent and are often so tame as to make poor targets.

Thus, today, the mainstay of grouse hunting is the justly famous ruffed grouse. After him, probably, come the sharp-tailed group and prairie chicken combined, then the dusky, or blue, grouse. After these big grouse come the ptarmigans, which are grouses of the Far North. Though we do not ever have ptarmigan hunting of any account within U.S. borders, these birds are well worth the attention of hunters who may be able to travel after them.

Since the four groups listed above form almost the entire grouse-hunting picture in America today, if the bird hunter learns to identify and hunt these, he will have no difficulty with other grouse species, especially because the habitats of these four are quite dissimilar. Identifications of the less populous grouses, and their special habits, can quickly be learned from hunters in their territory, or from a single day of experience with them.

Ruffed Grouse: A bird of the forest, weighing from one to one and one half pounds. Upper parts chestnut marked beautifully with black, gray, white, dark brown. Head with short crest, tail widely fan-shaped, held so in flight, when it acts as a rudder to steer the swift bird among thick slashing conifers and brush. Tail marked at its extremity with black band edged on either side by gray. A dark black-green ruff about the neck. Breast gray-white marked with bars.

199

The ruffed grouse is one of the world's finest game birds, and has often been called the King of the Game Birds. This fellow is no field or open-country inhabitant, but a bird of the deepest and most inaccessible thickets, copses, and forests. During colonial days the ruffed grouse was very tame and trusting of man, but he soon caught on to the meaning of gunfire, becoming one of the most wary and perhaps the trickiest of the game-bird clan. There are several subspecies, which stretch ruffed-grouse range clear across Canada and the northern U.S., into Alaska, and south in the eastern U.S. through Georgia. However, the concentration of the ruffed-grouse population is in the northeastern U.S., the Great Lakes region, the eastern provinces of Canada.

Here the birds are found in the slashing left from lumbering days, in deep cedar swamps, on oak-studded ridges, along old stone fences where tangles of vines grow, along the wooded mountain sides, and secluded in the alder thickets of wooded stream bottoms. Perhaps no other bird is capable of giving the hunter such a surprise when it flushes. One moment you are walking cautiously along through the deep woods, hearing no sound, and the next you are startled witless by the explosion of a bird at your feet, or behind you where you have just passed. The flush is usually very noisy, and the whir of wings in flight is easily heard at a distance. Always, if possible, the bird will put some obstacle between himself and the hunter the moment he flushes, and he is very seldom surprised feeding in the open, even in woods clearings.

Old Ruff spends his day about as follows. At dawn he drops down from his perch in some thick conifers, and as a rule actually walks outward to his favorite feeding ground. Sometimes, if food is scarce near his roosting place, he will fly some distance. But with good conditions he roosts fairly close to the berries, acorns, sumac, wild apples, strawberry leaves, etc., upon which he feeds. Half the morning is spent stoking his stomach. Then, with the sun warm on the slopes, he squats down to soak it up, or takes a dust bath, or goes to water. Never will he be found far from water, although it may be only a trickle of a stream. And seldom will he take siesta far from heavy cover to which he can dart swiftly if disturbed. In fact, if you come upon him sunning, and happen to approach from the cover, he will invariably flush under your feet, fly right *at* you, making for cover and confusing you at the same time.

By midafternoon he begins to feed again, stepping up the tempo until toward dusk, when he gets his drink and hikes for his secluded roost again. Thus, if you understand his well-regulated life, you will be able to locate him with fair ease. Hitting him, however, is a different matter. He appears to fly very fast, but actually does not get going much above 35 or 40 miles per hour. His take-off is so quick and noisy, and his adeptness at dodging in flight through the thickest cover so extreme, that he appears almost impossible to follow with a charge of shot. He is out of sight before many a gunner can train on him.

Seldom does he fly far, often only a few yards, and very often he may be marked down and flushed again and again. All this makes a dog practically a must, and it may be said that this bird lies to a dog perhaps the best of all game birds. When your dog points a ruffed grouse you somewhat avoid the confusion and start of the flush. However, the lone hunter who stalks his birds sometimes does very well, if he will be patient and train himself to expect that raucous whir every instant. The secret, of course, is to be constantly alert, to be able to handle a gun swiftly and calmly, and to train the eye to discount the confusion caused by the thick cover in which the shooting must be done. If a dog is used, the English setter is often preferred because his light color is easy to see in cover.

Since the grouse ranges quite widely, the successful hunter will carefully study the special section where his hunting is done, come to know every alder or wild-rose thicket, every rock-strewn slashing, every cedar copse, etc., which annually produces birds. He will come to know what, in his section, is the favorite haunt of the birds, and how best to approach each of the little oases so that telling shots may be made on a rise.

It is doubtful that in all wing shooting there is a greater thrill than ruffed-grouse hunting. Once a man has tasted it, though he may be only mildly successful he is certainly doomed to follow this grand bird for the remainder of his life.

Gun and load: Ruffed grouse are not especially hard to kill. Though any gun will do, the lighter weight double-barreled guns are often favorites. One barrel should be fairly open, the other choked down for a second shot at longer range if the close shot misses. Although the 12 and 16 gauges are used much, the 20 is often considered a good grouse gun. Either light or heavy powder charge, with shot size no larger than 7½ and preferably 8, makes the standard load.

Sharp-tailed Grouse: One of the "big grouses," weighing up to 2½ pounds. Plump, short of tail, and with the center tail feathers longer than the others, thus giving rise to the name. As with all the big grouses, the sharptail is without a noticeable crest. Toes serrated and legs "furry." Skin of feet and legs gray-green. Cock with pale-purplish air sacs (distended during mating ceremonies) along the neck. These sacs are of bare skin but are usually hidden by plumage. General color gray and brown, the wing feathers with white spots, the breast white or very light, with dark check marks, the rump whitish.

Prairie Chicken (Pinnated Grouse): Often confused with the sharptail, and vice versa, since their habitats are much alike. Easily set apart from the sharptail, as follows. Tail rounded, legs and feet deep yellow or reddish, air sacs yellow, cock with long neck feathers which are startlingly erect during mating ceremony. General color much darker than sharptail, with breast, rump, and tail *barred* with dark brown and grayish, the breast bars running crosswise.

Both of these birds—there are several subspecies of each—are birds of the prairies and the grasslands, the sharptail ranging much farther north, even well into Alaska. Originally both were fabulously abundant, from Arkansas and Texas far into the Canadian prairie provinces, and from the Rockies to Illinois. Market gunning and breaking of the prairie sod by intensive agriculture brought them low. Today there is still a bit of prairie-chicken shooting in the U.S., notably, at this writing, in Upper Michigan, and now and then in the Dakotas. The same is true of the sharptail. However, several mid-continent Canadian provinces still have excellent shooting. All told, the future of the prairie chicken looks dim, but that of the sharptail reasonably good in a few sections.

The chicken was originally a bird typical of the tree-less open grasslands. The sharptail lived there too, but also in the ragged fringes of wooded country, notably among northern willow flats, thin poplar slashing, etc., where large wild meadow openings were available. To-day both birds are sometimes found, as in Upper Michi-gan, in this same kind of territory—the jackpine, pop-lar, and willow barrens.

Methods: These two grand birds are so similar that methods of hunting them are almost identical. In fact, both are often discovered in the same covers, and at times nowadays even shot from the same flocks.

The birds, during hunting season, are generally found in coveys, or flocks, sometimes very large ones. The na-ture of the open cover makes them wary birds, but not especially tricky ones. On opening day they will usually lie well to a dog in the early morning, but if there is much shooting they may be very wild by nightfall, and often on the second day, or at least toward the end of the season, they neither lie well to dogs nor allow the close approach of even the best of stalkers.

They get away swiftly, always giving themselves away by cackling. Sometimes, in willows or deep grass, birds running on the ground will cackle, thus making their presence known when by keeping quiet they would have been passed by. Many hunters nowadays hunt without dogs, due to the fact that a wide ranging dog too often puts the jittery birds out of the grass beyond gun range. Shots, except in country such as that along the jackpine flats of the Lake Superior district, are in-variably wide open, with no obstacles. The birds make a large target, with a straight and constant, though fair-ly swift, line of flight. It takes a good shot and a calm shooter to withstand the excitement caused by the barrage of flushing covey wings. The sport, however, is of the most heady type, and the eating of the kill a feast for a gourmet.

Gun and load: Preferably a 12-gauge gun, fairly well choked down, for shots are inclined toward the long side. Shells should contain a heavy powder charge, with shot size of No. 6 to No. 7½. Some gunners even use No. 5.

Dusky Grouse (Blue Grouse): There are several different races and subspecies, all varying only slightly, such as the Sooty and the Sierra Grouses. Big birds (up to as much as four pounds) of the high, timbered country of the Rockies, from Arizona to Oregon, Colorado to British Columbia, and north into Alaska. A dark, gray-brown or "sooty" colored bird, with fine markings of a bluish cast; the tail fan-shaped, its color dark, almost to black, with a gray outer band.

Methods: These birds are in many ways western mountain cousins of the ruffed grouse. Though sometimes they follow the food supply down into the low valleys, they are essentially birds of the big timber in high elevations—woods grouse most at home among the alpine meadows where berries and wild thorn apples abound, and in the dark spruce forests where they spend a good deal of time in the trees.

In many portions of their range, especially remote and little-hunted sections, they are inordinately tame, which has been the cause of many being brought to bag by a light rifle. However, when hunted with a dog, or when stalked in the big timber where they have learned about guns, they are sensational game, probably swifter of wing than their smaller cousin, the ruffed grouse. The flight is straighter than that of Old Ruff, but mainly because there is less need for dodging brush and thickly set slashing. It is also very often downhill, which adds to the speed and also makes shooting difficult. The bird lies well to a dog, is a master at placing itself on the opposite side of a tree from a gunner, and is an all-round fine game bird under today's circumstances.

Gun and load: These birds require a fairly heavy gun because of many long shots, and their large size. Any gun will do, but a 12 is preferable, with No. 6 or No. 7½ shot, backed up by a healthy powder charge.

Ptarmigan: There are three main species: the willow ptarmigan, which ranges all the way across Canada, the white-tailed and rock ptarmigan both of which are mainly found in the far northwestern sections of Canada, and on throughout Alaska. A very few ptarmigan are found in the high elevations of the U.S., but there is little if any hunting to speak of for them. In summer all of these birds are of various mottled brown shades, often showing some white. In winter they change to a protective white plumage, making them difficult to see against the snow. The willow ptarmigan, best known and most easily available to a majority of U.S. gunners who may get into the lower Canadian provinces, retains several black tail feathers during winter which show against the snow for a sighting target.

Methods: Ptarmigan can be hunted either with or without a dog. Main reason for mention of them here is that in many parts of Canada they are very abundant. During fall they are partially migratory, coming down from the Far North in great flocks to feed at lower levels of elevation and latitude. They are fine game birds, lie well to a dog in the willow or blueberry thickets, and have the interesting habit of circling in a flock after flushing and even after being shot at, swinging back like pigeons past the gunner again. There is every reason to believe that in years to come many U.S. gunners will make bird-hunting trips into Canada after ptarmigan just as many big-game hunters do after antlered game. Certainly the ptarmigan has much to offer and should be seriously considered by many a U.S. shotgun enthusiast who has opportunity to travel after him. Gun and load as for other average grouse hunting.

THE WOODCOCK

THIS UNIQUE BIRD, which stands as a link between the true upland birds and the wading, or shore, birds of the marshes, is a target which has excited gunners and gourmets for centuries. He is at once beautiful and laughable in demeanor, eccentric and sternly logical in his daily life. Perhaps no other game bird is, in his relationship to hunters, such a mystery or such an intriguing customer.

The woodcock is of quail size, though longer and thinner. The back feathers are of gorgeous woodland browns, interlaced with black markings. The breast is the softest buff; the stubby tail, when spread, black and white below. The eyes of this fellow are set high, almost atop his head, and protrude slightly, making him appear to look everywhere at once in a pop-eyed, alert fashion. His bill is four inches long and quite thick at the base. It is also somewhat soft, as compared with the hard beaks of seed-eating birds. The woodcock is migratory, concentrating in New Brunswick, Nova

Scotia, New England, and the Great Lakes regions for nesting, and with the heaviest winter concentration usually in Louisiana.

Methods: Woodcock hunting is a gamble at best. You either catch the migration squarely, and stumble upon one of the scattered thickets where these birds so secretively consort, or you simply keep on trying for years with very little result. But once you've had a taste of it, you'll find it very difficult to eliminate the annual search from your program. Most of the better sessions with woodcock occur in the eastern Canadian provinces, New England, Pennsylvania, and Michigan.

Actually, success hinges basically upon knowing woodcock feeding habits. The diet is almost entirely of earthworms, which it probes after with its long, soft bill. This means that even a light frost, which slightly hardens the ground, will empty a covert of birds overnight, sending them farther south. Since they migrate at night, and do a lot of their feeding at night, the mystery is enhanced. Abundant earthworms, in soft loam, or hidden beneath leaves in birch or alder thickets, are the first requirement. But since the woodcock likes thin ground cover but fairly close cover overhead, this still further restricts his favorite feeding grounds. He likes his feet damp, but not wet. This explains the preponderance of good shooting in the alder thickets along stream bottoms.

No one can tell you exactly where to find woodcock. You simply have to learn to recognize likely cover, and keep searching. If birds are present, you will know it by the white splotches from the droppings on the ground and by the holes they've punched with their bills. Happily, once you find a covert they use or have used, you can be assured that there's a good chance it will hold birds year after year—if you happen to catch the migration, or catch the local birds before they leave. They have an uncanny way of locating these tiny covers each year.

Woodcock lie well to a dog, and a dog is most important in the extremely heavy cover where the shooting must be done, both for locating the game and for retrieving. The flight is not swift, but the flush is noisy, and birds often allow you almost to step on them, flush straight up, and down again within a few yards, even though shot at. They are masters of concealment. You need to shoot quickly, and be ever alert. The sport is altogether delightful, and the eating strictly in the super class.

Gun and load: Any gauge will do, but use a cylinder bore or only modified choke by all means, for most shots are at close range. A light gun which handles swiftly is advantageous; so is a short barrel, for work in the brush. Woodcock are not hard to kill. Thus, a load with light powder charge, and shot no larger than No. 8, preferably smaller, is best.

THE WILD TURKEY

SURELY IT would not be necessary to describe the wild turkey, for in appearance he is very nearly identical to the birds of our farmyards and our Thanksgiving tables. This fellow stands his ground against all odds as our largest and perhaps grandest game bird, even though very few of us ever get an opportunity to hunt him in the present day.

Once awesomely abundant throughout all of the

eastern U.S. and across the continent through Arizona, the wild turkey only a few years ago appeared headed almost for extinction. But game management methods have worked recent wonders with it. Today the turkey is doing well in numerous states of its original range and also in some new areas to which it has been transplanted. Most hunters can arrange nowadays to get a crack at a wild turkey.

Methods: Although fairly plentiful, turkeys are found only in rather small sections of their general range. Thus the first requirement is that the prospective gunner locate a turkey stronghold. By nonresidents that can be done by writing to the conservation department of the state involved, and asking for information as to good locations. Once on the grounds, local guides are invariably well worth their fees. Or, after inquiring of local residents about specific hunting grounds, the nonresident hunter can search for turkey sign. Each flock usually ranges over a square mile or more of territory, and no bird leaves a greater amount of sign—the large, unmistakable tracks in dust or soft earth, the huge windrows of scratchings in leaves, etc. In addition, feeding turkeys are rather noisy, scratching and talking to each other as they move.

The turkey is primarily a bird of the deep woods and swamps, and seldom is caught flat-footed in the open. He is also the most wary game bird in existence, with fabulously keen senses of sight and hearing. At the slightest unusual sight or sound the flock will fade ghostlike into the woods. They are exceedingly swift runners and will usually run rather than fly. But their habits are exceptionally meticulous. Each day the flock, or an old bachelor gobbler, follows a strict routine, covering some distance in its feeding, watering, and its trek back to the roost (which is always high in some special clump of trees), and invariably showing up punctually at each point of the long circle. Thus, one popular hunting method is to quietly observe this exact routine, then for the hunter to secrete himself and waylay his bird.

Pointing dogs are of no use, for the turkey will seldom lie to a dog. However, a dog is often used to locate and scatter a flock; then the hunter goes to that spot, hides, and uses a turkey call. It must always be sounded very sparingly so that the birds do not become suspicious. After a time the scattered flock will try to get together again, converging upon the point from which they took flight.

Good callers can also set themselves up in a blind and call up a turkey from a flock feeding near by. Calls can be purchased or homemade. However, the calling of turkeys is a high art, and it is best for the tyro either to let the guide do it or to get hold of a locally made call and learn the art from an old hand at the game in that particular section.

"Roosting" is another method. This consists of keeping watch of a flock until the roost site is located. Then, after they have flown up into the trees for the night, the hunter goes just at dusk, stalking with extreme caution until he gets within gun range. Although this sounds simple, it is a most difficult operation. It is, however, outlawed in some states, due to the fact that unsportsmanlike individuals have been known to wound and lose numerous birds from a single flock during an after-dark shoot on moonlight nights.

The main requisite of turkey hunting is that the hunter be a top-notch woodsman, and not underestimate the amazing wariness and intelligence of his game. Absolute silence is required; so is perfect camouflage. There must be no slightest movement in the blind. The turkey is well aware that man is his worst enemy. He avoids man like the plague—most of the time with exasperating success.

Gun and load: Some states require by law that a rifle be used and specify that no rifle smaller than a certain caliber be carried. Though a heavy rifle, as for deer, is not necessary, the lower-powered .22 loads should not be used. When a shotgun is used—which of course requires that the gunner be much closer to his bird—it is best to use the 12 or 16 gauge, loaded with shells carrying a heavy powder charge and shot of either No. 4 or No. 2. The turkey takes a lot of killing. Thus head shots are most desirable.

THE DOVES

THERE ARE three legal dove species in the U.S.: the mourning dove, the white-winged dove, the band-tailed pigeon. Though the last is called "pigeon," there is really no distinction to be made generally between "doves" and "pigeons." It has for years been usual to call the larger dove species pigeons, the smaller one doves. Oddly, today the mourning dove has become, by numbers annually killed, our No. 1 game bird.

Curiously, though these birds have had little publicity over the years as game birds, there is no doubt but that they are the most difficult targets which the wingshooter can find. Dove shooting is the sportiest kind of shooting, and it is nowadays conceded by experienced gunners that the doves are without question our most exciting upland game birds, lack of publicity notwithstanding. They are also delicious eating. In addition, since the mourning dove has extremely wide distribution and is extremely abundant, it will in coming years become more and more important to gunners. It is easy to locate, generally distributed near inhabited sections, and the hunting, from a physical point of view, is so easy as to be appealing to the most lethargic gunner.

Mourning Dove: A bird weighing about 4 ounces, soft gray on upper parts, pale pinkish-buff below. Two sub-species, eastern and western, the western one much lighter in color as a rule, and generally a bit larger. Tail pointed—the only U.S. member of the family with such a tail. Feet pink. This dove breeds in every state in the Union and in southern Canada. Northern birds begin migration early, in loose flocks, and join locally raised southern birds to form large concentrations wherever feed is most abundant. Shooting is legal during set seasons in all southern states, in the West Coast states, and occasionally in states such as Nebraska, Montana, Minnesota, etc.

Methods: Dogs are not used for dove hunting, except as retrievers. The flocks usually have a special roosting place, from which they fly out at dawn to feed in farm and weed fields. Beans, peanuts, corn, wheat, etc., are favorite foods, also such wild plants as mullein and foxtail. They do not scratch for food or take it from the stalk, but pick up loose feed from the ground.

By midmorning the feeding is finished, after which the birds retire to light foliated brush and trees for their siesta. During these hours shooting is usually slow, and the birds very wary. Feeding begins again in mid-

213

afternoon and continues on toward dusk. Then the birds rush for water, and from there to roost.

Thus several hunting methods have become popular. The sportiest is pass shooting as the loose flocks and singles, which usually follow a definite route from roost to feed, feed to water, and water to roost, wing overhead at high speed, dipping and swerving prettily. This is very difficult shooting, however, and requires that the gunner be a crack shot if he hopes to score.

The most popular methods therefore have been called feeding-field shoots and waterhole shoots. Usually a number of gunners take part, and the "shoot" becomes quite a festive and hilarious affair, with much shooting and much missing. A group of hunters surrounds a field which has been established as a favorite feeding place of the birds. Each hunter keeps partially concealed under a tree, or in brush or grass, and takes the birds as they come in or leave. Curiously, doves seldom flare away at such a barrage but run straight through it. If such a field—or waterhole—is too heavily shot, over a period of days, of course the doves will leave. But if rested between shoots, a field will usually hold birds for several weeks, sometimes in fabulous numbers.

The lone gunner, or a pair of hunters, sometimes may get very nice dove shooting by locating a stubble or weed field where birds are feeding. By walking into the wind, slowly, carefully, birds hidden and feeding in the weeds or stubble may be approached within gun range and flushed. Often, if the field is large, missed birds will fly back and alight in the other end of it. Thus a single large field can sometimes be combed back and forth with excellent results and some most enjoyable shooting. This jump shooting is by no means as difficult as pass or feeding-field shooting, for the flushed birds take more time to get under way. A full-flight dove winging over, however, is a tough proposition. His speed is amazing. His dipping, rolling, swerving flight makes proper lead a well-nigh insoluble problem.

Gun and load: There is no special dove gun and load. Though the 20 and .410 gauges are satisfactory for a good shot, the 12 is none too large. Seldom does average dove shooting furnish a majority of close-in shots. Therefore the gun should be considerably choked, or, in the case of double-barreled guns, the second barrel closely choked. Shot size around No. 8 or No. 9, though for long shots No. 7½ or even No. 6 does well. A light powder charge is satisfactory except for pass shooting.

White-winged Dove: Slightly larger than the mourning dove, with a bill noticeably down-curved. A white patch on each wing on the upper side and the fairly long though rounded tail easily set this species apart from the mourning dove.

The whitewing is actually a species of Mexico and Central America, a tropical dove of arid, desert regions. The northern fringe of its range, however, includes southern Arizona and southwestern Texas, where it nests abundantly in summer but from which sections it migrates back into Mexico about September. Although there is whitewing shooting only in this extremely restricted U.S. range, and only for a short time each season, the experience of a whitewing shoot is an unforgettable one. The shooting is much like that on mourning doves, as far as methods are concerned, but with an atmosphere of its own. On passes the whitewing usually flies higher than his smaller relative and can be a most exasperating fellow to deal with at such times. But he is certainly a bird worth traveling many miles after, even for only a single day of shooting. Gun and load as for the mourning dove, except on pass shooting where a well-choked gun with heavily loaded No. 6 shot is required.

Band-tailed Pigeon: As large as or larger than the homing pigeon of city streets. Tail squared, with a dusky band toward the end. General color over-all bluish with iridescent greens and wines. A white half collar at the back of the neck. A bird of the big timber of high western mountain regions. Ranges from British Columbia to Mexico, Colorado to Arizona and New Mexico. Legal shooting usual nowadays only from British Columbia down the West Coast of the U.S.

In early days the bandtail was extremely abundant and much hunted for market during fall and spring migrations. Today only a remnant of the former numbers is left. During fall migrations the birds travel southward but seldom with definite flight lanes. They follow the high ridges and valleys, and the river valleys, casting about in large flocks wherever the food supply is best. Mild weather and good feeding in a certain area will hold them for an unpredictable period. Thus bandtail shooting is something of a gamble. One season it will be excellent in some certain location. Then for several years perhaps hardly a bird will show up. West Coast farmers and fruit growers complain at times that the birds do great damage to crops.

The bandtail can be decoyed fairly well, and this practice is common at such locations as the seed-pea growing communities around Puget Sound, the decoys being set on the fringes of good feeding locations. The main and most popular method, however, is pass shooting. When heavy flights are on, the birds follow the valleys and often cut through a low notch in the mountains on their way to feed or roost. Or, in rolling country they fly up and over ridges in roller-coaster fashion. Hunters take stations near the notch passes or at the ridge tops and try their luck at full-flight birds. The ridge-top locations on a fly-way mean the birds can be taken as they lose speed on the up-flight. They are tremendously swift, require a heavy load of No. 6 or No. 7½ shot from a well-choked gun—and the closest attention to judgment of range and lead.

Bandtail shooting is, in fact, one of the most sensationally exciting sports to be had in all U.S. gunning. It is also one of the most difficult endeavors known to wingshooters.

The birds feed on acorns, grain of various kinds, fruit, and pine nuts. Their love for pine nuts has made high-country shooting among the "big sticks" a popular method for many hunters. During midday birds will choose tall, bare stubs on which to perch, and some "plinking" enthusiasts pick them off with a .22. Or, as they feed here and there among the piñons they are stalked by the shotgunners. This, however, requires even a far more quiet and expert stalk than for deer. But however you manage to surprise him with your charge, the bandtail, though a gamble, is a fit bird to bear the responsibility of closing this upland game-bird chapter. He is truly one of America's all-time greats among game birds.

Chapter Four

Hunting Lowland
Game Birds

When this country was a youngster, it was one of the world's most fabulous strongholds of all kinds of waterfowl and birds of the marshes. Our long coast lines, our hundreds of thousands of lakes and streams, our millions of acres of marsh lands made super-congenial breeding and feeding habitats for this grand galaxy of game birds.

Market hunters in those days were in their glory. It was nothing to wade into a marsh, shoot blindly into huge, compact masses of waterfowl which took wing, and bring down a dozen at a time. The shore birds—curlews, plover, snipe, etc.—were present in such abundance that with the oversized shotguns of the period fifty or more downed at a single shot was not even worthy of bragging about. It seemed then inconceivable that this plenitude would not continue forever.

But later, as agriculture began to take hold, more and more marshes were drained. Cities sprang up on the shores of our large lakes and streams, and along our coast lines, in the places where the waterfowl nested. As the process continued, the birds of the watery habitats dwindled more and more. Where upland birds could move back for a time into the wilder and more remote places as civilization pressed ahead and gobbled up their original homes, the marsh birds found themselves with nowhere to go. First to decline drastically were the shore birds, for most of these are not very prolific. Finally they faced extinction, and it was necessary to take them off the game list almost entirely. There is today a bit of shooting here and there on a single member of their large tribe only, the Wilson's snipe, or jacksnipe.

The ducks and geese, prolific birds by nature as regards the number of eggs they lay, might conceivably have done better had we recognized their plight in time. But we did not. Daily limits, after the law stepped in to assist them, were still high, and scattered market gunning still continued. But worst of all, concentrated agriculture succeeded foolishly in draining most of the U.S. marshes capable of holding large concentrations of nesting waterfowl. We had not yet come to understand that we should utilize to better advantage the land already drained rather than think in terms of acquiring more tillable soil.

The ducks and geese were slowly forced out, until

few really important large nesting areas are left to them today within U.S. borders. Even on the great Canadian breeding grounds, much of their summer habitat was destroyed. Meanwhile, since they are migratory, they had to put up with being gunned over thousands of miles of their migration route during the long duck seasons. Predators waxed fat and went their way with little effective control, while the ducks and geese were drastically controlled both by available nesting sites and over-gunning.

At last we woke up—barely in time to save our entire national waterfowl crop from complete extinction. Federal and state and private agencies went all out to save what was left. Thus, today, we at least know how to save the birds from extinction, and we are still able meanwhile to have a minimum of shooting.

All in all, the waterfowl picture is not good, even though many of us do succeed in filling our limits each fall. A great share of the best hunting grounds—more each year—are under lease or owned outright by wealthy hunters and hunting clubs. The average duck hunter thus finds it constantly more difficult, and more expensive in both time and money, to get even reasonably good shooting. However, one bright spot is the fact that today waterfowl are so thoroughly managed by various agencies that each season's success, or lack of it, can be and is fairly well predicted beforehand. And, with the daily limit very low, the average hunter who must put up with fewer ideal locations still has in many places as good a chance to fill his limit as those who belong to the clubs. He simply has to stay in his blind a little longer, whereas the club hunter often spoils his day by filling his legal limit during the opening barrage!

Today we must buy a federal duck stamp each year, in addition to our state license, in order to hunt waterfowl. But every hunter should be glad to do so, for this money goes directly to assist the continuance of his sport. There is still a great deal of good lowland hunting to be had. But it would be very foolish to write of lowland bird hunting today as if all were well with its future. The one thing every lowland gunner must keep constantly in mind is the deplorable history which is the forerunner of today's rather restricted sport. If we should fail to do so, it is no idle prophecy to say that within no more than a couple of decades lowland bird hunting will be entirely a matter of history!

THE DUCKS

THERE ARE A number of duck species in the U.S., and it becomes more and more important that hunters be able to recognize them. Already it has been necessary to restrict the shooting on a species or two, and from time to time it may become necessary during certain seasons to institute protective measures against certain others. In addition to the legal aspects, knowing your game is a source of great satisfaction to a gunner. Surely no duck hunter wants to come home with a limit and not be able to state under questioning what species of duck he has shot!

The habits of many of the species differ quite radically. For example, some migrate later than others; some decoy better than others; and some taste better than others. Thus, let us first have a quick look at the various more common and popular species and their generally outstanding habits as related to hunting, before we take up methods for bringing them to bag.

THE PUDDLE, OR POND, DUCKS are so-called as a group because they do their feeding in shallow water, either wading and scooping up food from the mud and weeds, or tipping tail-end up to grub bits of weed, etc., from a foot of water. It is these ducks at which the average duck hunter will do most of his shooting, for they will most often come within his gun range as he waits on river bank, the edge of pond or pothole, lake shore, or marsh.

The one habit common to all members of this group is that when taking to wing they spring straight up from the water, beating the air to gain altitude before setting their course. Every hunter should know this habit, especially if he intends to try "jump" shooting—that is, stalking. Among this group are some of the finest table birds, especially since they will, whenever possible, feed from inland grain fields.

Most drakes, or male ducks, of all species are far brighter in color than the females. But the molts of ducks often change their appearance so that species are difficult to identify quickly by sight. However, during hunting seasons the males have usually acquired most, if not all, of their full, bright plumage again. Thus the following descriptions are of ducks in full winter plumage, and for the most part only detailed descriptions of the males are given, since questionable females, shot from the same flocks from which easily identifiable males are taken, can usually be assumed to be of that species.

Mallard, or "greenhead": A fairly large duck, averaging about three pounds. Bill yellow, head iridescent green, white half collar in front, chestnut breast, light gray-white belly, orange legs and feet, back smooth gray and brownish, white-edged iridescent purple wing patch, rump green with several upcurled feathers in tail. Female mottled brown, with wing patch, orange legs and feet. Nesting and migration range combined blankets almost the entire U.S. Decoys well.

Black Duck: Average size about like mallard, or slightly larger. Male and female quite similar. Bill pale yellow or olive, head mottled medium buff, entire body mottled dark brown-black. Iridescent dark-blue wing patch. Feet either olive, or deep orange-red. Range predominantly eastern and throughout the Great Lakes region, and running down to include the entire Gulf Coast of the U.S. Very wary, but decoys well otherwise.

Pintail: Smaller than the above, averaging about two pounds. Long neck. Bill blue-black, head and part of neck deep chestnut, with pearl-white running up from breast and throat into the neck color. Under parts pearl-white, sides and back laced by fine dark markings, much dark brown toward rump, wing patch of iridescent green and reddish, tail very long, slender, and pointed, feet blue-gray. Female mottled brown and buff, without the long tail but with neck long and slender. Range includes almost entire U.S. Wary, but decoys well.

Shoveler: Also called "Spoonbill" and "Broadbill." It is not necessary to describe this duck, whose body coloring is faintly reminiscent of the mallard, for it can always be identified by its bill. The bill is longer than the head, extremely wide, with the upper mandible noticeably overlapping and down-curved, and with the tip hooked. Bill color black or brown-orange. Average weight just over a pound. Range predominantly western, but a few throughout the U.S. Nowhere especially abundant. Decoys well.

Teal: Three main species—blue-winged, green-winged, and cinnamon. All very small ducks, seldom weighing more than a pound. The first species with much blue on head and wing; the second with green likewise; the third with entire head, neck, and breast cinnamon in color. All very swift, tiny ducks of the rivers and marshes. Range: blue-winged, most of the U.S. except West Coast; green-winged, most of the U.S.; cinnamon, West Coast and Rocky Mountain region mainly. The Teals are always easily identified by their very small size. Decoy very readily.

Baldpate, or American Widgeon: Average weight roughly two pounds. Bill bluish with black tip, forehead white, back of head green, neck daintily mottled buff, breast and sides pale pinkish-chestnut, belly pearl-white, back darker than breast and finely laced with darker markings, dark iridescent green at tips of flight feathers and about rump. Fairly well distributed over the U. S., but usually found abundant during migration only spottily. Very wary and nervous. Will decoy but extremely shy and suspicious.

Wood Duck: Very small. Unmistakable because of its startlingly brilliant and varied colorings, and its long crest which lies back over the neck. Range predominantly from Mississippi River eastward. Some nesting in the Northwest. Rather tame, decoys easily. The Wood Duck should not be, and is not today, a "game" duck because of its scarcity. But it appears on the game list, usually one bird being the limit, simply to avoid illegal shooting due to wrong identification in flight. All hunters should be urged to pass up this beautiful and friendly little bird, so that its extinction may be avoided.

The foregoing are the most common of the puddle ducks, and the species which form the greatest share of the shooting in this group. There are, however, several other species, notably: the Florida Duck, which is somewhat similar in appearance to the female mallard; the Gadwall, nowhere abundant, mildly reminiscent of the Baldpate in stance and color pattern, even though the colors differ; the European Widgeon, a "visitor" in the U.S. who looks quite similar to the Baldpate and is often confused with that species; the New Mexican Duck and the Mottled Duck. Any of these ducks can easily be identified from books on the subject, but because of their lack of general abundance they hardly rate detailed descriptions here.

THE DIVING, OR DEEP-WATER, DUCKS are, as their group name implies, birds of the open water and of deep water. Although they come into the marshes, their feeding is done almost entirely by diving beneath the surface in deeper water and feeding on underwater vegetation and shellfish. Many of them decoy well, and many are inclined to gather in large flocks, or "rafts," on large lakes and along the seacoasts. The shooting for ducks of this group differs from that for the pond ducks mainly by taking place over open water, or along the edges of large marshes giving on open water, rather than in the marsh ponds and potholes.

One of the main differences in habits between these and the pond ducks is that instead of springing straight up into flight, the divers take a half-running, half-flying start along the water surface, then lift themselves as does an airplane at take-off. This is important for a hunter to know, for it makes for quite radical differences in ranges and angles between the two groups when they are flushed. In addition, as a group the diving ducks might be spoken of as hardier birds. For example, most of them nest in general much farther north than the pond and puddle ducks. And they do not migrate in force as quickly as their marsh relatives. Most of them wait in the far north until low temperatures and snow force them to be on their way. Thus the shooting for these open-water species is likely to be best during the middle or late portions of the season.

There are a larger number of species in this group, but the bulk of species names falls among the Scoters and Eiders of salt water. Thus, the common species of diving ducks found inland, especially those found in abundance, are relatively few in number. Only the most important are described here.

Scaups: Two distinct species: the Greater Scaup, commonly called "broadbill," and the Lesser Scaup, commonly called "bluebill." The broadbill is larger, weighing about two pounds, while the bluebill usually weighs under two pounds but seldom less than a pound and a half. Both have bluish bills, blue-black breasts, white under parts, lace-marked grayish and dark upper parts. The head of the Greater Scaup tends toward very dark iridescent green; that of the Lesser Scaup dark iridescent black-purple. Females of both species are less distinctly marked. The Lesser variety ranges widely over most of the U.S. during migration, but the Greater Scaup, with his very broad bill, is predominantly a duck of salt water, along both coasts, and sparingly around the eastern portion of the Great Lakes. These are late migrants. The Greater Scaup decoys readily, as does the Lesser, although the Lesser is usually more nervous both while in flight and when coming in to decoys.

Ring-necked Duck: Often confused with the Scaups, to which it is quite similar. This duck might better be officially called "ring bill," as he is colloquially, for seldom is the brownish neck ring of the male plainly visible, while the whitish ring about the bill near its tip easily identifies it. Ranges along the Pacific Coast, migrates down across the Great Lakes area to winter in the Deep South and Gulf states. Averages about two pounds. Not an especially wary bird, and will decoy readily.

Redhead: One of the best "eating" ducks. Weighs an average of two pounds, but sometimes goes to three. Head rust red, bill bluish with black tip, breast dark gray, back lighter, with fine lacings, under parts gray-white. Female gray-brown. Ranges throughout most of the U.S. during migration. A very unwary and easily decoyed species, which makes fine shooting during mid and late season because of its rafting habits.

Canvasback: Sometimes confused with the redhead, and vice versa, but quite without reason. Though the general body coloring is strikingly similar, and the head of the male about the same red shade, the bill is its identification tag. It is long, black, narrow toward the tip, and on an almost straight plane with the sloping forehead. This is a top-place "eating" duck, and one of large size, often weighing up to three pounds. Usually occurs in large flocks, as late migrants. Slow at take-off, but extremely swift when in full flight. A very suspicious and wary bird, but one with an insatiable curiosity, which leads it to decoy well if the setup is properly made and the hunter well concealed. Though canvasbacks range widely over the U.S., their main hunting-season abundance is along the full length of both coasts, with scattered flocks about the Great Lakes.

Golden-eye: Two species, American and Barrows, the first being the species best known to hunters because of its wide although thin distribution over a great share of the U.S. Commonly called "whistler," because of the sound its wings make when the bird is in full flight. Weighs roughly two pounds. A very suspicious, nervous species, at times difficult to decoy. Easily identified by the predominantly white body with black and white on the back, the yellow feet, and the iridescent green head of the male, which is furnished with a rounder crest and a large, round white spot on either side at base of the very short bill. Barrows Golden-eye looks rather similar, except that the iridescent head color is purple, and cheek marking is not round, but in the form of a half-moon patch.

Bufflehead, or "butterball": Often weighs less than a pound and is never larger than a teal. Though among the divers, this duck takes flight from a vertical spring, like the puddle ducks. Widely distributed over the entire U.S., but nowhere abundant nowadays. Extremely trusting, and decoys readily. Unmistakably identified by its small size, its white under parts, much white in wings, pink feet, short bill, and crested head. The crest is rounded; cheeks, forehead, and back of the head are dark iridescent greenish-blue with highlights of red and yellow, but top of the crown is white, and this portion forms a wide, deep V coming down almost to the bill.

The diving ducks so far mentioned are the most important on the hunter's bill of fare in this group. Others include the Old Squaw and the Harlequin Duck, neither of which is much hunted, the first because it is predominantly a northern species, the latter because it ranges only in small spots, chiefly along the West Coast, and because it is inclined to taste fishy. There is also the little Ruddy Duck, and perhaps one or two more meagerly populous species.

One other group of ducks important to certain groups of hunters are the Scoters and Eiders. The Eiders, of which there are several species, are the birds from which eider down is taken. They are all ducks of the Far North, a few of them coming into our range only along the seacoasts of the Canadian west and east, and casually along the Pacific Northwest and upper New England. The Scoters are fairly large, drab-colored ducks of salt water, somewhat strong of taste. They are hunted to some extent along the New England Coast and the Pacific Coast, but do not nowadays form any sizable portion of the annual duck kill, and are therefore quite unimportant to the average waterfowler.

In addition to these, there are three species of Mergansers, or "fish ducks," very commonly seen, and often shot, by duck hunters. Sometimes called "sheldrake" along the New England Coast, these ducks make mighty strong eating, although they are beautiful birds. They are very swift fliers which tax a gunner's skill. They are the American, Red-breasted, and Hooded Mergansers. The fish ducks can be unmistakably identified by their very narrow, hooked, saw-toothed bills, which enable them to hold on to the slippery small fish which form their main source of food. This strange bill has also caused the fish ducks to be called "saw-bills" in many sections.

THE GEese

WILD GEese are set apart from the ducks by their larger size, long necks, honking cries, and the fact that male and female wear identical plumage. Although they migrate southward along with the ducks, and over the same territory, most of them nest in concentration farther to the north than many of the ducks. And though they utilize the marshes and the waterways, a great deal of their actual feeding is done during migration in open fields such as the wheat and corn stubble of the Midwest.

Geese are in general exceedingly intelligent and wary birds, among the most difficult of all waterfowl to bring to bag consistently. Once awesomely abundant, the same conditions which brought the ducks low have drastically affected the goose population. However, we still do have very fine goose shooting in a number of locations along their migratory routes throughout the U.S. All told, this shooting stands among the very top gunning sports in America. It requires a fine craft on the part of the hunter and furnishes an exceptional thrill to those who are successful, as well as some of the best eating to be found among game birds.

It is important nowadays that prospective goose hunters are well acquainted with the different species and able to identify them quickly, even on the wing, for declines in goose population make it necessary from year to year to restrict shooting on certain species. Thus, in the following paragraphs, brief species descriptions and ranges are given which should easily make it possible for any goose hunter to stay within the law.

Canada Goose: This is the bird every hunter envisions when he thinks of goose hunting. There are several subspecies, differing for the most part, and noticeably to the average hunter, only in size. The Common Canada is the largest, weighing upwards of ten pounds average, often much larger. Range, throughout the U.S. The Western Canada is about the same size, but usually somewhat darker. Range, along the West Coast. The Lesser Canada is slightly smaller, has a shorter neck, ranges down the West Coast and the western Gulf Coast. The Cackling Goose, another subspecies, is smaller yet, and is mainly a West Coast bird. Richardson's Goose is the miniature of the tribe, has a high voice, and migrates down the western Mississippi Valley. All of these birds can be unmistakably identified as a group by the following markings: Bill, legs, and feet black; head and neck black except for a broad patch of white which sweeps under the throat and covers both cheeks; body gray of varying shades, rear belly white, with black and white tail feathers.

All of the other species of geese have quite restricted ranges, both for breeding and during migration. However, some hunters do find good shooting for them, and some stragglers turn up among the Canada Goose flights. Thus they are all listed below.

Blue Goose: Fairly large goose, with pink bill, legs, and feet. Back of the bill and forward of the eyes the feathers are pinkish tan. Remainder of the head, and the neck, are dull white. General body color gray-blue, of a lighter shade than the Canadas. Migrates down the western Mississippi Valley to winter in southern Louisiana and along the west Texas Gulf Coast.

Ross's Goose: Smallest of the geese, weighing about three pounds. Nests in small area of Far North, migrates into U.S. at Montana border, crosses Rockies to winter in California. Extremely fine eating. Not abundant. A grayish-white bird with pink bill and feet. See below.

Snow Goose, or "wavey": Two subspecies, Greater and Lesser. Good-sized geese, which look almost pure white from a distance. The bill and feet are pink. In flight, the black wing tips show plainly. Ross's goose, above, is simply a miniature of the snow goose tribe. In the U.S. the Greater Snow Goose is known in the East, where it winters along the mid-Atlantic Coast. The Lesser variety winters along the western Gulf Coast. Not especially wary birds, easily called and decoyed, as opposed to the very shrewd, hard-to-decoy Canadas. Nowhere especially abundant nowadays.

White-fronted Goose: Called "specklebelly," also "laughing goose," because of its peculiar cry. A species common only in the West and along the western Gulf Coast. A good-sized goose with mottled pinkish bill, yellow feet, general head, neck, and body color tan and gray, but the belly with dark brown speckles and uneven markings.

Emperor Goose: An exceedingly wary goose of the Far North, where it winters in the Alaskan Islands. Body mottled gray, feet yellow, throat and chin very dark brown, head white with orange tinge.

These listings, for all practical purposes, cover the true goose tribe. Hunters should be very careful, however, when snow geese are in their range, not to confuse them with the various swans, which are still in evidence in small flocks from time to time. The swans, even in flight, are unmistakable because of their large size, very long necks, and their all-white bodies and *wings*. Also the feet and legs are black, while those of the snow geese are pink.

The group of birds called *Brant* also belongs in the goose group. They are really medium-sized geese of *salt water,* and thus are never found inland. One species, the American Brant, migrates down the Atlantic Coast, wintering as far south as North Carolina. The other, the Black Brant, migrates down the West Coast. Both look rather similar, and though smaller than the Canada Goose, the two brants are faintly reminiscent of the Canada in color. However, the white cheek and throat swath are missing. The head is entirely black, the neck and upper breast also, except for a frontal throat patch dully striped with black and white. This readily identifies them. The brants usually weigh from three to four pounds. These birds are rather wild, but much less so than the Canada goose. They decoy rather well and can always be hunted over water, for they are aquatic feeders, never going inland to the fields.

WATERFOWL GUNS

WHEN IT comes to choosing a gun for hunting waterfowl, one must use a different approach from that taken with the upland birds. It must be remembered that, by and large, all waterfowl are heavy of body, and that their coats of down and feathers are very thick. In addition, the ranges at which waterfowl are shot will in general be longer than those for upland birds. The very fact that the shooting is open, with the birds limned against the flat sky, makes judgment of distance difficult, so that many shots are taken which should be passed up because they are definitely out of range. In reference to this it should be said that so many lost cripples and wounded ducks result from poor range judgment that every duck and goose hunter should make it a practice not to shoot until he can readily distinguish every marking on his bird, or even see its *eyes*. Such shots will always be within range.

Besides the long shots and the toughness of the birds, their high flight (at least when passing birds are shot at) and their swift flight make it imperative that the hunter be certain of killing the bird stone dead in the air. Thus a heavy gun immediately becomes of paramount concern. Although 20 and 16 gauges are in use here and there, the 12 (or even the 10) is the best waterfowl gun. Since the shooting is open and the gun may be swung into action without obstructions in the way, a long barrel is best, and it should be choked down well, so that the greatest range and most compact pattern are assured.

Gun action is a matter of personal choice, but here again the maximum of fire power should be considered. Though the double is a popular duck gun, the automatic and pump actions are preferred by many. This is because the double offers but two quick shots, while the pump or automatic offers more. It is nowadays illegal to use for waterfowl hunting a gun capable of firing more than three shots without reloading. Thus the magazine of a five-shot pump gun, for example, must be plugged. However, that extra third shot is very often important. A duck' merely winged with the first shot hits the water and begins to swim rapidly away, making for marsh cover if possible. Killing a duck on the water is more difficult sometimes than killing one in the air. The third shot may mean the difference between a duck only wounded and one irretrievably lost, especially when the hunter does not have a retrieving dog at hand. A dog, as well as that third shot, is for this reason extremely important.

As to loads, the powder charge should always be heavy, and the shot size large enough to insure potent damage from each pellet. Although some hunters, shooting over close-in decoys, use No. 7½ shot, under average conditions a larger size is preferable. No. 6, No. 5, and No. 4 are most popular. For geese, nothing smaller than No. 4 should be used, and many hunters drop back even to size No. 2, which under long-range shooting circumstances can be extremely effective.

HUNTING METHODS

SCIENTISTS, through patient banding and research operations, have discovered that waterfowl have rather definite migratory flight lanes. There are four of these, very broad general lanes which are followed by both ducks and geese. These are the Pacific Flyway, which follows a broad swath down the entire West Coast; the Central Flyway, which lies between the Rockies and the Mississippi Valley; the Mississippi Flyway, which follows the broad river valley; the Atlantic Flyway, which brings birds down across the Great Lakes region, and from eastern Canada, curves around east of the Great Smokies, and blankets the entire East Coast, the Florida Peninsula, and the West Indies.

Obviously, the prospective waterfowl gunner must plan his hunting in relation to the best feeding and watering places which occur along the flyway in which he is situated. The Atlantic Coast, from Nova Scotia to the Carolinas, offers some of the best hunting for both pond and diving ducks, and also geese. The St. Lawrence waterways, and the Great Lakes region also offer excellent sport, but around the Great Lakes the shooting is inclined to be spotty because of the myriad small bodies of water which break up heavy waterfowl concentrations. The prairie provinces of Canada and the plains states such as the Dakotas furnish fabulous hunting at times, much of it dry-land hunting for birds which flock by thousands to feed in the stubble fields. The river bottoms in Illinois are famous for waterfowling, and so are such spots as the flooded lowland country of eastern and southern Arkansas. The latter offers sensational hunting for ducks such as the mallard in flooded woodlands, where birds are plentiful and the trees form obstacles to a swinging gun. The Gulf Coast of Texas, Louisiana, etc., is also a topnotch location for all kinds of waterfowl shooting, and here the hunting is for the most part straight marsh hunting. The same is true in the Salton Sea area of California, and in the central and northern portions of California. Farther north along the West Coast, the shooting is more like that along the upper East Coast, part of it in the marshes, part over open water. Even the desert is not without some very good duck shooting at times, when tanks and irrigation ponds fill up with migrants sorely in need of places to rest and feed.

In other words, there is in almost every section of the U.S. some waterfowl shooting to be had. But the hunter who chooses to make a real issue of it will do best to pick his location carefully in relation to its past fame and present conditions.

Only in "jump" shooting are waterfowl flushed in the manner of upland birds. This shooting is high sport, and is the method followed by a great many hunters who are not especially waterfowl enthusiasts but who try to get in a day or two of sport, and a bird or two, each year. This hunting is almost entirely for the pond ducks, and the best of it occurs during the first half of the season, before hard frosts have laid the reeds and other vegetation low. The hunter simply dons hip boots or waders and enters a marsh, walking into the wind if at all possible, covering the marsh slowly, ever alert.

Ducks such as black ducks, mallards, teal, etc., will often be found hiding and feeding in the deep vegetation, usually where there is water enough at least to float them, but sometimes where the ground is only wet. By cautious movement, the gunner comes upon the birds unaware of his presence. They flush the moment they hear or see him, and he gets shooting much like upland shooting. This same "sneak" method of stalking is used around the tiny ponds and potholes where the puddle ducks consort. It's good sport, and the shooting is fairly easy on these flushing birds. But nowadays it is not usual to kill any great number of birds by this chance method.

Of all waterfowl hunting, pass shooting provides the most difficult and thrilling sport. It requires no more equipment than that for jump shooting. But it does require a good knowledge of the area in which the shooting is to be done, and of course not all areas provide it. When ducks are spending nights in a marsh and flying out at dawn to feed in some particular location such as a grain field, they usually follow a definite route. After they have fed full, they return to the marsh, or fly on across it to open water if such is available. Later in the day they fly back to the feeding ground, and toward dusk return to the marsh once more.

Thus, if a gunner knows of such a flyway, he stations himself advantageously somewhere along it, well concealed, and shoots at the full-flight birds as they wing over. The same type of shooting may often be had along rivers, where the birds tend to trade back and forth, flying up and down the stream perhaps all day, especially if the weather is bad or if many hunters are out and the constant barrage tends to keep them on the wing. It should be obvious, of course, that as usual a good retriever is very important to this operation.

Perfect concealment is also paramount. This is true of all duck hunting. Waterfowl have amazingly keen eyesight and a wariness which causes them to shy from the least unusual object or change in a habitat with which they are familiar. It is not enough simply to be dressed in drab brown or olive green hunting togs. A hunter must also be well hidden, and must keep his face from showing as ducks fly toward or over him. He must also be exceedingly cautious about making the slightest movement. The birds, from their high vantage point, can sweep the landscape with their gaze. Their eyes pick out danger easily from a far greater distance than many a hunter realizes or imagines.

Since pass and jump shooting are both somewhat of a gamble in most instances, shooting waterfowl over decoys has over the years been the standard and most popular method. Centuries ago it was discovered that waterfowl were among the few birds that would come to the gunner if he set out a "stool" of decoys fashioned in their likeness. In conjunction with the decoys, since waterfowl "talk" to each other a great deal, hunters learned to use duck and goose calls. Thus, when a gunner built a blind of reeds or other material for concealment, set out a number of decoys in a place which appeared to be a good feeding ground, hid in the blind, and waited for a flock to come winging over, he called their attention to the artificial decoys with blowing *sparingly* on his call. By careful work, and experience, he soon learned to pull the curious flocks down within gun range. Today by far the greatest share of really serious waterfowl hunting is done by this method.

If he hunts on a shallow marsh, the hunter can do without a duck boat. But to do very much duck hunting a boat is really necessary. The usual duck boat is a craft built for one, or no more than two, men. It is pointed on each end, very low to the water, as a rule covered part way fore and aft. This tiny, light, tippy craft can be poled or sculled easily through thick vegetation. It can also be camouflaged by covering it with reeds and building a border of standing reeds around its cockpit. The reeds can be strung on chicken wire.

For the pond and marsh ducks, no great number of decoys is necessary. A dozen, or two dozen, set in natural positions around a small pothole or bayou in a marsh, will draw down the singles, pairs, and small flocks passing over. Decoys can be purchased in sporting goods stores. If they are not weighted on the bottom when purchased, they should be weighted by the owner. A small piece of lead (these weights can also be purchased) is fixed to the bottom of each decoy so that it rides smoothly even in rough water, without tipping over. Anchors are also necessary for decoys, and can be purchased. The anchor is simply a small metal gadget attached to a stout cord. The cord must be long enough to reach bottom in the water being hunted. When the decoy is tossed out, the anchor goes with it to keep the decoy from floating away in wind or current.

For the pond ducks, many hunters use no special decoy setup. They simply scatter a dozen or so decoys here and there, in singles and pairs, in a position where they will be easily visible to all ducks flying over, yet near enough to the blind to make for proper shooting range when the birds attempt to settle among the decoys, or "blocks" as they are often called. The decoy set, however, should be placed so that incoming birds will be able to land against the wind. The kind of decoys used should also match the species of ducks most abundant. In other words, since decoys may be purchased in any pattern, or replica of any species, it is best to use mallard decoys when mallards are most abundant, etc.

The kind of decoy—what they're made of—is not especially important. Each locality has its favorite type. Some are of fiber, some of balsa wood, some of cedar, some of rubber, some merely silhouette cutouts stuck into the mud on a stake. Best advice is to follow the method of setup and the type of decoy and general usage most popular in the region where the hunt takes place. Old hands thereabouts will know what works best in that section.

For the diving ducks, which often gather in huge rafts and must be shot over large bodies of open water, from large, well-camouflaged boats doctored up to look like floating islands of reeds, in general many more decoys are needed. These diving ducks, if "rafting," will usually pay no heed to a dozen decoys, but will come in only to a set of from thirty to a hundred. At many duck hunting camps, decoys can be rented at so much per dozen for a day. This is the best bet for the average hunter who does not care to invest in a large number, or have the task of toting them around.

Such large decoy sets are usually carefully planned "stools." Every old hand at open-water hunting will have his ideas as to the type of setup which will bring the ducks in best. Some use, for example, what is called a "pipestem" set. This consists of setting a long curving line of decoys out into open water in the shape of a pipestem. Sometimes this set stretches several hundred yards out. It grows wider as it comes marshward and, in a quieter cove, spreads out into a large stool like the bowl of a pipe. Thus, the birds flying far out are attracted to the line of decoys which appear to be swimming shoreward. The birds follow down the line, see the huge "pipe bowl" and settle in to the calls of the hunters. There are many such carefully planned types of sets. The tyro will do well to note these refinements of the old-time waterfowlers, and copy them.

In using a call, it is best to study the directions which come with it when it is purchased, so that you may know, if you've never used one, exactly what sounds to make, or how much or little the call should be used under various circumstances. Much can also be learned from hunting with old hands. Or, nowadays, phonograph records can be purchased which give detailed instruction by actual sound.

Duck hunting, then, as may be readily seen, can be as complicated or as simple as you choose to make it. It must be carefully noted, however, that in general the hunter who takes the most pains, outfits himself the most elaborately, and works with the greatest caution and care for meticulous detail will have the best success. So also will the hunter who watches the weather and is willing to put up with those days most unpleasant for humans. On so-called "bluebird" days, when the air is calm and the sun warm and bright, waterfowl fly little. They are inclined to stay out of the marshes, out in deep water, where they are difficult to get at. They also are difficult to decoy at such times. On bad days, however, when rain or sleet is pelting down and an icy wind making the reeds of the blind rattle, the birds will be on the wing, trading restlessly back and forth, and ready to swing into decoys and calls that they would scorn on a pleasant day.

Goose hunting is reasonably similar to duck hunting, and in fact sometimes exact methods may be used, or a goose or two knocked down when only ducks are expected. In general, however, geese are far more wary, and their habit of feeding in open fields makes them exceedingly difficult birds with which to come within gun range. The usual procedure is to set out goose decoys very carefully in wheat stubble or fields of shocked corn. If in a field of shocked corn known to be a feeding ground for geese, then the hunter conceals himself completely within a corn shock. In open wheat stubble—or on sand bars in the big rivers where geese alight to rest —a pit must be dug for concealment. This must be done most carefully and meticulously. All dirt must be carried away or smoothed down, no obvious disturbance made in the field. The pit must have a cover, camouflaged to look like a bit of the ground. The hunter sets out decoys, gets into the pit before dawn, or during midafternoon, and waits for the feeders to come in. He keeps the "lid" on, allowing himself only the slightest peephole to observe incoming birds. When the birds are within range, he heaves up the cover and blazes away. This kind of goose shooting, as with all goose shooting, is a tricky affair. The beginner can learn far more of its refinements from experienced hands at the game than he could from a hundred books on the subject.

All told, although waterfowl hunting is a somewhat complicated business, it is one of the finest and most exciting and enjoyable gun sports known to man. It is truly worth whatever trouble and inconvenience and discomfort comes with it, and is a wonderful hobby for those who are so situated as to be able to partake of it. Today every hunter who partakes of it should think of it in that light, and so work to conserve the birds which make it possible that this grand gunning occupation may continue permanently, even though it must continue on the much-lessened scale to which declines in the annual waterfowl crop have brought it.

RAILS AND RAIL HUNTING

RAIL SHOOTING is one of the most curious of all gunning sports. Because the birds are so difficult to find and flush, there is little inland rail hunting nowadays. But there is still a good bit of excellent shooting to be had along the tidal rivers of the coasts, and the salt marshes from Connecticut to Florida. Here the hunting is accomplished successfully by watching the tides. The birds gather in these marshes in early fall, most of them as migrants, and they feed out over the thick vegetation at low tide. As the tide begins to come in, they are crowded inland. Now a boat poled slowly through the matted vegetation will put them up before the gun.

The usual procedure is for the hunter to hire a boatman who knows the business of rail shooting. This guide stands at the back end of the boat, on a small platform, and pushes it with a pole. The gunner sits in the middle of the boat, sometimes on a bolted-down swivel chair, swinging on the birds as they flutter up beside the boat. This shooting is most unusual, and from the unsteady boat rather tricky. Both guide and gunner must watch very carefully where each bird falls, for rails are difficult to find after they are downed.

In the South, the birds are called "marsh hens," and are sometimes hunted with dogs at high tide along the marsh edges. The dog chases them through the thick growth, routing them out before the gun. In the Gulf Coast rice fields, hunters sometimes follow the rice-cutting combines. Birds skulking in the rice are slowly herded into the last patch of grain still standing. When it falls before the combine, they flush. This is a common method on the highly prized, large King Rail.

Chapter Five

Hunting Small Game Animals and Varmints

If any group of creatures could be said to form the basis of gunning sport for every hunter, everywhere, the honor would unquestionably fall to the small game animals, some of the fur animals, and the so-called predators and varmints. By their abundance, their extremely wide ranges, and the ease with which they may be taken, such animals as the rabbits and squirrels made themselves famous as "meat in the pot" centuries ago. And while furnishing good eating, they also made possible extremely pleasant sport for literally millions of people everywhere. Today, even though we have progressed far in the refinements of hunting, those same common and traditional little beasts still hold top place in the favor of the great majority of hunters.

All told, none of these lesser huntsman's targets should be overlooked by the would-be hunter. There is very fine and exciting sport of a very special kind to be had with each. None of it is complicated, or expensive, and all of it together is available to more hunters than are any other type of gunning. Indeed, each of these "lesser gamesters" is well worth a close-focus look.

RABBITS

THERE ARE numerous species of rabbits in the U.S. Technically some of these so-called "rabbits" are hares. This makes no difference as far as the hunter is concerned.

Most popular and abundant species is the cottontail, distributed over almost the entire U.S., and well known to every outdoorsman. His small size, and the white lower side of his short, fluffy tail, identify him. There are several species of like size called brush rabbits, most of them western in distribution. There are also the swamp rabbits of the South, somewhat larger as a rule than the cottontail, and with hind feet partly webbed. These rabbits, curiously, take to water readily.

Among the larger U.S. rabbit species are the varying hare, or snowshoe rabbit of the northern portions of the U.S., and the various long-legged jack rabbits of the western plains and desert. The jack rabbits are hunted very little, except by small-rifle enthusiasts who like to try their skill on running targets, or who spot the jacks through a scope and bag them sitting, at long range. But the snowshoe of the snow country is a prime game animal to many a northern resident.

This big fellow turns white in winter, except for the tips of his ears. He doesn't live in burrows, or hole up when chased, as does the cottontail. Indeed not! He is a long-distance runner who will give rabbit hounds a merry chase round and round the cedar or tamarack swamps which are his chosen habitats, a chase sometimes lasting for hours. Some hunters try stalking him, without dogs. This is especially good sport when an open winter with little or no snow causes the white hares to stand out plainly in the brush. Hunting with dogs, however, is by far the best sport. Beagle hounds are a good choice, although in places where the snow is deep larger, heavier dogs stand the gaff better.

The snowshoe can run at great speed, but if slow dogs are used he will travel at a more moderate pace. The circles he makes are likely to be long, sometimes a mile or more, and about all the hunter can do is to station himself in a clearing, or on a knoll where he can get a good view, listen to the dogs, and keep watch some distance ahead to try for a shot when the game shows up. The shots are as a rule fairly long. A 12-gauge shotgun is undoubtedly the best gun for this work, and if it is well choked down, all the better. Number 6 shot is a good size, for these big fellows, especially at a distance, take a lot of lead. Some of the best hunting grounds are in the northern Great Lakes region. No special knowledge or technique is necessary for this hunting. If there is snow on the ground, tracks are readily found. If not, dogs will find the hares anyway. The dog-less hunter simply chooses a likely looking piece of cover and starts walking. But it is best to look for snowshoe rabbits in fairly wild locations. They are not, as a rule, commonly found around farm buildings and gardens, as are the cottontails. It is also best to hunt the snowshoes early in winter. Once the snow is deep, they have a habit of feeding on cedar and other bark, which makes the flesh bitter to the taste.

Hunting the extremely popular cottontail is even easier than hunting snowshoes, and the reason for his tremendous popularity is that here is one game animal easily available to practically everybody. The cottontail likes old orchards, abandoned farms, swales where grass and weeds grow tall, briar patches, brushy bottoms, etc. On sunny days he will be out soaking it up, often crouched close to the ground right out in the open. In midwinter, such days make excellent hunting days. When the weather is nasty, he will be under brush piles, in hollow logs, under stumps, the edges of cut-banks, etc.

Many hunters prefer simply to go afield without a dog, and to walk slowly, kicking every brush pile, pausing here and there to peer into hedgerows, crisscrossing the grassy fields in the hope of "kicking up" a bunny. It's not a bad method. The hunting is pleasant work, and many a rabbit is bagged in this fashion. The best sport, however, is to use either a beagle or basset hound, or several small hounds running in a pack. Dogs that work slowly are advantageous, for cottontails, if hard pressed, will duck into a burrow or beneath a stump. A slow dog will keep them moving casually along, and give the hunter ample opportunity for a shot.

The cottontail usually has several well-marked trails that he follows in his daily routine. If there is tracking snow, these trails will be evident. Once the dogs start a rabbit, the hunter should take up a stand on one of these trails, for chances are the rabbit will eventually circle back and follow the trail past the hunter. If no trails are sighted, then the hunter should conceal himself and wait quietly at the spot where the rabbit was put up by the dogs. Invariably, on his first circle, or shortly after, the rabbit will come hopping along back to the very point from which he was jumped. This is his method of making sure whether or not the dogs are still on his trail, and of trying to fool them. The hunter who waits patiently will usually be rewarded with a shot.

Some rabbit hunters like to use a .22 rifle, but rifles may often be dangerous in heavily settled country, and a running cottontail is no target for the average rifle shot. A shotgun, therefore, is a better choice. The gauge makes little difference. Shot size No. 7½ makes a good load.

Of late, it has been found, many rabbits in certain sections are carriers of tularemia, a disease dangerous to humans. It is contracted by skinning or handling a sick rabbit with the bare hands, especially easily if the hands have scratches or abrasions of any kind. Thus, none but lively, obviously healthy rabbits should be used for food, and it is an excellent idea to wear rubber gloves while cleaning rabbits, to wash the hands thoroughly afterward, whether or not gloves are used, and to see to it always that rabbits are thoroughly cooked.

SQUIRRELS

THE VARIOUS squirrels—gray squirrel, fox squirrel, red squirrel, black squirrel—are probably next in general popularity with the majority of hunters. There are several other species, most of them rather rare. Of the squirrels mentioned, the gray and fox squirrels are the prime targets. The red squirrel is generally considered too small to bother with, and though the black squirrel is an excellent customer, he is rather rare nowadays, and in many sections entirely protected. Actually, the so-called black squirrel is but a color phase of the gray.

As with the rabbits, squirrel hunting is popular not because it takes great skill or knowledge, but because squirrels are available almost everywhere, make delicious eating, and provide some of the most pleasant and relaxing days afield it is possible for a sportsman to have. In the hills of Missouri, Arkansas, and in the ridges and lowlands of other southern states, squirrel hunting has always been one of the top activities of gunners. Several states, such as Arkansas and Missouri, usually have spring as well as fall seasons. But squirrel hunting, though traditional in the South, is by no means restricted to that territory. Southern Indiana and Illinois are good squirrel-hunting locations; likewise the Great Lakes states, New England, and the Midwest. In fact, almost anywhere in the U.S. one can find the opportunity to try his hand at gathering the wherewithal for a squirrel potpie.

In farm country, patches of woods bordering on corn and other grain fields make good habitats for squirrels. In wilder country, the oak ridges and flats, beech and maple woods, any stands of timber where nuts abound are the ticket. Here squirrel nests of leaves may be sighted in the trees, and "cuttings" (the debris left where squirrels have been shelling nuts) will be evident beneath the trees.

There are several standard methods of squirrel hunt-

ing, and old-time squirrel hunters are most vociferous
about which is best. Some of them stalk their game, simply going into a good patch of squirrel woods and walking slowly, quiet as an Indian, keeping watch in the
trees, on the ground, on the tops of stumps and logs,
until they catch a squirrel off guard. This is something
of a fine art, for squirrels are often very wary. However,
the stalker, even though he may frighten his game,
usually gets a glimpse of it as it races along a branch
or up a tree. He then tries for a shot, or slowly circles
the tree until he can get a sight of the squirrel.

Squirrels will always attempt to stay on the opposite
side of the tree from a hunter. Thus, two hunters working together have a better chance, once the squirrel in
question is aware of their presence. Squirrels will usually lie close and flat against a branch, if other hiding
places are not available. And so the schooled hunter
will look very carefully, knowing well that a squirrel
can hide in places where it would seem impossible for
him to be concealed. His tail, or his ears, will usually
give him away.

As popular as stalking is the method of simply going
quietly into a squirrel woods, choosing an inconspicuous spot by a stump or log, sitting down, and waiting,
still and motionless. The spot chosen should be one
which commands a wide view of the surrounding woods.
Even though feeding squirrels may have seen the hunter
approaching, and have gone into hiding, after a time
they forget their fear and come out again. The hunter
waits until he sees a squirrel move, or until he hears the
sound of claws on bark, or of cuttings dropping from a
tree into the dry leaves below. Once he has his squirrel
located, he carefully raises his gun and blazes away.

But unless he has merely wounded the squirrel and thus finds it necessary to go to it and finish it off, he will let the dead game lie, and stay quietly at his stand. For, curiously, even after a gunshot which has downed one of their number, squirrels in the vicinity will usually soon come out again for a curious look around, or to begin feeding again. Thus, from one good position a hunter can often bag several squirrels simply by remaining quiet for several hours. Some hunters use squirrel calls, which can be purchased nowadays from sporting-goods stores. These are worked as the hunter sits quietly waiting, and are often very effective.

A few squirrel hunters use dogs. Such dogs, as a rule, are mongrels who have learned to run through the woods and locate a tree with a squirrel in it, or to chase a squirrel up a tree. Some bark, some simply sit and look up a tree, indicating to the hunter that his game awaits him there. Fox terriers and other small, quick dogs are often used for this work. But training them seems to have no definite procedure. A dog either learns to be a good squirrel dog by going hunting with his master, or he doesn't.

The best times of day for this sport are early morning right after dawn, when the squirrels begin their breakfast hour, or late in the afternoon when they are feeding heavily before darkness chases them to bed. Bright, warm days are also best, for during cold or wet weather the animals hesitate to leave their nests and hollow trees. Though many squirrel hunters sneer at the idea of using a shotgun, the average hunter chooses the scattergun in preference to the rifle, in order to be able to hit squirrels running swiftly through the trees better. However, a .22 rifle makes a fine implement if one sits it out, waiting for a squirrel to show, for such shots will usually be at sitting squirrels. The hide of a squirrel is tough, and therefore, though shotgun gauge makes little difference, a fairly heavy load and fairly large shot should be used.

NIGHT HUNTING

OF ALL THE sports beloved by U.S. hound men, night hunting for fur animals undoubtedly stands at or very near the top. Though many of us have never been out at night to chase raccoons, possums—even skunks— with one or more hounds, it is an activity to which no other kind of hunting can be compared. The atmosphere and tradition of it lend a tang to this sport which, to the enthusiast, makes all other sport pale by comparison.

Not many hunters, it is true, care much about running the malodorous black-and-white skunk with their dogs. But there are a few who make a practice of it, not so much for the sport as for the dividend in cash from a collection of skunk pelts. There is nothing especially difficult or complicated about this sport. If skunks are known to be in the vicinity, hounds trained not to be choosy in what fur animals they will trail are simply taken out in the evening and followed until they locate a track. Warm fall evenings, after frosts have made the fur prime, are best, or midwinter periods when thaws have brought the hibernating skunks from their burrows. The chase is usually of short duration. A flashlight and a light rifle are carried to dispatch the game.

Night hunting for the gray-furred, bare-tailed nocturnal opossum is more popular, and is an exceptionally pleasant way to spend an evening. The opossum is an animal weighing from 4 to 10 pounds. It is slow, and not especially brilliant in its maneuvering before a dog. Through the Ozarks and the Great Smokies, and in many other sections east of the Mississippi, running hounds at night on possum trails is one of those things that every outdoorsman hankers for when frosty nights roll around each fall. But the possum is hunted in other sections also, for he is distributed to some extent over almost all of the U.S.

The kind of dog used is quite unimportant. Almost any hound will follow a possum trail. Further, the choice of places to hunt is seldom of great import. The opossum feeds on such a variety of fare that he may be anywhere, from the chicken coop to the oak ridges and the wild persimmon patches. Some hunters take a gun and flashlight or lantern along. Some simply wait for the dogs to give tongue with the bark that says the possum is up a tree; then they race toward the sound, build a fire of leaves beneath the tree, climb it, and knock the animal down with a club.

Hunting raccoons, however, is likely to be something quite different. Of all night hunting, this is the sport which draws the big crowd of hound men. It is no game for those who don't care for sport on the rugged side, or for those who don't want to give some time and thought to proper training of their dogs.

The raccoon, of which there are numerous subspecies throughout its territory, ranges from Maine to Florida, from Minnesota to the Gulf, and even down into the Southwest. They weigh anywhere from 8 to 20-odd pounds. No doubt everyone is familiar with their appearance—the quizzical narrow face with its black mask about the cheeks and eyes, the thick brown-grizzled fur, the beautiful ringed tail.

In the North the raccoon frequents stream bottoms and thick woods, the edges of corn fields bordered by wood lots. In the South it is commonly found in swamps, around lake shores, rivers, and bayous. Its food runs the gamut, from birds, mice, clams and oysters to green corn, acorns, berries, and farmers' chickens.

In scouting for good raccoon territory, it is a good idea to search along the muddy edges of streams and ponds. Here tracks are sure to be found, if raccoons are in the vicinity. Availability of food will be a great factor in hunting success, and thus the hunter should scout feeding possibilities also. Their feeding is done at night: Thus the sport of running hounds on their trails after dark. The dog should be scrupulously trained to run raccoons only. Usually this can be accomplished by running a young dog in the beginning with an older, experienced coon dog, and by sharply reprimanding him for running other game. If you are lucky enough to get hold of what is known as a "cold trailer" (a dog with a nose keen enough to start on a track made hours before and follow it through), it will be possible to run raccoons in the daytime as well as at night. Most dogs, however, require a fairly fresh track, no more than an hour or so old at the most.

Some few coon hunters prefer what are called "silent trailers"—dogs which do not give tongue until the coon is cornered or treed. Such hounds are often able to tree more raccoons than tonguing hounds because of the surprise element in their chase. However, since the music of the hounds is one of the most enjoyable parts of the chase, most coon hunters prefer a dog with a good voice and one not averse to using it.

It is doubtful if there is a more intelligent and crafty animal than the raccoon. He knows, and uses, every trick to throw the dogs off his trail. He will take to water when hard pressed, and is perfectly capable of drowning almost any hound which dares to follow and corner him in deep water. He turns this trick by treading water and ducking the dog's head under with his handlike front feet. He is also, if large, a formidable antagonist for the average coon hound. Though most good dogs are capable of killing their prey, many a dog gets serious lacerations to prove his spunk and courage.

Given a proper dog of one of the big-hound strains, such as the black-and-tan, and territory in which raccoons are abundant, there is no special method except to get out in the best of the territory, in a spot where coons may be feeding in the evening, and get the dog started on a trail. Some hunters roam the woods until a strike is made. Some put the dogs on a back road and drive slowly along until a track crossing the road is struck, whereupon they leave the car and follow the hounds.

But the tyro should not take that last phrase lightly! Following the hounds on a coon trail may, if you're lucky, be only a short chase, the sound of trail bellowing broken suddenly by the excited, staccato tree bark of the dogs only an eighth of a mile away over easy ground. Or it may mean a chase which goes on for hours, over the roughest of rocky terrain, the most impenetrable of brush and bottoms.

But no matter how tough and long the going, the

hunter should never leave his dog or dogs at the tree without getting to them as quickly as he can. Nor should he ever leave them on a long trail and go back to the car, nor try to call them off. Rugged it can be, but in late fall when the leaves are down, the fur prime, and the coon meat fat and delicious for a roast, there's nothing like it. To a lover of hounds and hound music, this is indeed the acme of sport!

BOBCATS AND FOXES

THE BOBCAT and the various foxes are covered under the same heading here primarily because the methods of hunting them are fairly similar, and because most average hunters often fail to realize how many of each of these animals reside in their areas or how much sport can be had in coursing them with hounds. No doubt the fox-hunting enthusiast, however, would feel somewhat annoyed to find his special game classed with the bobcat. But this would be simply because he fails to realize that hunting bobcats can be altogether as much sport as fox hunting, and sometimes more!

The bobcat, bay lynx, or wildcat, as he is variously known, ranges over practically all of the U.S. He is a tawny fellow with slightly tufted ears, a stub tail, and an uncanny ability for keeping out of sight. In the desert states he is usually of a pale sand-gray color, but in the North more yellow. He may weigh anywhere from 15 to 50 pounds.

In many communities the bobcat is a serious predator on game birds and animals, young fawns, lambs, poultry, etc. Yet very often he will live his exceedingly secretive life out in the deep thickets, cedar swamps, brushy ravines, and forested hills quite close to civilization without being detected. Though he has been accused of attacking man, there is no proof to back up the old tales, and actually the bobcat is perhaps more chary of having his presence known than any fox.

During the last decade or two, bobcat hunting with hounds has become a rather popular sport in many parts of the country. In the northern and western states the animal usually trees quickly, but in the South the chase may last for hours. It takes a dog, or dogs, of rugged stature and determination, especially in deep snow in the North. Also, in snow country, the hunter usually needs a pair of snowshoes, for the hunt will surely require slogging around in the thickest kind of going, where snow drifts are deep. Either a light rifle or a shotgun loaded with buckshot or No. 2 shot can be used to dispatch the cat when it trees, or to fire at it as it crosses thicket openings with the hounds baying behind.

Usual procedure, in cat country up north, is to drive back roads until a track is located, then to put down the hounds, post several hunters at advantageous points around the cedar swamp or woods where the cat is being run, and wait until he comes within gun range or is treed. Another method often followed by lone hunters is to walk with the hound on leash until a track is struck in the snow. The hound is then released. Once the direction of the chase is ascertained, the hunter attempts to keep ahead of the hound, watch for the cat to circle, and shoot it. In the South, very often a pack of dogs is run on a bobcat, and no guns used. The dogs run the cat until they catch it and kill it—or until the cat beats them at the game and goes free. In states

258

where there is a bounty on bobcats, needless to say the hunter wishes to make sure of the cat by carrying a gun. All told, bobcat hunting is good sport, rugged enough to please the toughest of sportsmen, and exciting to a high degree. Early morning, when trails are still hot and fresh, is the best time to start a hunt.

Due to a smaller bobcat population than that of foxes, however, the fox is top game for hound men who like daytime hunting. Of course, there are numerous hunters, in states such as Missouri, Tennessee, and Arkansas, who like to run foxes at night with their hounds, not with the idea of killing the fox, but simply for the fun of listening to the hounds. There are also a few fox-hunting clubs still existing in the U.S., especially along the Atlantic Coast in Maryland and Virginia, where the old sport of riding horses to a pack of foxhounds on trail is still practiced.

The Walker hound is the prized foxhound, but various other large hounds are often just as good. They should definitely be trained not to run deer. Procedure is much like the various methods used for bobcat hunting, except that a fox, if not killed on its first few circles, may well lead the hounds many miles away, where they may become lost, or are stolen.

For this reason, still-hunting of foxes has become a popular sport in many northern sections, especially in the Great Lakes region and New England. This is done when there is a good tracking snow, and is a matter simply of finding a fox track and patiently following it, with utmost quiet and care, until the fox is put from his daytime bed and a shot is offered. Still-hunting takes a master stalker.

In addition, where foxes are plentiful, as they are in

259

much of the pheasant and bird country today, drives are often organized by groups of hunters. Sometimes slow dogs are used. Sometimes the hunters simply line up and beat over a large area of woods or swale, while other hunters are stationed at its far side, ready to shoot any fox which emerges. A study of the terrain, which will often locate trails and old roads habitually followed by foxes in their daily food-hunting route, is advantageous in offering the best possibilities for a shot.

Though many Southerners will not allow foxes to be killed, considering them too valuable as objects of "tomorrow night's chase," fox hunting in many of the northern states, with a kill at the end of the chase, is to be encouraged. It is not only great sport but lends a helping hand to our harassed game birds. There are several fox species scattered throughout the U.S. The gray fox and red fox are the two most important and abundant. Of these, the red fox is by far the most game, and the one which has become a source of worry to conservationists in states such as Illinois, Pennsylvania, Michigan, etc. Easily recognized by his long, full-furred brush, and his rusty-red coat, he is an extremely intelligent and amazingly crafty little beast of 8 to 12 pounds, an animal to be admired, to be sure, but one which must also be kept within reasonable limits of abundance, what with bird-hunting pressures high, in order to keep some semblance of balance in nature.

VARMINT HUNTING

DURING RECENT years enthusiasts of the light, high-powered rifle have brought a very old hunting method into high popularity and have made of it what might be termed a new sport. It is varmint hunting and consists of stalking various animals not generally considered game animals and shooting them usually at long distances. The animals which figure most generally in the varmint category are the woodchuck or ground hog, the prairie dog, the badger, and the coyote. As previously mentioned in the section on rabbit hunting, the large scrawny antelope jack rabbits of the desert and plains also are hunted in this manner; so are pests such as the abundant western ground squirrels.

Actually, the sport of varmint hunting is a means for the rifleman to use a live target for his shooting practice. It also makes possible "live" shooting during spring and summer, when game seasons are closed. And in most instances it helps to rid the countryside of unwanted varmints and pests.

Of the various varmint targets, the woodchuck is probably the most popular. This well-known little burrow digger of fields and wood lots ranges over most of the U.S. He is, however, most abundant in the East and Midwest, where he feeds on farm crops, especially clover, lives along fence rows, wood lots, around old stone piles, etc., digging his burrows near such places, or in the open fields. He is an exceptionally shrewd little customer, weighing upwards of ten or more pounds. His eyesight is very keen, and he is seldom found far from a burrow, into which he will duck the moment he spies an enemy.

The two most popular and successful methods of ground-hog hunting are as follows: Either the hunter locates a network of burrows, conceals himself near by, and waits for the furry tenant to get over his fright and emerge for a look around, or else the hunter carries a good binocular, travels either on foot or in a car, scanning the territory for distant ground hogs. When one is thus located, a most careful stalk must be made if the hunter expects to get within shooting range. The stalk, in fact, often entails worming along on one's belly for several hundred yards.

The sport, for varmint enthusiasts, consists in the making of long-range shots. A good stalker can sometimes get close enough to make the use of any ordinary .22 rifle effective. But the popularity of woodchuck shooting, of late, has brought about the development of several special rifles usually called varmint rifles. All of these guns and their loads are of the high velocity, flat trajectory type. Good examples are: the .220 Swift, the .257 Roberts, the .22 Hornet, the .250-3000. A telescope sight is advantageous in most chuck shooting, and is, in fact, requisite to success where the chucks have been much hunted and have thus become extremely wary. Bright, warm days usually bring the best hunting.

In some states, the woodchuck has been given the status of a game animal, and is protected by a closed season during a portion of the year. The hunter should therefore check his state laws before indiscriminate shooting. When possible, late spring and summer are the best hunting times for this wary little beast. Although the hide is worthless, some states pay woodchuck bounties. And for those who like to try new dishes a young woodchuck doesn't make half-bad eating.

The diminutive prairie dog of the dry, treeless plains is next in popularity among varminters. He resembles the woodchuck, but is much smaller. In some sections prairie dogs do great damage to crops, and their control is therefore necessary, for the prairie dog lives in colonies, some of which become huge gatherings of several hundred individuals, with burrow systems pocking the soil over many acres.

Unfortunately for the varmint hunter, the prairie dog cannot be stalked in the same manner as the ground hog, for the simple reason that almost no cover exists in his habitats to conceal the hunter. Luckily, however, the prairie dog is more of a curious personality than the woodchuck. As a hunter approaches a colony, a lookout will be heard to whistle. Other "dogs" now take up the cry and all of them run for their burrows. But as a rule they do not dive blindly in. Usually each will sit erect on his burrow mound, looking sharply around to see what all the fuss is about.

The hunter who is in position to shoot and can handle his arm accurately at long distances now begins to line up his sights. A scope is advantageous for this hunting, just as with woodchucks. However, if the range is still too long, the old-time prairie-dog hunter will often walk in plain sight, straight toward the prairie-dog colony. If the colony is spread over a large area, he will walk right through it. As he does so, many a curious "dog" will pop out of his burrow after he has passed, to have a look at the enemy. The shrewd hunter will now turn, and get in some mighty good rifle practice at these jack-in-the-box targets. It is best to choose early morning or late afternoon for prairie-dog hunting, for during the heat of the day most of the animals stay below ground.

Stalking the badger and the coyote, both animals of the plains and deserts, is sport quite similar to those covered above. It is simply a matter of getting into territory where either animal may be spotted either with the naked eye or with a binocular, and of making long-range shots with a scope-sighted rifle. To say "simply a matter of," however, is an understatement, for an animal such as the coyote is an exceedingly canny beast, located more by chance than good stalking ability, and the hunter is usually as much surprised to sight his game as the game is to see the hunter.

Under no circumstances should a varminter use his rifle in country where it may be dangerous to residents, and before any shot is made the hunter should be positive that no livestock, person, or farm building is within range. For safety it is best to use a high-velocity rifle, whose bullet will be more apt to disintegrate upon contact with a rock or twig, than to use low-velocity loads which have a tendency to ricochet.

CROWS

THE PROBLEM in crow shooting has always been to get close enough to the birds for a telling shot, for if there ever was a wily creature who could exasperate a gunner, the crow is it! His eyesight is exceedingly keen, and since man is his most important enemy he is suspicious of every human movement, and of everything connected with humans. However, the natural gregariousness of the crow, his hatred of owls, and his penchant for constant "talking" have been his undoing. Upon these crow characteristics the sport of crow shooting is based. And a mighty exciting sport it is, with no limits and no seasons.

During fall and winter crows begin migration, and

often at this time, especially in the Midwest and the Plains states, they gather at congenial roosting sites in fabulous concentrations. Although fairly good crow shooting can be had almost anywhere in the U.S. at any season, and at practically any location, the vicinity of a huge roost concentration makes for top shooting.

It is practically useless to attempt to stalk single crows or flocks of crows. The popular methods used are calling, and decoying, or a combination of the two. A hunter may simply drive around until he sees a flock of crows in a field, pass on by, conceal his car on a side road, conceal himself in a natural blind, and begin using his crow call. Or he can locate a roost site, conceal himself along one of the flyways leading to it, and work the call when crows are flying out from the roost in the morning or returning to it at night. Whichever method is used, it is of utmost importance that both car and hunter are completely out of sight of the crows, and that the call (which can be purchased in any sporting-goods store) is worked properly, according to the directions which come with it. Crow calling even then takes some practice and experience, but anyone can do it effectively after a few trials. Calls that sound as if a crow is in difficulty, or angry at some enemy, are most effective in bringing crow brethren to the "rescue."

Since the crow and the owl are sworn enemies, a stuffed owl or an owl decoy set up in a conspicuous place near a spot which crows frequent will bring them sailing in to do battle. Often, in conjunction with the owl decoy, a dozen crow decoys are perched about in bushes near by. And the hunter, concealed within gun range, works his call raucously and frantically to alert all passing crows. Both owl and crow decoys can be purchased from sporting-goods stores.

A good shooting site should not be used every day, else the crows will soon catch on and be driven from the vicinity. But the sound of the gun, if the hunter stays completely hidden, will not necessarily drive birds away, especially when they are plentiful. That is, during any one session of shooting, often crows will continue to pour in at the sound of the call or the sight of the decoys, no matter how much shooting is done.

It is surprising what a difficult target the crow can be at times. He appears to fly slowly, because of his characteristic wing motion. But his pace is fairly swift, and when he is diving toward a calling hunter, or toward a stuffed owl, he really turns on the steam. This is good sport, which can be had at any time of the year; it is excellent wing-shooting practice; and the destruction of the ever-abundant crow is unquestionably a great aid to various facets of conservation. Any shotgun can be used, but crows take a lot of killing, and therefore a 12-gauge gun, loaded with at least No. 6 shot, with a heavy powder charge, makes the best crow-shooting weapon.

Chapter Six

Hunting Big Game

*T*he hunting of big-game animals is a sport completely in a class by itself. To enthusiasts, many of whom are also avid hunters of small game and birds, the stalking and shooting of a big-game animal is the culmination of all lifelong sporting ambitions. Yet, curiously, out of our hundreds of thousands of hunters, there are a great many who have tried big-game hunting and found it not to their liking, and many others to whom the thought of killing large game is downright distasteful and who therefore never even think of going after big game.

However, the enthusiasts of the rugged stalk and the heavy rifle have many valid arguments and a loud voice in affairs of American sport. There is no question but that the hunting of big game is a thrill to which nothing else can compare. The dense forests, the awesome mountains, the great distances of the wilderness lend an aura of nostalgia backed by long tradition which makes the task of outwitting large animals of keen intelligence an exciting endeavor, an occupation with appeal of a quite different and expansive sort from that of flushing birds from near-home coverts or running hounds at night.

The big-game picture on a varied-diet scale in the U.S. today is far from bright or encouraging, and there is every indication that it will steadily become worse, due to hunting pressures and the pressures of civilization. Nonetheless, for those who are willing to save for a real big-game hunting trip, Canada and Alaska still offer superb possibilities, and for those who cannot go long distances to hunt, happily we do still have an abundance of deer. U.S. big-game hunters have, in fact, become for the most part a great army of deer hunters, with a national herd of some several millions of animals on which to base their sport, and a 70-30 chance over a great territory for bringing home the venison each fall.

Deer hunting, therefore, stands out as the most important subject to be covered in this chapter. And, since many of the much coveted big-game targets are now extinct or on the restricted list in the U.S., we will also have a look at the hunting for such game in Canada and Alaska, where opportunity still thrives.

WHERE TO SHOOT at big game is, however, a subject which must be touched on first. The old hand at this sport will know that no matter how large his animal target there are but few points of aim at it which will be productive of instant kills. To the beginner, this is something that all too often, and inexcusably, must be learned the hard way.

On running shots, of course, not all hunters can score a killing shot. But it is unforgivable for either an experienced or a tyro hunter to become excited, when standing or slowly moving big game is sighted, and simply fire blindly at the general outline of the animal. Such shooting not only very often causes much suffering to the beast, but makes it necessary for the hunter to go through the ordeal of a long search in trailing the wounded creature—if indeed he does not lose it entirely, while it crawls away to hide and die uselessly.

Although some targets may be easier than others, and the point of aim may change slightly as one shifts from deer to bears, etc., in general nothing but a bit of thinking about simple anatomy is necessary for the hunter to understand where killing shots must be placed. In general, the brain of all animals lies in the crown of the head, slightly above a line between the ear and the eye. A shot expertly placed here brings an instant kill, given proper gun, load, and range. But this shot is a very small target, and therefore is to be avoided by beginners at least.

Neck shots, which break the spine or sever the large artery, are good choices, and spoil little of the meat. A spine shot just forward of the haunches also kills instantly, but this is a hard shot to judge, and may ruin much meat. The neck shot, likewise, can easily be misjudged, especially at long ranges.

In general, then, unless there is no opportunity presented for it, the best shot is a shoulder shot, not too high.This shot not only breaks the shoulder, and perhaps both shoulders, but if properly placed, hits the heart and the lungs. It means invariably an instantaneous kill, and a very small amount of usable meat spoiled.

Paunch and "gut" shots should be avoided at all costs; so, generally speaking, should shots made straight from the rear. These will seriously and mortally wound, but there is no telling how far the animal may travel before it dies. When any big-game animal is wounded badly yet runs, the wise hunter will not follow immediately, but will wait a half hour. This insures that the wounded animal will quickly lie down, and each time it does so it will stiffen up and getting up will be that much more difficult. For example, a wounded deer followed immediately may travel several miles, while the same one not molested may lie down and die within a quarter-mile of the spot where it was shot. When bear hunting, any wounded specimen should be approached with extreme caution. Wounded bears, even when mortally wounded, can be extremely dangerous.

DEER HUNTING

ALTHOUGH THERE are several subspecies of our various deer species in the U.S., these are inconsequential to the hunter. The *type* species are but three, as follows.

Whitetail Deer: Ranges over all of the U.S. excepting the west slope of the Rockies and an east-west strip of the interior U.S. running from southwestern Ohio into a portion of lower Nebraska, down into southern Colorado, Utah, and Nevada. Most abundant in New England and Great Lakes region, although well distributed throughout the South, Texas, Arizona. Abundant also across southern Canada to the Rockies. Prefers thick, brushy woods and swamps, with openings and forest edges for feeding.

General color of the whitetail gray-tan, merging with white on the belly. Whitetail in heavily forested coniferous regions usually darker than those in second-growth birch and poplar; and whitetails of the plains and deserts usually very pale. Easily identified by the tail, which is tan on top and pure white below, and held straight up when the deer is running. Size of whitetails varies greatly, according to region and subspecies: those of New England and the Great Lakes often run to from 200 to 300 pounds; those of Florida much smaller; the Arizona desert whitetail not much more than "fawn" size.

Mule Deer: Ranges from the Dakotas and northwest Texas west throughout the Rockies; south well down into Mexico; north well up into the central Canadian provinces. Found in a variety of habitats, from desert to mountain forests, but generally speaking a deer of rugged mountain terrain with more open, coniferous forests broken by mountain parks and meadows, aspen copses, canyons and gullies.

General color much darker than the whitetail, with antlers branched and carrying points on the branches, as opposed to the simple antlers of the whitetail. Easily identified by the tail, which is narrow, as opposed to the wide "flag" of the whitetail, black at the *tip,* and not held erect when the deer runs, but held flat down between the haunches. Forehead with a distinct black patch. Averages much larger than the whitetail, commonly weighing up to 300 pounds, and occasionally going to 400. Chunky, slightly awkward as compared to the graceful whitetail. Ears very large, tipped with dark or black hair.

Blacktail Deer: Smallest range of the three basic species: confined to the West Coast, from central California north to upper British Columbia. East, in Washington and Oregon to the top of the Cascades, and in California to the peak of the Sierra. A species much like the whitetail in habitat preferences, for it commonly sticks to the brushy and thickly forested sections which have clearings and openings in which they may feed.

Sometimes unnecessarily confused with the mule deer, which it somewhat resembles. Its color, however, is similar to the whitetail, except usually darker, and with a black swath along the back. Smaller than the mule deer, with a general top weight seldom over 200 pounds. Most easily set apart from the mule deer by its tail, which is *wide,* black on top *throughout its length,* with a white border, white beneath, and held straight up like that of the whitetail, when running.

THE HUNTING OF DEER, all told, varies little from species to species except as the specific terrain makes it necessary for hunters to follow slightly differing methods for best success. It is a hard and fast rule that deer hunting, like all big-game hunting, should be done upwind, that is, *into* the wind if at all possible. Deer have keen noses and excellent hearing. These two senses are more important to them than their eyesight, although it is obvious that noticeable movement will "spook" a deer within sight range of them.

In the West, especially when hunting mule deer, traveling is often via horseback, for the difficult mountain terrain makes a long walking hunt out of the question when a hunter gets into the back-country. In white-tail and blacktail hunting, where the terrain is some-what less rugged as a rule and much thick woods and brush are encountered, walking is the approved manner of "transportation."

Basically, in all deer hunting, there are three main methods in use: driving; still-hunting; stalking. Of these, the last, though on the whole not as popular as the first two, is by far the most interesting, thrilling, and sporting.

Driving is most commonly used in the heavily popu-lated states where large herds of whitetails thrive, and where many hunters are in the woods, and large par-ties of hunters often go out together. Actually, it is downright dangerous. A party of hunters goes into a section known to contain deer, and, choosing a place where the deer are likely to be bedded down or in hid-ing during the day, they post some of the party at one side of a swamp or section of woods, while the rest en-ter from the other side and walk through. The drivers are not supposed to do any shooting, but simply to make their presence obvious by noisy movement, so that any deer ahead of them will be moved upwind toward the posted sentinels with waiting guns.

The making of a good drive is not a simple procedure. A stretch of cover must be chosen expertly. This re-quires a good knowledge of deer habits. Generally speaking, deer feed very early in the morning, move into cover and either stand or bed down during the day, from around 8:30 A.M. until mid-P.M., then begin moving out again to feed toward dusk. On cold days they will invariably choose slopes where the sun strikes warmly; they dislike cold rain and stay in thick cover at such times; wind makes them nervous and jumpy, as does a noisy stream (which they often avoid) because it interferes with listening for sounds of danger. Such are basic deer habits, all of which, of course, are subject to change according to factors at any time quite unknown to the hunter.

Thus, when a spot is chosen for a drive, all such factors must be considered, and in addition the drive must center on a stretch of cover that will give the deer little choice as to which way to move. Also, the view of the posted gunners must be carefully considered. Each must be able to keep well hidden, yet in a position to have as wide a range of vision as possible and reasonably unobstructed opportunity for a shot.

Again, though driving is very common, it can be exceedingly dangerous, for often the gunner will be shooting toward the drivers, or not knowing where the drivers are. Never under any circumstances should such a gunner shoot at mere movement. He must see the whole deer, and be positive of his target.

In still-hunting, which is a very common method used by the lone hunter or by a small party, the hunter simply takes up a stand along a well-used deer trail, an old logging road, at the peak of a ridge overlooking a likely canyon, or in any other spot where a deer moving about may be apt to pass. He refrains from smoking, from movement, from making any sound whatever, keeps well concealed, and waits for luck to bring him a target. In nasty or cold weather, needless to say, this manner of hunting is an uncomfortable business. However, to the patient hunter it regularly pays off.

Stalking, as has been said, is the most active and exciting of deer hunting methods. It makes little difference where the hunt takes place, whether in the brushy stream bottoms of New England, the high mountains of the West, or the desert. The mounted hunter rides quietly and carefully, keeping to the ridges and the shadows, pausing often to scan the canyons and mountain sides with his binocular. When he locates a deer, he dismounts, if the range is too great, and finishes the stalk on foot, always mindful of wind direction and the whimsy of wind currents in the mountains.

In flat country, or brushy country, the stalker afoot needs snow, or a wet woods, to do his best. A dry woods, with no snow, makes noisy walking. The lone hunter, or a pair of hunters working together, move with extreme caution, following deer tracks in snow or deer trails on dry ground, ever alert, pausing every few paces to peer carefully through the brush. A good stalker often jumps a deer from his bed within a few feet of him—unless he fails to see it, and passes by only to have the prize buck of all time crash noisily out behind him, or sneak away quietly and low to the ground.

To sum up, it may be said of driving deer that it is much more a method of meat hunting than of real sport. Still-hunting, though it requires a good knowledge of deer habits and especially of *local* deer habits and a thorough knowledge of the section which is being hunted, is a tame sport in that there is little activity connected with it, and that most still-hunting shots are, by the nature of the hunt, easy ones. Stalking, though rather difficult in brushy country, is perfect for the big country of the West, and, no matter where it is attempted, requires first of all that the hunter be a good *woodsman*. That is the basis of all good sport with a gun. A deer hunter who can become successful at stalking has something to be proud of both in venison and woodscraft!

DEER GUNS AND LOADS are a varied lot. Many bird hunters who are casual deer hunters make a shotgun do double duty, using a shell loaded with No. 00 buckshot, or one loaded with shotgun slugs. Either of these loads is readily available in deer country. The shotgun deer hunter must understand, however, that 50 to 75 yards is his top range. Buckshot will not give an effective pattern at much over that or have enough killing power. Slugs (which do not, as is popularly and falsely reported, harm a shotgun barrel) are murderous loads, but not very accurate in some guns, and certainly not consistently accurate over 75 yards.

As to rifles, there is no such thing as the perfect deer rifle. A very great many calibers and loads make excellent deer guns. However, light calibers should be strictly crossed off the list, and for hunting in brushy terrain in all states where the average shots at deer are fairly short, the hunter should shy from high-velocity loads. Generally speaking, a bullet weighing from 150 to 170 or 180 grains, shot in a gun such as the .303 Savage, .32 Winchester Special, .30 Remington, or .30-'06 is a good all-round weapon for deer hunting in the East, or on the West Coast. For mountain hunting of mule deer, probably the best basic example of a good rifle for the purpose is the .270, with a 150-grain bullet. For mountain, plains, and desert hunting, a telescope sight is most advantageous. For heavily wooded country, with brushy terrain, almost all deer shots are made at no more than 100 yards, and the telescope, while occasionally useful, is by no means requisite. It can, in fact, be a nuisance under such conditions.

OTHER HORNED AND
ANTLERED GAME

IN THE U.S. proper, the hunter who lives in the West has an opportunity regularly nowadays to hunt over a fairly wide area two other hoofed species of big game in addition to deer. These are the antelope and the elk. By taking in territory in Mexico, Canada, and Alaska, it is possible, any year when opportunity to travel allows, to add to those trophies the mountain sheep, mountain goat, moose, and caribou. The rifleman who is familiar with deer hunting will have a very good foundation for these other sports. However, there are certain important differences in hunting methods brought about by the wide differences in habits and habitats among these various animals. And for the best results something must be known about proper weapons.

Antelope: Once fabulously abundant over the Plains states, the pronghorn antelope declined until, a few years ago, it was nearly extinct. Today, however, due to careful control of shooting and campaigns against the coyote, which preys heavily upon antelope fawns, the pronghorn has made a remarkable comeback. The present range extends throughout the Southwest, down into Mexico, up through the West Coast states, east to the western portion of the Dakotas, Nebraska, Kansas, and north into some of the prairie provinces. Wyoming is currently the center of antelope abundance.

The pronghorn is an animal of open, rolling plains

country, of the sage flats and the sparsely wooded sections. Weight from 60 to 100 pounds. Color, rich tan above, white below, with large white rump patches, brown bars on the throat. The white rump hairs are erected as a warning signal of danger to other antelope when an enemy is sighted.

The pronghorn is the swiftest of all our game animals, with a speed at a full run of over 60 miles per hour. It also has the most amazing eyesight of any game. These characteristics, plus the open country where it must be hunted, make this one of the most intriguing of all big-game hunting endeavors. However, the animal also has an insatiable curiosity, which has often led to its downfall. Early hunters often bagged antelope by hanging a white cloth on a bush, concealing themselves, and waiting until a herd came to investigate. However, to offset curiosity, the antelope is a very high-strung, jumpy little beast, and must thus be approached very gingerly.

A telescope sight and a good binocular or spotting scope are must items of equipment of the antelope hunter. Although some hunters drive a car across the plains toward a herd which has been spotted through the glass, try to head them off, then leap out and take running shots, this method is illegal in most sections. So also, in most areas, is the method of a group of hunters hunting on horseback, surrounding a herd, putting it to flight toward waiting guns. Some hunters do drive in a car until a herd is spotted at a long distance, then through the glass pick out an animal and try for long shots.

This method is somewhat more sporting, for it usually entails a stalk after the trophy has been chosen.

Whether hunting from a car, a horse, or on foot, the stalk is the best method, requiring a real test of the hunter's skill. After a herd is spotted, every effort at perfect concealment is made in order not to spook it. The hunter begins his stalk upwind, taking advantage of every slightest rise or depression, every bush or tree. Often he must worm his way along on his belly for several hundred yards, keeping completely out of sight, for the herd will spot the slightest movement from as far away as he can see with his glass.

Once within shooting range, extreme care must be taken in judging the distance, and in getting off the shot. If the animals do run, it is necessary for the gunner to learn to lead them just as he would a bird in flight, due to their great speed. In addition, once a shot is made, the hunter should make absolutely sure he has not wounded an animal, and not be too quick to think he has missed if his target appears to have gone flying away unscathed. A wounded antelope often runs a mile or more before crumpling. For this reason, a proper gun and careful holding to assure an instantaneous kill are to be desired above all else.

At the extreme ranges at which antelope often must be shot (up to 400 yards), flat trajectory is all important. But shocking power must not be sacrificed. If the rifle has been used on game at closer ranges, sighted in, say at 100 yards, it should be resighted at 200, at least, and the hunter should know exactly what both the gun and its load will do at those ranges. A soft-nosed bullet of not over 100 grains weight will be best, and the best example of a perfect antelope rifle is the .270. Other rifles which approximate the performance of the .270 may be used, such as the .250/3000, but the performance of the .270 should be considered as a basis from which to plan what gun will best suit your purpose and convenience.

Elk: A large member of the deer group, often weighing upwards of 1000 pounds. Typified by the extremely high, spreading antlers of the male, the bulky body and slender legs, the heavy neck mane. Color dark tan or dark brown, mingled with brown-gray on back and sides. Rump patches gray-white. Present range from Montana to New Mexico and Arizona, with some in the prairie provinces of Canada. Some stocked herds under control here and there, notably in northern Michigan, and one of the Alaskan islands. Also a few elk "oases" in such areas as the Dakotas, California. Since most of the herds are rather carefully controlled, a hunter must watch the various state game laws for open seasons from year to year.

Because the elk is so large, and must be for the most part hunted in extremely rugged, high mountain country of the Rockies, the usual procedure is to begin an elk hunt by planning a long trek via horseback, with extra pack horses in tow to transport meat and trophy back to civilization. Since the animals are found as a rule in the high, open timber, or in the alpine meadows close to cover, long shots are the rule. Elk also are great wanderers, and the horseman may find it necessary to change his camp site several times in order to keep up with a herd on the move, once elk sign is struck.

Usual methods are either to stalk a herd while mounted, or to begin the stalk on foot once fresh sign is located. Needless to say, the stalk must be made into the wind, for the elk has a keen nose. A knowledge of the terrain is essential, and for the stranger to the territory this makes a good guide most important. When large parties of hunters are out, sometimes they split up after a herd is located, some taking stands as in deer hunting, down-wind from the herd, the others making a drive on horseback, from the other side, down-wind. Early morning or late afternoon is the best time to find elk feeding in the open.

A good binocular is requisite, for locating the game at long distances in the mountains, and a telescope sight a *must*. Elk, being large, heavy, and having great stamina, take a lot of killing. The shot must be extremely well placed. Never should a chance be taken which may mean a gut shot, for though the elk will probably eventually die, the hunter will seldom know when or where. Never should an elk hunter go under-gunned. A heavy bullet, up to 180 grains, is definitely called for. Good examples of the perfect elk rifle are the .300 and the .348, with some leeway on either side. Needless to say, in most instances, because of the usual long ranges, flat trajectory and great shocking power and range are prime requisites.

Moose: Largest of the deer family. Weight of the bull up to very near a ton, but averaging from 1000 to 1500 pounds. Several subspecies, all very much alike as far as hunters are concerned. The huge, wide-spreading antlers with prongs set about a large, flattened palm quickly identify the bull, and the humped snout identifies either sex. Color dark brown. A beast of the forest and the lake country, in cold climates. Once abundant across much of northern U.S. Now confined to most of Canada, much of Alaska, and, in the U.S., to a small area in Montana, Wyoming, Idaho, where hunting is occasionally legal in fall, and to small oases in New

England, Minnesota, Michigan. A browser on willow, aspen, etc., and a feeder on many aquatic plants of the lakes and marshes, such as pond lilies. These feeding habits give a strong cue as to where to look for moose in their territory.

The moose is one of the all-time grand prizes of the ambitious big-game hunter. A wary beast, but one not so inclined to run quickly or fade from sight as the deer, and the bulls when in rut are, in fact, often dangerous, inclined to charge the hunter. Two methods of hunting are most generally used, either calling or a combination of still-hunting and stalking, but the fact that moose are hunted both in western mountain country and in the thick woods of the East makes different approaches to these methods necessary according to terrain.

For example, in the mountains a hunter may walk the ridges, keeping always in position to survey great stretches of valleys and river bottoms. In flat country, it is best to search the marshes, pond edges, etc., from the best vantage point that is at hand, keeping the survey point always down-wind from a potential target. Quiet is essential, for the moose is a "listener," depending to a great extent upon his ears to tell him of the approach of an enemy. In addition, the search must be very carefully made. Many tyro moose hunters expect, because of the size of the game, to have it stand out plainly. This may be true. Many a moose has been sighted through a glass from a ridge two miles away. But when one is standing quietly in brush, or especially among big trees of evergreen forests, it is amazingly difficult to see without close scrutiny. When there is snow on the ground, and a favorable wind, tracking is an excellent way of hunting.

The problem of getting a downed moose out of the woods must always be considered. Therefore, packhorse train hunting, or hunting near old logging roads, etc., is a good idea. However, much hunting is also done from canoes because of the fact that the moose stays around water so habitually. A canoe means a quiet approach to likely places and a means of packing out trophy and meat a bit at a time. Needless to say, for those who do not live in moose country or have never hunted them, a guide is practically a *must*. A guide is entirely requisite if calling is to be attempted, unless of course the hunter is an old hand at the game.

Calling is attempted fairly late in the season, after the bulls are fully in rut. Native guides usually employ a horn of birch bark, and imitate the call of a cow moose. The bull makes grunting answer, and approaches the sound—maybe. Old bulls are exceedingly suspicious, and may take several hours to "case" the territory silently before coming out into shooting range and position, although a young bull usually is more likely to let his heart rule his head. In the lake country, a canoe can be used to advantage for calling. In mountainous western country, calling can be employed in conjunction with the still-hunt and stalk.

It should be obvious that a heavy bull will take a lot of lead. Bullets of 180 to 220 grains are mandatory. Although now and then, in certain sections of moose range, close shots are common, it is best as a general rule to have the gun equipped with telescope sight, and let the load be of the high-velocity type. The .30-'06 with very heavy bullet or one of the magnum calibers such as the .300 are good examples of rifles in the moose category. For the hunter who wants an all-purpose rifle for various big game, from western deer and antelope to moose, the .270, so often mentioned, but shooting a heavy bullet, is a reasonably good choice—not the perfect moose gun, but one which can serve all big-game purposes as well as, and perhaps better than, any other.

Caribou: Three species, all more or less alike except in size and general coloring: Mountain Caribou, very dark (almost black), largest of the three, the bulls averaging 400 to 800 pounds; Woodland Caribou, somewhat lighter in both coloration and weight; Barren Ground Caribou, averaging to 350 pounds and the lightest in color. All three have various subspecies. Notable among these is the Peary Caribou of the Arctic (one of the Barren Ground subspecies) which is very nearly white.

Range of the caribou—which is a close relative of the reindeer—once came well down into the U.S., especially in New England. Currently the range covers most of Canada, including Newfoundland (where very good hunting may be had), Alaska, portions of Greenland, etc. The Prairie Provinces of Canada are for the most part an exception.

Caribou are easily identified by their antlers, which are very high and spreading, curve backward, then forward again, and are widely palmated, especially toward the tips, with numerous flat points protruding. In addition there are wide, flattened "brow tines" coming forward and down above the forehead. Curiously, both male and female bear antlers. This is the only member of the deer family that possesses this characteristic.

Although the distribution of caribou is wide, their gregarious habits and seasonal migrations make it important for the prospective hunter to ascertain before-hand exactly where his best chances will be, and at what time of year. To U.S. hunters, a guide is requisite, and of course an outfitter must see to all preparations such as transportation into the caribou country and means of getting both men and trophies out. The hunting may be in high, rocky, difficult terrain or on the barren grounds of the Far North, depending upon the species hunted and the time of the year. The woodland and mountain species make for the most sporty hunting, for with these a herd must be located in the high and forested country, the partial stalk made, the specimen chosen, and the final portion of the stalk completed. This last can prove to be a difficult task, and must be done very carefully, against the wind of course. Barren Ground Caribou are usually hunted by taking a stand, or setting up a camp, near the migration route which the animals travel to winter feed.

It is a prime rule never to go undergunned. Here again, the .270 makes a good gun, with a load of per-haps a 130- to 150-grain bullet. Even the old .30/30 may be satisfactory, but a rifle capable of firing higher velocity loads with flat trajectory will usually be wanted in caribou country. Obviously, a telescope sight will be wanted on such a hunt.

Mountain Sheep: Weight from 150 to 300 pounds. Two basic species, with many subspecies. The Bighorn, with subspecies geographically divided according to local habitat, is the one known in the U.S. This includes the Rocky Mountain Bighorn, Desert Bighorn, Texas Bighorn, etc. The other single species, found along with the Bighorn north of our borders, may for all practical purposes be divided into two. These are the

Black, or Stone, Sheep of northern British Columbia and the Yukon Territory, and the White, or Dall, Sheep of British Columbia and Alaska. All told, the complete range of mountain sheep is from northern Alaska down through the Rockies into Mexico. At one time the Bighorn was plentiful as far east as Nebraska and the Dakotas. Today we have only remnants of the early herds anywhere in the U.S., with no hunting except occasionally and in very restricted sections of one or two western states such as Wyoming and Idaho. Actually the sheep should have full protection everywhere in the U.S., for their struggle against civilization is a difficult one, and they have often been on the verge of complete extinction. They are, however, fairly abundant north of the U.S., and good hunting may be had in their northern ranges.

Mountain sheep have thick hair, not wool as the name might infer. Their great, curving horns are their trademark. General color is as follows: Bighorn, light gray-tan; Stone Sheep, very dark, appearing sometimes black from a distance; Dall Sheep, white. All have characteristic white or very light rump patches.

Mountain-sheep meat is considered one of the finest of wild meats, and the head of a good ram probably the ace trophy of every big-game hunter. This last is not only because of comparative rarity nowadays but because these animals choose such inaccessible places as their habitats, and because the awesomely cautious stalk necessary to bag one, in the fabulously rugged high country which is the sheep's home, make a trophy come hard. The animals depend little on scent or hearing for protection, but have eyesight like that of an eagle, invariably choose places for feeding and bedding where they cannot possibly be surprised at close range, and are capable of racing down nearly perpendicular cliffs where no man could possibly follow, hurdling chasms, bounding over rock slides.

Hunting sheep requires a top-notch guide—and a hunter who can "take it," and who can shoot expertly at long ranges. It is undoubtedly the most hazardous and difficult of all North American big-game hunting. Nowadays, no guide would take out a hunter who merely wanted *any* sheep, or one who wanted it solely for meat. Sheep hunting has become strictly trophy hunting for a good ram head, which means a head with large and perfect horns. This side of sheep hunting makes it necessary to hunt during the pre-rutting season (late summer and early fall in the North) for at this time of year the rams keep to themselves, usually in small groups. It is then that legal hunting seasons are open.

Although a ram *may* be spooked by winding a hunter, many hunters pay little attention to the direction of the wind, for a great many guides feel that sheep noses are much less than keen. Nor does the noise of a rock knocked loose and hurtling down a mountain alert a sheep to any great degree. They are used to the sound. The caution that is vitally important is that the hunter not show himself at all, except from a very great distance.

Sheep hunting, therefore, becomes something of a precision game. First, since sheep may use certain mountains year after year, but never be found on other mountains, or ranges, in the general vicinity, the guide must be completely familiar with the territory, and know which hangout consistently produces. Next, when a mountain has been carefully surveyed through the glass, then climbed, both hunter and guide must be experts at using binoculars. They must recognize the signs of sheep, such as worn trails across shale deposits, at a distance, using a glass, and they must be absolutely certain that sheep are or are not in the field of view. Many a good ram has been missed because he lay quietly on a ledge and was taken at a great distance, through the binocular, as a rock—if indeed he was noticed at all.

After the ram with a desired head is located, it is all a matter of expert stalking and neither spooking the ram (or others in the vicinity, which may spook him) nor killing yourself by falling off a mountain during the process. A feeding ram should be "waited out"—that is, the hunter should simply sit until the ram goes to bed down. Once bedded, he'll stay there for some time, and the stalk can be started, after extremely careful planning. One of the prime rules is this: Never, once the stalk is begun, be tempted into trying to get another look to make sure the ram is there. If you do, he will probably still be there—but only for a moment!

The best in a binocular is needed. In addition, a spotting scope is advantageous; likewise a telescope sight. An expert stalker often gets close shots, and, due to the type of country and ram habits, shots over 250 yards are seldom necessary, although it is paramount to be prepared for anything. Here again, the .270, with a moderately light bullet, makes a fine gun, or at least a basis of performance from which to choose a gun.

Mountain Goat: An animal of the highest, most inaccessible country of the northern Rockies, from southern Alaska down into Washington, Idaho, Montana. Weight to 300 pounds. Color white, coat long and silky, horns very slender, black, straight, from 6 to 12 inches long.

The mountain goat never has been an especially exciting game animal. The meat is not particularly appealing, the head has never been as popular as a trophy as has that of the sheep. In addition, the going is often even rougher and more dangerous to acquire one, as far as the climbing is concerned, than for mountain sheep. But most of all, the goat shows few real game characteristics. Many individuals show little fear of man, and when they do "run away" from their stalker, the "running" is usually done at a slow walk or at best an awkward trot. All told, the goat is a rather stoical character who depends almost entirely upon his climbing ability and his rugged domain for safety. If, in hunting, you approach one from above, he usually gets very much alarmed. Approached from below, he simply starts climbing when he sights his enemy, and keeps it up at no great speed until he forces the hunter to call it quits.

At one time the range of the mountain goat in the U.S. was much larger than at present. However, in the mountain fastnesses still left to him, there seems to be little danger of his extinction, mainly because he is not greatly molested either by hunters or predators. Usually Montana and Idaho have open season on goats each year, and there is excellent hunting for them on north into British Columbia, the Yukon, and Alaska. Most hunters, however, take them only incidentally, while hunting other big game.

Any accomplished sheep hunter will do all right when he turns to goats, but he will find one major difference in stalking. The mountain goat depends little on his ears, but unlike the sheep, uses his nose more than his eyes. Thus, wind direction is a factor to consider. Waiting for a feeding goat to bed down before beginning the stalk is the best way of saving a long and difficult climb for nothing.

Goats show an amazing stamina in carrying lead without going down, and therefore no hunter should go undergunned. However, in general, the same equipment is required as for sheep—good binoculars, perhaps a spotting scope also, telescope sight, and a rifle in the .270 or .300 category, with load up to a 150-grain bullet.

BEARS

FEW HUNTERS go bear hunting for the meat involved. The hide and head make good trophies, and the sport of the hunt is the thing. In the South and Southeast, bears are often hunted with dogs. This makes for a good and interesting chase. But northern hunters, feeling that the bear doesn't have a chance, have always objected to the use of dogs in this manner. In fact, bear hunting with dogs in most sections of the North is illegal.

Some states and provinces have both spring and fall bear seasons; some do not protect bears at all; and in some localities, where bears have multiplied to the point of becoming pests, hunters are encouraged to shoot them at any time of year. Brief descriptions of our several bear species follow.

Black Bear: Range includes almost the entire U.S., Canada, and Alaska, but nowadays the U.S. range is one of spotty abundance, wherever conditions are congenial. Color black, with a white throat patch, but there are many variations, from light to dark brown, gray, even dirty-white. Weight from 100 to 600 pounds, average 200 to 300. Sectional differences in stockiness or leanness of build.

Brown Bear: The islands and southern coast of Alaska, on down into British Columbia. Many subspecies. Color usually a uniform dark brown. A very large bear, weighing from 500 to 1500 or more pounds.

Grizzly Bear: Ranges from throughout most of Alaska and western Canada throughout the Rockies and on down into Mexico. Not at all plentiful in the U.S. nowadays, and for the most part rather closely controlled and protected. Many subspecies. Much variation in color, from very dark (almost black) to very pale (yellowish or creamy), but the type characterized by a brown underfur overlaid by long grizzled or silver-tipped hairs. A noticeable hump above the shoulders. Very long claws. Size about as for the brown bear.

Polar Bear: The white bear of the Arctic ice floes.

All species of bears are more or less individualists, and therefore potentially dangerous. Almost all of them are lone wanderers, and are seldom seen in groups except when cubs are still following their mother, or when especially good feeding conditions bring a group of bears into the same range. On the whole, all bears see poorly, but their noses and ears are very keen. They are peaceable in a sense, wanting to be let alone, and preferring escape rather than a fight. But no one can ever say when a bear considers that he has been "bottled up," and when he will fight rather than run. Therefore, even with the common black bear, the tyro bear hunter should not be too ready to take chances. And never should a hunter be too anxious to follow a wounded bear into thick brush, or to race to a downed bear which he thinks is dead.

Bears look awkward, but are amazingly swift when occasion demands. And all of them are extremely powerful, killing with blows from their heavy front paws, or by ripping with their claws. They are both vegetarians and meat eaters, and the range of any individual bear will always be based upon feeding conditions in the area.

When dogs are used on black bears, the bear is either treed and shot or hunters take stands around the swamp or the ridges where the hunt takes place, waiting for the dogs to move the bear out where a shot may be had. Stalking of bears, however, or tracking them in the snow, is the usual and most sporting procedure. A lot of it, however, is pure luck. The hunter must first of all locate a section where bear sign is in evidence, which shows that a bear is living on that range. From here, if he is in mountain country, he can use a good glass to keep watch for the feeding bear, after which the stalk is begun, or, in flat, brushy country he simply hunts quietly, always into the wind, hoping to surprise his game and get a shot.

Hunts for the big brown and grizzly bears are occasions which definitely call for a good guide familiar with the territory and with the ways of these bears. And of course a hunt for a polar bear is an undertaking of such magnitude and expense that it hardly rates space here. Hunting the big browns and grizzlies of Canada and Alaska is much like the hunting of other big game: a pack trip into bear country, careful binocular surveys of the area from a vantage point, much waiting and watching until a target is sighted and the final stalk begun.

For the common black bear, almost any deer rifle will do. In the West this will mean the rifle is usually carrying a scope sight. In the East, under brush hunting conditions, the scope is not necessary, although sometimes advantageous. For the big brown and grizzly bears, a heavier rifle and load is needed than for any other North American big game. Lighter rifles may turn the trick, but can hardly, in general, be considered safe. Bullets of from 220 to 300 grains are preferred, and the heaviest calibers, such as the .348 Winchester or the .375 H. & H. Magnum, telescope sighted.

MOUNTAIN LION

THE COUGAR, puma, or mountain lion, big, tawny cat with the long tail, once ranged over almost all of the U.S., but is now for the most part confined to the all but inaccessible big swamps of the Southeast, and to the Rocky Mountains.

The hunting is done with dogs, hounds specially bred and trained for the tough job of running mountain lions in the rough mountain and desert terrain of the Southwest. Since this type of hunting requires either that the hunter own a pack of lion hounds, or employ a guide with hounds to take him out, there is little point in describing its details here. Suffice it to say that it is a very exciting and rugged pastime, and that those who have the opportunity should certainly not pass up a chance to try it. Conservation departments of several western states, such as Arizona and Washington, can furnish contacts for the prospective hunter. Also, several guides owning lion-hunting hound packs advertise regularly in the outdoor magazines. In addition to the hunting in the U.S., there is good mountain-lion hunting to be had in Mexico, and there, in certain sections, the jaguar may also be hunted with the same pack of dogs.

WILD HOGS

MANY HUNTERS are not fully aware of the possibilities for hunting wild boar in the U.S. All of the true wild boars in our territory came from stock originally imported from Europe, Asia, and Africa. In North Carolina and Tennessee, in the Tellico Mountain district, there is good boar hunting to be had, under state conservation department supervision. This hunting is done with packs of specially bred and trained boar hounds. There is a small oasis of wild boars in New Hampshire, another in Texas, another in California, and others in the islands off the California coast. It is best, when planning a hunt for wild boar in any of these areas, to contact the conservation department of the state involved. From this source full information as to local conditions and laws may be had.

Boar hunting is an exciting business, and can be a dangerous one. A really big boar will weigh well up toward 400 pounds, has vicious tusks, and is a most unpredictable wilderness character. Though some still-hunting and stalking is done, most of the sporty hunting is with dogs. The hunter should go prepared to do some rugged hiking, and should always carry a heavy rifle and know how to use it. For the true wild boar, a guide is always requisite unless the hunter is already familiar with the country and the sport. Therefore, no further details are necessary here. The sport falls under the heading of off-trail endeavors, and is mainly for the purpose of acquiring a trophy head.

The only native wild hog of the U.S. is the little peccary, or javelina of the Southwest. It is small, seldom weighing over 50 to 70 pounds, and travels in droves in the dry brush and desert country of such states as Texas and Arizona, where open seasons still exist. In the past there has not been much sport hunting for these game little wild pigs, but recently new interest has been shown in the sport. Conservation departments of Texas and Arizona will give full details to prospective hunters.

The hunting is of the still-hunting and stalking variety. The usual procedure is to ride a horse out into country known to harbor the little wild pigs, and, once sign is located—their tracks and rootings—to dismount and start stalking a feeding drove. The animal is very swift, a master at racing through the brush or desert growth without being seen. It is sometimes called musk hog because of a scent gland in its back, and often a drove can be smelled before being sighted. Or they will be heard moving about in the brush as they feed. Their eyesight is not keen, but they are constantly listening and testing the air for danger.

Although a really heavy rifle is unnecessary, no hunter should go after peccaries with a rifle too light. The medium calibers do very well, and a rifle used for deer will pass the javelina test very adequately.

Chapter Seven

Calling Predators, Pests, and Game

For centuries hunters have known how to call ducks and geese, how to bring a wild gobbler to them with a call, and how to use the bark horn to intrigue a bull moose. Long before white men came to this continent Indians also knew how to "squeak up" foxes, to rattle antlers to attract buck deer in rut, and even how to call muskrats close to their canoes by making squeaking sounds with the lips pressed to the back of the hand.

Over the years, however, only a few of the facets of this mysterious art of calling were thoroughly explored on a popular basis. Calling waterfowl, turkeys, and crows became standard procedure. Now and then someone would claim he could call a fox by making mouselike squeaks. Usually such claimants were scoffed at. Now, however, it is well known that all predators can be called. Within the past few years the sport of calling them has grown so swiftly that today more people hunt foxes with a call than ever hunted them with dogs. Thousands of hunters make a hobby of calling coyotes and bobcats. Some have succeeded in calling lions, and even black bears and wolves.

The art has not stopped there. Many deer calls are now on the market. Some work rather well under certain conditions. Much more research needs to be done to perfect not only deer calling, but all animal calling. It is now beginning to be understood that all animals and birds can no doubt be called, if only we learn the secrets of the how-to. Already, however, animal calling has become so important to the hunting scene that every hunter should know at least a little bit about it.

For example, hunters quite commonly "bugle" for elk, using either homemade or purchased calls. This is a specialized undertaking, and must be done when bulls are in rut. The several deer calls on the market work in several different ways. Each has instructions for its proper operation. Most make a low-pitched *blatt,* supposedly representing the voice of doe or fawn. Some work on an entirely different principle, appealing to a deer's natural curiosity. Such calls, pitched to represent the sound a deer in difficulty might possibly make, are blown loudly and incessantly. Yet in real life deer seldom make such sounds. Nonetheless, mule deer especially will come to such calls rather well, particularly in areas where they are not hunted hard. Whitetail deer do not respond as well to this type of call. In fact, it will often "spook" them from cover. Thus, some hunters have taken deliberately to using such calls on whitetails, to get them on the move and into the open.

All makers of deer calls as well as of predator and other calls have recordings for sale, which teach by example how to use the call for best results. There is, therefore, no need to go into detail here.

It is in the predator field that greatest progress has been made. The predator call as currently perfected supposedly represents the sound made by some forage animal—such as a rabbit—in great anguish or distress. Thus, the appeal is not to any sex desire, as in elk or moose calling, but to the killer or feeding instinct. Procedure is about as follows:

The caller, after coyotes, let us say, puts on a camouflage suit—another popular development for all kinds of hunting but sparked mainly by the upsurge in predator calling—and selects a place where he knows coyotes live, and where he can see for some distance all around. If he wishes to do a thorough job of it, he may even use a camouflage headnet to pull over his head and face. He can see out through it, but his face does not stand out to frighten an animal.

Gun across his lap, he blows the call long and loud, modulating it from screams of pain to low wails of great agony. A coyote as much as a half-mile away will come if it hears the sound. It may come running at full speed, hackles raised and eyes burning. Usually it will circle, if there is any breeze at all, to get the wind on the position of the sound. It will of course smell the hunter as it does this, and the shot will have to be taken quickly. On still days, however, coyotes, or foxes or bobcats—the three larger predators most gullible to the call—will often come to within mere feet of the hunter. If the animal hesitates at some distance, the caller lowers the volume of his calling. He may even switch to a minor squeak and thus "talk" his target right on in to him.

Coyotes and foxes often come on the run. Bobcats do not. They come sneaking, and take much longer as a rule. The caller ordinarily operates for about 15 minutes at any one spot for coyotes or foxes, then moves on at least a half-mile before calling again. He should stay longer when trying for bobcats, and he must watch very closely as a general rule for a sign of the cat peering from heavy brush. For all these animals some callers get best results by incessant calling; others call very sparingly, with long pauses between bursts. Much depends on how much calling is being done in the vicinity. If the animals have been "whistled at" a lot, they become far more cautious.

An interesting and most effective variation is night calling. Most of the predators, natural night hunters, come better and with less caution at night. Also, raccoons (special calls for them are on the market) come readily. At night the usual procedure is for the caller to move quietly to a selected spot, wearing a headlamp with its beam turned up so it will cast a glow in a wide circle but will not strike approaching animals in the eyes. He holds in one hand a strong spotlight or flashlight. (There are other procedures, but this is the best, used by most experts at the game.) Behind the caller, back to back, stand his two companions, scoped rifles ready. They may of course use shotguns, but ranges often are too long.

Now the caller begins his wailing, and as he does so he turns slowly from side to side, sweeping the area with the glow from his headlamp. When he picks up the returned glow from the eyes of an approaching animal, he stops turning his head. The shooters know he has spotted game. They seldom can see the glow of the eyes. One must be directly behind the headlamp to see this. They watch the spotlight hand of the caller. When he raises it, they get set. When its beam stabs into the night it will pinpoint the animal.

If it is a coyote, it will be running immediately. A fox will usually run, too. A bobcat, oddly, may stand a moment or two. Picking any of these animals up in a scope while a light attempts to follow them is a most difficult and sporting operation. Raccoons will usually stand pretty well, and fur hunters are now using calls to some extent instead of hounds or traps. Other animals, such as the ringtail of the southwest, come to the call very readily at night.

In daytime, hawks can be called, and in later afternoon horned owls are gullible. There are special hawk calls on the market, but hawks and owls will also come to fox and coyote calls. Magpies and crows also may be called the same way.

In addition to the predator calls, this new field has developed special calls for the quail hunter and the pheasant hunter. The idea of these calls is to get the bird to reply, and thus locate it. For example, when a covey of bobwhite quail is scattered, a whistle of the call will generally elicit an answer, and lead the hunter straight to the singles. Coveys may also be located by the caller pretending he is a lone quail seeking company. Blue, or scaled, quail, and western valley, or California, quail can be handled the same way.

Over the next few years no doubt there will be broad development of the calling art and many refinements of currently existing methods. Today, however, animal and bird calling has come a long way, and the hunter who will study professional recordings made by expert callers, and put in a bit of practice with whatever type of call he chooses, will find a vast new area of hunting enjoyment and success opened to him.

Chapter Eight

Hunting with Bow and Arrow

During the past two decades that ancient weapon, the bow, has been developed through modern research and manufacturing methods into a most effective hunting implement. It has also gained astonishing popularity. Today there are at least a million sportsmen who hunt exclusively with bow and arrow, having given up guns entirely. Some hunt small game such as rabbits and squirrels. A few are so proficient that they shoot game birds on the wing. The main realm of hunting archery, however, is in the big-game field. Such expert archers as Fred Bear, renowned as the father of the current popularity of bow hunting, and the world's foremost manufacturer of hunting-archery equipment, have killed with the bow everything from elk and mountain sheep to moose, antelope, and grizzly bear.

The beginner, therefore, must understand first of all that the bow, properly handled and with proper hunting arrows such as the now standard and uniquely deadly razorhead type, is a most lethal weapon. However, he must also understand that for the most part he must get very close to his game. Though an arrow shot from a powerful bow is capable of killing game at some distance (kills of big game have been made over a hundred yards), arrow trajectory describes a very high arc and accurate aiming at long distances is all but impossible. Thirty yards is considered a good average shot. Fifty or sixty is average maximum.

It is often difficult for gun hunters to understand, when first they shoot a bow, that an arrow, unlike a bullet, has almost no shocking power. It has, however, a most unusual penetration capability, compared to the rather slow speed (around 200 feet per second) at which it travels. It kills by cutting blood vessels and so severely wounding that an animal quickly bleeds to death. Penetration as compared to weight and speed may be illustrated as follows. Hold an inch-thick slice of steak suspended horizontally in midair. Hold a bullet a couple of feet above it. Drop the bullet and it simply plops atop the meat. Repeat with a hunting arrow and the arrow will go right through.

Fundamentally, hunting with a bow is a fairly simple operation that becomes intriguingly complicated as one progresses. Equipment required to begin is only a bow, a few arrows, and a quiver in which to carry them. Several manufacturers make what is called a "bow quiver," an attachment that fits onto the bow itself and holds 3 or 4 arrows parallel to the bow between bow and bowstring. Leather quivers are carried by a sling upon one's back.

There are numerous types of arrows. There are blunts —blunt pointed arrows—for hunting small game. These are designed to kill by the force of the blow, not necessarily by their penetration. Big-game hunting arrows all are designed with fairly large cutting heads of varying styles. There are also, of course, practice arrows, fish-shooting arrows, etc. Modern arrows are made of wood, of hollow fiberglas, of aluminum. Hollow glass arrows are the current trend. There are various weights in arrows, and lengths also. The beginner need not concern himself too much with this. A standard-weight 28-inch arrow will undoubtedly be what he needs.

Bows also are made of varying materials, but here again laminated fiberglas, usually with a wood core, seems to be best. Most popular is the so-called "recurved" bow. There are different lengths in bows. There are also heavy bows—literally heavy—and light bows, "fast" bows and "slow" bows. What the beginner must settle first to his best advantage is the so-called "weight" of bow best suited to him. Weights run all the way from 15 to 100 pounds. The term thus used means the number of pounds pull on the bowstring required to draw a standard arrow full draw, that is, with its head back to the bow.

Youngsters should begin with very light bows. An adult should not start with the most powerful, even though he finds he can draw it to full draw. He should start with, say, a bow of 28 to 35 pounds, and practice with it, shooting at a target no more than thirty feet. Proper shooting technique is with the bow arm extended, elbow not quite fully straight. The bow hand should grip solidly but with wrist cocked slightly outward, instead of inward. In other words, the hand should not be *pushing* the bow from between its grip and the string, and the wrist should be well out of the way of the twanging string when it is released. With feet well planted, and body turned so that the bow-arm side is toward the target (the shooter does not *face* the target), the string arm now makes the draw.

The arrow has been nocked in proper position on the string so that it is level with and at right angles to the bow. It is laid across the little outcrop on the bow, if it has one, or across the top of the bow hand—gently, loosely—and on the side of the bow from which the bow hand grips. The draw is made quickly and smoothly. The bow arm stays extended and solid. The tips of the first three fingers of the draw hand pull the string, the first finger just above the arrow, the second two just below. The fingers do not squeeze against the arrow. They hold it, if at all, very lightly. The draw hand comes back to the side of the face. The aim is instantly made and the string released, sending the arrow on its way. Never should the archer attempt to *hold* the string back, that is, hold the bow at full draw, while he aims. The arm cannot hold without trembling.

Most bow hunters nowadays shoot with what is called instinctive aiming. That is, they look at the target, not along the arrow. It is a good idea to begin by practicing proper draw technique. Many expert hunters, however, break all the standard rules once they become proficient shooters. In hunting situations they find they must. Fundamentals given here are meant simply as a general guide.

A leather wrist guard and an archer's shooting glove are standard equipment for both beginners and accomplished shooters. The bowstring hitting the wrist can give severe abrasions, and the string soon makes fingertips of the hand raw.

When shooting is first begun, the prospective hunter must learn what his arrow trajectory is at various distances, and compensate for it with his aiming. In other words, he must come to judge fairly accurately, or else he will shoot what he thinks is point-blank at a deer at twenty paces—but the arrow will fly over its back. After much target shooting has been done, the 28- or 35-pound bow may seem too "mushy" in action. This simply means the shooter has built up muscles not ordinarily used, has begun to perfect the technique of his draw, and is ready for a heavier bow. He now tries one of perhaps 48 or 56 pounds. Such bows are perfectly adequate hunting weapons, and many archers never go beyond them. These weights, they discover, are about their maximum. Others will eventually work up to 60-, 65-, or 70-pound bows. This is about tops. A very few archers have built up to and learned to handle still heavier bows. There is little advantage, and often great disadvantage, in hunting with a weapon that is too heavy.

Big-game bow-hunting methods do not differ from those used in rifle-hunting—except that the archer must get so much closer. This is a tremendous exception, and on it hinges the great sport and the challenge and satisfaction involved. In other words, the whole problem in hunting with a bow is to get within proper shooting distance. It requires that a hunter become most proficient in still-hunting and stalking, and above all keen in judgment as regards placing himself where the game is most likely to *come to him*.

There are three general techniques used by most bow hunters. Prowling quietly through the woods until game is sighted is first. Staying on a stand is second. Stalking an animal is third. Ordinarily the stalking is an outgrowth of one of the other methods. Game sighted while still-hunting or prowling is not likely to be close enough for a shot—as it might be to a rifleman. Thus, after the sighting, either while standing or still-hunting, the stalk must be made. The most successful stalk technique will always be one that places the hunter in good shooting position in the line of travel the animal is following so that it comes to him. This of course is not always possible. When it is not, the full stalk must be most carefully made.

Sharp arrows with multiple blades are a must for successful big-game hunting. The blades must also be *kept* sharp by the hunter. When an animal is shot at, the hunter must find the arrow if he has not seen it hit the animal. If he cannot find it, he must assume he has made a hit, then search diligently for blood. Since an arrow kills by hemorrhage, a wounded animal must be given time to lie down and bleed to death. From a half-hour to an hour or more is proper waiting time for the archer.

The archer will soon discover that he must hunt with far more patience and with far greater care than gun hunters use. He must play the breeze with extreme care, too, for his slightest scent will give him away at the short distance separating him from his target. He must consider, too, the limitations of the arrow where obstacles such as brush are concerned. A bullet may plow right through. An arrow will be deflected.

The bow hunter must practice shooting from many, and many awkward, positions. He must learn to get an arrow off quickly when opportunity is presented. He must pay very close attention to leading moving game. A deer out at 40 yards will require at least 10 feet of lead if he is even loping along. Of course arrow weight and the cast of the bow (how fast that particular bow sends its arrow) will affect lead. The hunter must know what his equipment will and won't do.

Of utmost importance, too, is the clothing of the archer. Every item must be selected for how quiet it will be when the hunter moves. Camouflage suits are often very useful, if of soft material and without starch. Time and place selected for hunting are also considerations. When rain or snow makes quiet going, or wind covers the noise of the prowling archer, the odds are in his favor.

All told, however, just as in rifle hunting, the most important requirement of all is that the archer have vast patience and determination—and shoot not at a whole animal, but at the spot where a quick kill will occur. To this end, much practice plus calm, quick shooting when opportunity is presented will bring the greatest amount of success.

BIBLIOGRAPHY

Bibliography

FISHING

Brooks, Joe, *Complete Book of Fly Fishing*. New York: Outdoor Life Publishing Company, 1958.

Bueno, Bill (ed.), *The American Fisherman's Guide*. Englewood Cliffs, N.J.: Prentice-Hall, Inc., 1952.

Dahne, Robert A., *Salt Water Fishing*. New York: Henry Holt and Company, 1950.

Dalrymple, Byron, *Fishing in the United States*. Englewood Cliffs, N.J.: Prentice-Hall, Inc., 1959.

——, *Ice Fishing for Everybody*. New York; Lantern Press, Inc., 1948.

LaMonte, Francesca, *Marine Game Fishes of the World*. New York; Doubleday & Company, 1952.

——, *North American Game Fishes*. New York; Doubleday & Company, 1945.

McNally, Tom (ed.), *Fishermen's Digest*. Chicago: The Gun Digest Company, 1958.

Roedel, Phil M., *Common Ocean Fishes of the California Coast* (Bulletin No. 91). Sacramento: California Department of Fish and Game, 1953.

HUNTING

Amber, John T. (ed.), *Gun Digest*. Chicago: The Gun Digest Company, 1959.

Cahalane, Victor H., *Mammals of North America*. New York: The Macmillan Company, 1947.

Elliot, David, *Training Gun Dogs to Retrieve*. New York: Henry Holt and Company, 1952.

Fitz, Grancel, *North American Head Hunting*. New York: Oxford University Press, 1957.

Kortright, F. H., *The Ducks, Geese and Swans of North America*. Washington, D.C.: Wildlife Management Institute, 1953.

O'Connor, Jack, *Outdoor Life Shooting Book*. New York: Outdoor Life Publishing Company, 1957.

Ormond, Clyde, *Hunting Our Biggest Game*. Harrisburg, Pa.: The Stackpole Company, 1956.

——, *Hunting Our Medium Size Game*. Harrisburg, Pa.: The Stackpole Company, 1958.

Trueblood, Ted, *The Hunter's Handbook*. New York: Thomas Y. Crowell Company, 1954.

GENERAL

Angier, Bradford, *Living Off the Country: How to Stay Alive in the Woods*. Harrisburg, Pa.: The Stackpole Company, 1956.

Kesting, Ted (ed.), *The Outdoor Encyclopedia*. New York: A. S. Barnes and Company, 1957.

INDEX

INDEX

Action
rifle, 138-39
shotgun, 153
Albacore, 111
Amberjack, 111-12, 123
American brant, 233
American merganser, 229
Ammunition, rifle, 140-44
Angling. *See* Fishing
Antelope, 277-81
Anti-backlash reel, 7
Atlantic salmon, 36

Badger, 263-64
Bait
ice-fishing, 74-5
natural (chart), 30
natural, for trout, 41
salt-water, 96-8
Bait casting, 5-13, 95
Bait-fishing, 28-31
black bass, 45
pickerel, 48
surf, 89-90
Band-tailed pigeon, 212-13, 216-17
Barometric pressure, 104
Barracuda, 112
Barred perch, 126
Barred pickerel, 47-8
Barren ground caribou, 284
Barrow's golden eye, 228

Bass, 43-5
black, 43-4
California white sea, 113-14
ice-fishing for, 77
sea, 124
striped, 112-13
white, 56-7
yellow, 56-7
Basset, 173
for pheasant, 195
Bay lynx, 257
Beagle, 166, 173-74
for pheasant, 195
for rabbit, 247
Bear, 290-93
Belt, surf, 90-1
Big game, 267-95
Big-game fish, 106-10
Bighorn, 285-86
Binoculars, 147
Birds, speed of flight, 158
Black bass, 43-4
ice-fishing for, 77
Black bear, 290-91, 293
Black brant, 233
Black crappie, 53-4
Black drum, 127-28
Black duck, 223
Black sheep, 285-86
Black-and-tan hound, 173
Blackfish, 124, 128
Black-spotted trout, 40

Blacktail deer, 272
Bloodhound, 173
Blue goose, 231-32
Blue marlin, 108
  tackle, 109
Blue quail, 191
Blue sunfish, 51
Bluefin tuna, 107-8
Bluefish, 114-15
Bluegill, 50
  ice-fishing for, 77
Boar, wild, 294-95
Boat, duck, 239
Bobcat, 257-59
  calling, 296-300
Bobwhite quail, 187-91
Bonefish, 115-16
Bonito, 116
Boots, 31
Bottom fish, 123-30
Bottom fishing, salt-water, 94
Bow and arrow hunting, 301-7
  arrow types, 302-3, 306
    sizes, 302-3
  bow weights, 303-5
  techniques, 305-6
Bowfin, 63-4
Brant, 233
Bream, 50
Brittany spaniel, 171
Broadbill (duck), 223-24
Broadbill (swordfish), 108
  tackle, 109
Brook trout, 39
Brown bear, 291, 292-93
Brown trout, 39
Bufflehead, 228
Bullet rifle, 140-43
Burbot, 64
Butterball, 228

Cackling goose, 231

Caliber, rifle, 137-38, 139-40,
  142-44
California bonito, 116
California halibut, 129
California quail, 191
California white sea bass, 113-
  14
Calling, 296
  bobcats, 298-99
  coyotes, 298-99
  crow, 265-66, 300
  deer, 297
  duck, 241
  fox, 298-99
  hawk, 300
  horned owl, 300
  magpie, 300
  moose, 283
  night calling, 299
  pheasant, 300
  predators, 297-98
  quail, 300
  raccoon, 299-300
  ringtail, 300
  squirrel, 252
  waterfowl, 239
  wild turkey, 209-13
Canada goose, 231
Canvasback, 227-28
Caribou, 284-85
Carp, 61
Cartridge, rifle, 140-43
Casting
  bait, 5-13
  fly, 13-23
  salt-water, 95-6
  surf, 88, 90
Catfish, 59-61
Center fire ammunition, 163
Cero, 117
Chain pickerel, 47
Channel bass, 114

Chesapeake Bay retriever, 171-72
Chinook salmon, 37-8
Choke, shotgun, 154-56
Chukar partridge, 197-98
Chum pot, 95
Chumming
    for bluefish, 114
    in ice-fishing, 74
    in still-fishing, 94-5
Clothing, for keeping warm, 66
Clumber spaniel, 171
Cocker spaniel, 170-71
Cod, 127
    fresh-water, 64
Coho salmon, 37
Common bonito, 116-17
Common croaker, 128
Common jack, 118-19
Common pompano, 120
Common sunfish, 50-1
Cottontail rabbit, 246, 248-49
Cougar, 293-94
Coyote, 263-64
    calling, 296-97
Crab-eater, 117-18
Crappie, 53-4
    ice-fishing for, 77
Creek sunfish, 51-2
Creels, 21
Croaker, 128
Crow, 264-66
    calling, 265-66, 300
Curly-coated retriever, 172
Cusk, 64
    ice-fishing for, 77
Cut-throat trout, 40

Dall sheep, 286
Decoy
    crow, 265-66

waterfowl, 238, 239-42, 242-43
Deer, 270-77, 279-86
    calling, 297
    hunting, 272-76
    killing shots, 268-70, 281
Desert bighorn, 285
Dog, 164-83
    for bobcat, 258-59
    for fox, 260
    for mountain lion, 293-94
    for opossum, 254
    for pheasant, 194-95
    for quail, 188-89, 192
    for rabbit, 247, 248
    for raccoon, 255-57
    for skunk, 253
    for squirrel, 252
    training, 166-69, 174-83
Dogfish, 63-4
Dolly Varden trout, 40
Dolphin, 118
Dove, 185
    band-tailed pigeon, 212-13, 216-17
    mourning, 212-15
    white-winged, 212, 215-16
Dressing, line, 20
Drum
    black, 127-28
    fresh-water, 62-3
    red, 114
Duck, 221-30
    calling, 241
    decoys for, 238-39, 239-42
    deep-water, 225-30
    diving, 225-30
    pond, 222-25
    puddle, 222-25
Duck boat, 239
Dusky grouse, 205-6

Ebb tide, 105
Eider, 229
Elk, 280-81
Emperor goose, 232
English setter, 169
  for ruffed grouse, 202
European gray partridge, 196-97

Fish
  fresh-water, 33-64
  salt-water, 103-30
  See also under name of fish
Fish duck, 229-30
Fish-finder rig, 89
Fishing, 3-130
  fresh-water, 3-64
  ice, 65-78
  salt-water, 79-130
Flies, 17-9
  dry, 17, 18
  ice, 75-6
  for salt-water casting, 96
  wet, 17-8, 40-1
  See also Fly-fishing
Floating lures, 10-1
Flood tide, 105
Flounder, 129
Fly casting, salt-water, 95-6
Fly-fishing, 13-23
  for Atlantic salmon, 36
  for black bass, 45
  method, 20-1, 21-3
  for pickerel, 48
Force training, 181-82
Fox, 257, 259-60
  calling, 298-99
Foxhound, 259
Free-spool reel, 7
Fresh-water cod, 64
Fresh-water drum, 62-3

Fresh-water fish, 33-64
  See also under name of fish
Fresh-water ling, 64

Gambel's quail, 191
Game birds
  lowland, 218-44
  upland, 184-217
Game fish, 36-49, 103-30
Gauge, shotgun, 152-53
Geese. *See* Goose
Goat, mountain, 288-89
Goggle-eye (rock bass), 54-6
Golden retriever, 172
Golden-eye, 228
Goose, 230-33
  decoys for, 242-43
Gordon setter, 169
Gray grunt, 126
Grayling, 43
Greater scaup, 226-27
Greater snow goose, 232
Green sunfish, 51
Greenhead, 223
Grizzly bear, 291, 292-93
Ground hog. *See* Woodchuck
Groupers, 124-25
Grouse, 198-207
Grunts, 126
Gun
  for antelope, 279-80
  for bear, 293
  for caribou, 285
  for crow, 266
  for deer, 276-77
  for dusky grouse, 206
  for elk, 281
  for mountain goat, 290
  for mountain sheep, 288
  for mourning dove, 215
  for partridge, 198
  for pheasant, 196

for prairie chicken, 205
for quail, 190-91, 192
for rabbit, 247, 249
rifle, 136-51
for ruffed grouse, 202
safety with, 161-63
shotgun, 151-60
for squirrel, 252-53
for waterfowl, 233-35
for wild turkey, 212
for woodchuck, 262
for woodcock, 209

Halibut, 129
Harlequin duck, 229
Hawk, calling, 300
Heath hen, 198
High tide, 104
Hog, wild, 294-95
Hooded merganser, 229
Hooks, 30
  salt-water, 87
  use of (chart), 30
Horned owl, calling, 300
Hounds, 172-74
  See also Beagle
Hungarian partridge, 196-97
Hunting dogs, 164-83

Ice flies, 75-6
Ice-fishing, 65-78
Incoming tide, 104
Irish setter, 169
Irish water spaniel, 172

Jack, 118-19
Jack Crevalle, 118
Jack rabbit, 246
Javelina, 295
Jewfish, 124
"Jump" shooting, 237

Kamloops trout, 41, 42
King salmon, 37-8
Kingfish, 117-18
Knot, fly, 19

Labrador retriever, 172
Ladyfish, 119
Lake salmon, 36-7
Lake trout, 42-3
  ice-fishing for, 76
Landing net, 20-1
Landlocked salmon, 36-7
Largemouth (black bass), 44
Leaders
  bait-casting, 8
  fly-fishing, 15-6, 19
  salt-water, 86
  spinning, 26
Lesser Canada goose, 231
Lesser scaup, 226-27
Lesser snow goose, 232
Level-wind reel, 7
Lines
  bait-casting, 7-8; (chart), 9
  dressing for, 20
  fly, 14-5; (chart), 15
  ice-fishing, 72
  salt-water, 82-3, 83-4, 96
  spinning, 26
Ling, fresh-water, 64
Load
  shotgun, 156-57
  See also Gun (name of game)
Loch Leven trout, 39
Long-eared sunfish, 51
Low tide, 105
Lures
  bait-casting, 8-11
  "fly rod," 23
  ice-fishing, 75-6
  spinning, 26-7

Mackerel, 119-20
Magpie, calling, 300
Mallard, 223
Mangrove snapper, 125-26
Marlin, 108-10
Marsh hen, 244
Merganser, 229-30
Migration of waterfowl, 235
Moose, 281-84
  calling, 283
Mountain caribou, 284
Mountain goat, 288-90
Mountain lion, 293-94
Mountain pheasant, 193
Mountain quail, 191
Mountain sheep, 285-88
Mourning dove, 212-15
Mud pickerel, 47
Mudfish, 63-4
Mule deer, 271-72
Multiplying reel, 7
Muskellunge, 46
Muskie, 46
Muzzle velocity, 140-41

Net, landing, 20-1
Night calling, 299
Northern pike, 47
Northern porgy, 126

Oceanic bonito, 116
Old squaw, 229
Opossum, 253-54
O'Shaughnessy hooks, 87
Outgoing tide, 105
Oxygen content, and fishing, 104

Pacific pompano, 120
Pacific salmon, 37-8
Pacific yellowtail, 123

Pan fish, 50-9
  ice-fishing bait for, 74-5
Partridge, 196-98
Pass shooting, 237-38
Peary caribou, 284
Peccary, 295
Perch
  barred, 126
  ice-fishing for, 76-7
  Sacramento, 55-6
  sauger, 48-9
  striped, 126
  surf, 126
  walleyed pike, 48-9
  white, 58
  yellow, 56
Pheasant, 192-96
  calling, 300
Pickerel, 47
  ice-fishing for, 76
Pigeon, 185
Pigfish, 126
Pike, 47-9
  ice-fishing for, 76
Pinnated grouse, 203
Pintail, 223
Plug casting, salt-water, 95
Pointer, 169-70
  and pheasant, 195
Polar bear, 291
Pollock, 127
Pompano, 120
Pond duck, 222-25
Porgies, 126
Possum, 254-55
Prairie chicken, 199, 203-5
Prairie dog, 262-63
Predators, calling, 297-98
Pronghorn antelope, 277-80
Ptarmigan, 206-7
Puddle duck, 222-25
Puma, 293-94

Pumpkinseed (common sun-fish), 50-1

Quail, 187-92
  calling, 300

Rabbit, 246-49
Raccoon, 254-57
  calling, 299-300
Rail, 243-44
Rainbow trout, 39
Red drum, 114
Red fox, 260
Red snapper, 125-26
Red trout, 40
Redbreast (bluegill), 50
Red-breasted merganser, 229
Red-eared sunfish, 51
Red-eye (rock bass), 54-5
Redfish, 114
Redhead duck, 227
Red-legged partridge, 197-98
Red-spotted trout, 40
Reels, 7, 16, 24, 25, 71-2, 89, 95, 96
Reindeer. See Deer
Retriever, 171-72
Richardson's goose, 231
Rifle, 136-51
  varmint, 262
  See also Gun
Rifling, 136-37
Rig
  fish-finder, 89
  three-way, 89-90
Rim fire ammunition, 163
Ringneck, 192-96
Ring-necked duck, 227
Ringtail, calling, 300
Rock bass, 54-5
Rock ptarmigan, 206-7
Rockfish, 112-13, 124

Rocky Mountain bighorn, 285
Rod holder
  for surf still-fishing, 91
Rods, 6-7, 15, 25, 71-2, 81-2, 85, 88-9
  chart, 9
"Roosting," 211
Ross's goose, 232
Rough fish, 59-64
Round pompano, 120

Sacramento perch, 55-6
Safety
  with guns, 161-63
  in ice-fishing, 67-8
  tularemia, 249
  in varmint hunting, 264
Sage hen, 198-99
Sailfish, 110
Salmon, 36-8
  ice-fishing for, 77
Salt-water fish, 103-30
  See also under name of fish
Sargo, 126
Sauger, 48-9
Saw-bill, 229-30
Scaled quail, 191
Scaup, 226-27
Scoter, 229
Sea bass, 124
Sea trout, 122-23
Sebago salmon, 36-7
Setters, 169, 170
Shad, salt-water, 34
Sharp-tailed grouse, 202-5
Sheep, mountain, 285-88
Sheepshead, 62-3, 128-29
Sheldrake, 229
Shellcracker, 51
Shelter, ice-fishing, 66
Shocking power, 156-57

Shooting
  big game, 268-70
  "jump," 237
  pass, 237-38
  rifle, 148-49
  shotgun, 157-60
Shotgun, 151-60
  See also Gun
Shoveler, 223-24
Sierra grouse, 205
Sights, rifle, 144-47
Silver salmon, 37, 38
Sinkers, 29-30
  salt-water, 87
Sinking lures, 11
Skunk, 253
Slack tide, 105
Smallmouth (black bass), 44
Smelt, 58-9
  ice-fishing for, 76
Snap shooting, 159-60
Snapper, 125-26
Snapper blue, 114
Snook, 120-21
Snow goose, 232
Snowshoe rabbit, 246-48
Sooty grouse, 205
Spaniel, 170-71, 195
Spearing, 77-8
Speckled trout, 39, 122-23
Spike, for surf still-fishing, 91
Spinning, 23-8
  method, 28-9
  salt-water, 96
Spools. *See* Reels
Spoonbill duck, 223-24
Spotfin croaker, 128
Spotted weakfish, 122-23
Springer spaniel, 166, 171
Squirrel, 249-53
  calling, 252
Steelhead trout, 41-2

Still-fishing, 28-31
  salt-water, 94-5
  spike, 91-2
Still-hunting, for fox, 259-60
Stone sheep, 286
Striped bass, 112-13
Striped bonito, 116
Striped marlin, 108
  tackle, 109
Striped perch, 126
Striper (bass), 112-13
Sturgeon, spearing, 78
Suckers, 62
Summer flounder, 129
Sunfish family, 53-6
  See also True sunfish
Surf belt, 90-1
Surf casting, 88, 90
Surf perch, 126
Swamp rabbit, 246
Swan, 233
Swing shooting, 160
Swivels
  salt-water, 86-7
  surf bait-fishing, 89-90
Swordfish, 108
  tackle, 109

Tackle
  albacore, 111
  amberjack, 111-12
  bait-casting, 5-13
  barracuda, 112
  blue marlin, 109
  bluefin tuna, 107-8
  bluefish, 115
  bonefish, 116
  bonitos, 117
  California white sea bass, 114
  cero, 117
  channel bass, 114
  cod, 127

INDEX

dolphin, 118
fly-fishing, 13-23
fresh-water, 3-31
groupers, 125
"heavy," 85
ice-fishing, 70-3
jack, 119
jewfish, 124
kingfish, 117
mackerel, 119-20
"medium," 85
miscellaneous, 31
Pacific yellowtail, 123
pollock, 127
pompano, 120
salt-water, 79-92
sea bass, 124
snappers, 126
snook, 121
striped bass, 113
striped marlin, 109
surf, 88-9
swordfish, 109
tarpon, 121-22
wahoo, 122
weakfish, 123
white marlin, 110
Tarpon, 121-22
Tautog, 128
Teal, 224
Telescope sight, 146-48
  for woodchuck, 262
Temperature, and fishing, 103-4
Ten-pounder, 119
Texas bighorn, 285
Three-way rig, 89-90
Tide
  and fishing, 104-6
  and rail hunting, 243-44
  terminology, 104-5
Tide rips, 105
Tip-up, 72-3

Tobaccobox (sunfish), 51
Trajectory, of bullet, 140-43,
  145-46
Trolling, 8, 92-4
Trout, 38-43, 122-23
  ice-fishing for, 76
True sunfish, 50-3
  See also Sunfish
Tularemia, 249
Tuna, bluefin, 107-8
Turkey, wild, 209-12

Valley quail, 192
Varmint, 260-64
Varying hare, 246

Waders, 31
Wahoo, 122
Walker foxhound, 174, 259
Walleyed pike, 48-9
  ice-fishing for, 76
Warmouth bass, 54-5
Waterfowl, 218-44
  calling, 239
  decoys, 238-39, 239-41
  duck, 221-30
  geese, 230-33
  hunting methods, 235-43
  migratory lanes, 235
Wavey, 232
Weakfish, 122-23
Western trout, 40
Wet flies, for trout, 40-1
Whistler duck, 228
White bass, 56-7
White crappie, 53-4
White grunt, 126
White marlin, 109-10
White sheep, 286
Whitefish, ice-fishing for, 76
White-fronted goose, 232

323

INDEX

Whitetail deer, 270-71
White-tailed ptarmigan, 206-7
White-winged dove, 212-13, 215-16
Wild boar, 294-95
Wild hog, 294-95
Wild turkey, 209-12
  calling, 211
Wildcat, 257
Willow ptarmigan, 206-7
Winter flounder, 129

Woodchuck, 261-62
Woodcock, 185, 207-9
Woodland caribou, 284

Yellow bass, 56-7
Yellow grunt, 126
Yellow perch, 56
  ice-fishing for, 76-7
Yellowfin, 128
Yellowtail, 126
  Pacific, 123

GREAT SEA STORIES

ABOARD THE *FLYING SWAN* • C-191   35¢
   Stanley Wolpert. A violent novel of the men of the merchant marine.

CAPTAIN JUDAS • 1076   25¢
   F. van Wyck Mason. American seamen *vs.* the pirates of Tripoli.

CAROLINA CORSAIR • C-228   35¢
   Don Tracy. A roaring story about Blackbeard the Pirate.

THE DISTANT SHORE
   Jan de Hartog. Published in two parts — THE KEY (originally *Stella*) (2952) and THE SEA (953) — at 25c each. One of the most brilliant novels of World War Two.

GOLDEN ADMIRAL • C-165   35¢
   F. van Wyck Mason. Sir Francis Drake and the smashing of the power of Spain.

H.M.S. *ULYSSES* • M-4067   35¢
   Alistair MacLean. Combat at sea in the Arctic during World War Two.

THE MAPMAKER • M-4111   35¢
   Frank G. Slaughter. A novel based on the discoveries and adventures of the bold seamen employed by Prince Henry the Navigator.

MEN AGAINST THE SEA • 2358   25¢
   Charles Nordhoff and James Norman Hall. The most popular and exciting novel ever written about survival at sea.

MUTINY ON THE BOUNTY • C-34   35¢
   Charles Nordhoff and James Norman Hall. The famous story of Captain Bligh and Fletcher Christian.

RUN SILENT, RUN DEEP • M-4061   35¢
   Commander Edward L. Beach. "The best submarine yarn ever written..."

[MORE→]

THE SEA CHASE • 2652   25¢

> *Andrew Geer.* One ship—thirty men, one woman—against the British Navy.

THE SMOLDERING SEA • C-140   35¢

> *U. S. Andersen.* Wartime in the South Pacific.

SOUTH BY JAVA HEAD • M-4116   35¢

> *Alistair MacLean.* Escape from the Japanese in an open boat in the China Sea.

TWILIGHT FOR THE GODS • M-4091   35¢

> *Ernest Gann.* "A taut classic of the sea . . . a magnetic, exciting narrative."—*New York Herald Tribune*

THE WRECK OF THE *MARY DEARE* • M-4079 35¢

> *Hammond Innes.* An enthralling tale of a derelict ship.
